Individual forecasting and aggregate outcomes

"Rational expectations" examined

Edited by

Roman Frydman   *and*   **Edmund S. Phelps**
New York University   Columbia University

CAMBRIDGE UNIVERSITY PRESS

Cambridge
London   New York   New Rochelle
Melbourne   Sydney

Published by the Press Syndicate of the University of Cambridge
The Pitt Building, Trumpington Street, Cambridge CB2 1RP
32 East 57th Street, New York, NY 10022, USA
296 Beaconsfield Parade, Middle Park, Melbourne 3206, Australia

First published 1983

Printed in the United States of America

Library of Congress Cataloging in Publication Data
Main entry under title:
Individual forecasting and aggregate outcomes.
"Proceedings of the conference, Expectations
formation and economic disequilibrium, held in
New York City, December 4, 1981."
1. Rational expectations (Economic theory) –
Congresses. 2. Equilibrium (Economics) – Congresses.
I. Frydman, Roman, 1948– . II. Phelps, Edmund
HB172.5.I55   1984   330'.0724   83-10165
ISBN 0 521 25744 1

Contents

Contributors

Margaret Bray
Faculty of Economics and
    Politics
University of Cambridge

Clive Bull
Department of Economics
New York University

Phillip Cagan
Department of Economics
Columbia University

Guillermo A. Calvo
Department of Economics
Columbia University

Juan Carlos Di Tata
Columbia University
(Currently at International
    Monetary Fund)

George Evans
Department of Economics
Stanford University

Roman Frydman
Department of Economics
New York University

Jerry Green
Department of Economics
Harvard University

Frank Hahn
Faculty of Economics and
    Politics
University of Cambridge

Alan Kirman
Ecole des Hautes Etudes
    en Sciences Sociales
Universités d'Aix-Marseille
    II et III

Axel Leijonhufvud
Department of Economics
University of California
    at Los Angeles

Edmund S. Phelps
Department of Economics
Columbia University

Roy Radner
Bell Laboratories and
    New York University

John B. Taylor
Department of Economics
Princeton University

Robert M. Townsend
Graduate School of Industrial
    Organization
Carnegie–Mellon University

Preface

In this book we are publishing the proceedings of the conference "Expectations Formation and Economic Disequilibrium," held in New York City, December 4, 1981.

We are immensely grateful to the C. V. Starr Center for Applied Economics at New York University for inviting us to hold this conference under its auspices and for providing generous financial and organizational support. We are grateful also to New York University for providing facilities and hospitality to the participants at the conference.

We also want to express our deep appreciation to the authors and discussants whose contributions are published here for their participation in the conference and readiness to help in every way in the preparation of this book.

In addition to the authors and discussants whose work appears herein, the following persons also participated in the conference: Jess Benhabib, Franklin M. Fisher, Duncan Foley, Walter Heller, Peter Howitt, Pentti J. K. Kouri, Melvyn B. Krauss, Mark Lilla, Francisco L. Lopes, Fritz Machlup, Cathy Morrison, Robert A. Mundell, Ishaq M. Nadiri, Gerald P. O'Driscoll, Joseph Ostroy, Michael Parkin, James B. Ramsey, R. Robert Russell, Thomas J. Sargent, Mark Schankerman, Paul Wachtel, Bernard Wasow, Lawrence White, Clas Wihlborg, and Andreas Woergoetter. Their great interest in the subject and lively contributions to the discussion added much to the value of the conference.

Lastly, our thanks also go to Colin Day of Cambridge University Press for his steady help in expediting this book.

R. F. and E. S. P.

CHAPTER 1

Introduction

ROMAN FRYDMAN AND EDMUND S. PHELPS

Understanding the formation of individual expectations and the roles of information and knowledge in economic decisions has long been one of the most difficult and important problems in economics. Until the recent rational expectations movement, it was widely thought that expectations behavior contained psychological and sociological elements and hence could not be modeled with only the tools of individualistic optimization calculus and statistical decision theory.

1.1. Modern thought on expectations modeling

Knight, in his classic book, introduced the distinction between measurable uncertainty – which he called "risk" – and "true uncertainty," which cannot "by any method be reduced to an objective, quantitatively determined probability" (Knight, 1921, p. 321). For Knight, the uncertainty of events arises from their uniqueness:

Business decisions ... deal with situations which are far *too unique* ... for any sort of statistical tabulations to have any value for guidance. The conception of an objectively measurable probability or chance is simply inapplicable [Knight, 1921, pp. 231–2].

But there is some regularity in economic life. Although Knight's insistence on the unique aspects of each situation cannot be neglected, economics must also recognize the recurring elements. It must do so if it is to aspire to any explanatory power.

Keynes, too, spoke of uncertainty. Unique developments over the future – parameter shifts, in modern terms – make it impossible to assign an objective probability distribution to distant future states. In fact, Keynes noted that "[not] all probabilities are measurable" (Keynes, 1921, p. 34), because it is not generally possible to enumerate all possible states of the world (thus foreshadowing a problem for contract theory!).

Roman Frydman acknowledges the support and hospitality of the Hoover Institution, and Edmund Phelps acknowledges a research grant from the National Science Foundation, during the preparation of this Introduction. The authors are also grateful to Olivier Blanchard, Clive Bull, George Evans, Mark Schankerman, and Robert Townsend for helpful comments on portions of an early draft.

But Keynes brought in a new source of uncertainty, even when the near future is concerned. With his oft-quoted "beauty contest" example he sought to dramatize the role played by subjective guesses of "average opinion" in the formation of stock market prices (Keynes, 1936, p. 156). Because there is only the most "flimsy" basis for estimating average opinion, it is a factor that creates uncertainty about stock prices (Keynes, 1937, p. 214). The inability of agents to assign a probability distribution to average opinion, linking it to observed exogenous variables, rules out the existence of a direct and objective connection from the probability distribution of exogenous variables, whether or not ascertainable itself, to the probability distribution of stock prices.

It follows from the problem of average opinion that for an understanding of individual decisions in decentralized markets, computation of the solution to a maximization problem is not sufficient. The agents and the modeler alike also want the best feasible theory, to the extent that any theory is feasible, of how market expectations are formed.

Hayek (1948a,b) drew a now widely recognized distinction between the pure logic of choice and the "economic problem which society faces":

[It] is ... not merely a problem of how to allocate "given" resources – if given is taken to mean a single mind which deliberately solves the problem set by these "data." It is rather a problem ... of the utilization of knowledge which is not given to anyone in its totality. [Hayek, 1948b, pp. 77–8]

Anticipating some later developments, Hayek then distinguished between

the objective real facts, as the observing economist is supposed to know them [and data] in the subjective sense, as things known to the persons whose behavior we try to explain.... The data on which any one person will base his plans will be the expectation that other people will act in a particular way. [Hayek, 1948a, pp. 38–9]

Hayek's widely known emphasis on the division of knowledge further complicates the agents' forecasts of average opinion.

The postwar development of Keynesian economics largely ignored the role of information and expectations formation in explaining macroeconomic phenomena. Keynesian economics was cast into the Walrasian complete information approach, with "money illusion" being invoked to explain wage stickiness. The theory of maximizing individuals having perfect information drove these models.

1.1.1.   *Early models of the role of expectations*

A series of papers (Phelps et al., 1970) laid the foundations of an alternative macroeconomic theory, one based on the neoclassical theory of intertemporal maximization, but without the Walrasian postulate of complete information on the part of each agent concerning his choices. The formation of individual expectations thus played a crucial role in the new theory.

The basic development in Phelps et al. (1970) was the application to macroeconomic models of the costliness of transmitting and gathering wage and price data. That concept was introduced by Phelps (1968), with the firm setting wages without knowing the wages set by others; it was used again by Phelps (1969, 1970) in his "island parable" involving informationally isolated labor markets. As he put it, agents on each island

have to cope ignorant of the future and even much of the present. Isolated and apprehensive, these Pinteresque figures construct expectations of the state of the economy – over space and over time – and maximize relative to that imagined world. [Phelps, 1970, p. 22]

There was no presumption by these authors (Phelps et al., 1970) that an outside investigator could accurately model individual expectations about the "world imagined" on each island. Because individual decisions cannot be derived from the formal maximization framework alone, models of individual market behavior have to remain "open" in the sense that individual behavior can be analyzed only with some additional assumptions concerning the formation of individual expectations.

One such plausible assumption is that individuals, ignorant of the environment they face, form expectations according to some error-correcting, or adaptive, mechanism. Adopting that assumption, this new theory provided an analysis of price and employment dynamics under the condition of disequilibrium, of incorrect expectations – a condition inextricably linked with learning.

The original formulation of adaptive expectations by Cagan (1956), Friedman (1956), and Nerlove (1958) did not ascribe any optimality properties to adaptive forecasts. Subsequently, Muth (1960) showed that if the behavior of the forecasted variable is characterized by the particular moving average process, adaptive expectations (with the adaptation coefficient equal to a function of the parameters of this process) are optimal in the minimum mean square error sense. This result, however, did not play any role in the approach of Phelps et al. (nor did it influence Friedman's 1961 analysis of long and *variable* lags in the short-run effects of monetary policy). It was simply inapplicable to any analysis of economic decisions in which the stochastic processes governing the behavior of endogenous variables are not confined to be stationary processes and agents are not assumed to know the parameters of those processes.

It might be added in passing that this book is the logical sequel to Phelps et al. (1970): There the individual agent "models" the *conduct*, to use Hayek's term, of the other agents, but not the expectations function that generates that conduct. This book contemplates the agent's model of the other agents' model.

1.1.2. The recent hypothesis about expectations behavior

Muth (1961) later proposed a radical approach to the problem of modeling individual expectations. Muth advanced the rational expectations hypothesis (REH) "that expectations of firms (or, more generally, the subjective probability distribution of outcomes) tend to be distributed about the prediction of the theory (or the 'objective' probability distribution of outcomes)" (Muth, 1961, p. 316). The hypothesis that subjective forecasts are based on the "objective" distribution represented a radical departure from all previous approaches in the literature that stressed the importance of uncertainty – the various nonstationarities and the difficulties in ascertaining the plans of the other agents in individual economic decisions. Thus, it is not surprising that the REH was slow to influence macroeconomic research in the 1960s.[1]

In an important series of articles, Lucas (1972, 1973, 1975) formulated his own version of Phelps's island parable. Lucas retained the concept of local information. But he restricted the behavior of exogenous variables to stationary processes, and, strikingly, he postulated that all price expectations are rational in the sense of Muth. Hence, the new formulation, though an outgrowth of the old, contained a significant departure from the approach of Phelps et al.

In the development of his REH island model, Lucas (1973) presented a novel analysis of output–inflation trade-offs and built an equilibrium model of the business cycle (Lucas, 1975). Subsequently, Sargent and Wallace (1975) used the Lucas model to derive the striking policy ineffectiveness proposition.[2] The REH was drawn upon for a powerful critique of policy analysis with traditional Keynesian macroeconometric models (Lucas, 1976). The rational expectations approach has also been adopted in applied econometric research. Most notably, combining the stochastic optimization framework with the REH, Hansen and Sargent (1981) formulated econometric procedures for interpreting economic time series. Many other investigators have since adopted the REH, which has by now become the major approach to expectations in theoretical and applied economics.[3]

---

[1] Some examples are Lucas (1966) on investment behavior and Phelps (1965), Uzawa (1966), Hall (1967), and Arrow and Kurz (1969) on public finance. For Phelps and Uzawa, however, the rational expectations case was only hypothetical, to be used as a benchmark.

[2] It is now well known that the policy ineffectiveness proposition holds only under restrictive assumptions. See Fischer (1977), Phelps and Taylor (1977), Frydman (1981), Weiss (1982), and Di Tata (1982).

[3] A useful collection of studies using the REH is that of Lucas and Sargent (1981).

The attractive power of the REH for economic analysis is readily explicable. On the substantive level, the hypothesis seemed to offer an escape from the difficult challenge of understanding how the agents acting in the economy model reality and form their beliefs, apparently a problem in psychology and sociology as much as economics. On the methodological level, the REH (together with the minimum mean square error optimality criterion) seemed to integrate individual expectations formation with the maximization postulate of classical theory. Thus, the economist could use standard choice theoretic tools to treat acquisition of knowledge and information like any other economic decision.

There have nevertheless remained unresolved problems about the meaning of the REH and its applicability to modeling individual expectations in decentralized markets.

1.1.3. *Some difficulties with the rational expectations doctrine*

One of the fundamental problems in the formulation of the REH is the absence of any definitions of "the relevant economic theory" and "the objective probability distribution of outcomes." In applications of the REH this problem has been sidestepped by the assumption that "the relevant economic theory" is represented by the specific model being analyzed by the rational expectations theorist. Here it will be convenient to represent the model – any model – by its typical semireduced form that specifies the behavior of endogenous variables as a linear function of exogenous variables, disturbances, and the average of expectations (average opinion) of endogenous variables.[4]

Postponing until later a discussion of the consequences of the existence of plurality of theories and models, let us suppose, arguendo, that agents have somehow agreed on one model as representing "the relevant economic theory." However, universal agreement on the relevance of only one model is not sufficient for the formation of rational forecasts. The hypothesis that agents use equilibrium forecast functions of the model has no epistemological status or "operational meaning" unless and until it is shown that it is possible for the agents to learn the parameters of those functions.[5]

[4] To the exogenous variables we should add the lagged endogenous variables in "dynamic" models. In some treatments of expectations formation, average opinion is one of these predetermined variables.

[5] The difficulty with the assumption that agents know the relevant parameters of the model is particularly apparent in the econometric applications of the REH. Although an econometrician can, at best, obtain *estimates* of the parameters of the model, in the derivation of the reduced form he assumes that agents have known the *true values* of those parameters for the entire sample period.

In order to highlight the problems in modeling such learning processes, let us suppose that agents attempt to estimate the parameters of the minimum mean square error forecast function by running regressions of endogenous variables on exogenous variables. Because the average opinion is one of the variables appearing on the right-hand side in the "true" semireduced form, these regressions are misspecified.[6] Consequently, the resulting estimators are biased. Hence, individual agents cannot form optimal forecasts, in the minimum mean square error sense, on the basis of the universally agreed upon specification of the model and information available to them. If the agents cannot form optimal forecasts, the individual agents (and the economist) have no basis for imputing any particular forecast function to other agents. The indeterminacy of the average opinion follows *endogenously* in the model.[7] Furthermore, the indeterminacy of the average opinion implies that even if the parameters of the stochastic processes governing the behavior of exogenous variables are assumed to be known by agents, they have no basis for assigning "the objective" probability distribution to the behavior of endogenous variables. Thus, individual agents have to deal with uncertainty, in the sense of Knight and Keynes, when they form expectations in decentralized markets.

The agents' forecasting problem is further complicated when government policy alters the parameters of the processes governing the behavior of exogenous variables. In such a situation the average opinion problem arises even if agents are assumed somehow to know the true parameters of the model and the intended change in policy is announced. The problem is that although an individual agent may know and believe the government announcement, he does not know if other agents also know and believe in the change in policy. Thus, the assumption of rational expectations is not generally appropriate for the analysis of policy changes. In fact, where the rational expectations approach predicts instantaneous movement to a new equilibrium, the difficulties faced by agents in their expectations formation will lead to a protracted period of disequilibrium.

---

[6] In the models with Hayekian local information, some of the exogenous variables appearing in the model may not be directly observable by agents. This decentralization of information may further compound the misspecification problem.

[7] The *ex ante* indeterminacy of the average opinion will still remain if agents receive information on the average opinion from an opinion poll or other institution external to the market. The problem is that for this information on the average opinion to reflect accurately the actual forecasts used by agents, the external institution would have to disseminate it *ex post*, after the decisions made on the basis of those forecasts have been consummated (Frydman, 1982a).

Because agents face fundamental obstacles in forming rational forecasts, it is not surprising that economists have thus far found it impossible to specify *the* model generating self-fulfilling forecasts. As a result, many models coexist in the real world.

The existence of a plurality of models raises additional logical problems about the meaning and applicability of the REH. There are obviously as many *candidates* for "the objective probability distribution of outcomes" as there are models; hence, it is not generally true of every rational expectations model extant that all agents are basing their expectations on that particular model. Thus, even if it is assumed that every agent somehow knows the relevant parameters of the economist's model and uses it in forming his forecasts, it is not implied that all or any agents, acting alone and seeking to maximize utility, will be led to impute to other agents the utilization of the same model. Thus, even the apparently implausible assumption that every agent knows the true values of the parameters of the economist's model is not sufficient for the derivation of rational expectations. One has to impose an additional sociological condition that entails *perceived and actual unanimity of beliefs across all agents* in the model being analyzed by the economist. Moreover, this universal consensus cannot pertain to more than one model. Hence, it would be an incongruity if Keynesians, monetarists, and supply-siders were simultaneously marrying their models to the REH when in logic the REH can at any moment be faithful to at most one. Yet this linkage of expectations with the particular model being analyzed by the economist has been considered one of the important advantages of the REH. It was presumed to have freed economic analysis from the arbitrariness introduced by ad hoc expectational assumptions in the period preceding rational expectations literature.

1.2. Expectations analyses in this book

This book is devoted to an examination of some of the fundamental problems related to the relevance and coherence of the REH. The chapters included in this book consider the following problems: applicability of the REH in an analysis of changes in macroeconomic policy (Chapters 2 and 3); expectational stability (Chapter 4); connections between individual rationality, the possibility of learning, decentralization of markets, and the REH (Chapter 5); convergence to the rational expectations equilibrium (Chapters 6 and 7); alternative strategies in individual decision making for modeling the decisions of other agents and corresponding notions of equilibria (Chapters 8 and 9); reconsideration of monetarist and Keynesian theories in the light of rational expectations (Chapter 10).

The authors of these chapters conduct their analyses in a variety of models, both macroeconomic and microeconomic. In order to clarify relationships among the chapters we shall attempt to outline the essence of most of the arguments and results in the context of a reformulated version of the Lucas (1973) model. In our presentation we shall sometimes omit idiosyncratic features of individual chapters.[8] A unified treatment allows a more general perspective. It may also facilitate comparisons between problems considered in this volume and the standard analysis in the rational expectations literature.

1.2.1.   *A model*

We set up a reformulated version of the Lucas (1973) model: Suppliers are assumed to be located in a large number of scattered competitive markets, indexed by $z = 1, \ldots, N$. Demand is distributed unevenly across markets. Hence, prices of goods vary across markets.

The quantity supplied in market z, $y_t^s(z)$, is assumed to be governed by

$$y_t^s(z) = \alpha [P_t(z) - {}_tF_z P_t] + u_t^s(z) + v_t^s \tag{1}$$

where α is the supply parameter, $P_t(z)$ is the market clearing price in z at t, P_t is the general price level defined as an average (across markets) of $P_t(z)$, ${}_tF_z P_t$ is the average of individual forecasts of P_t in z. These forecasts utilize information in $I_t(z) = \{P_t(z), P_{t-1}, P_{t-2}, \ldots, M_{t-1}, M_{t-2}, \ldots\}$; $u_t^s(z)$ is a local supply shock, $u_t^s(z) \sim N(0, \sigma_{u^s}^2)$, $\sum_{z=1}^{N} u_t^s(z) = 0$; v_t^s is an aggregate supply shock, $v_t^s \sim N(0, \sigma_{v^s}^2)$. All variables are expressed in logarithms, and $y_t^s(z)$ is measured relative to the natural rate of output.

We shall let ${}_tF_z P_t$ denote the (average) forecast of the general price level P_t, based on information including the current price in market z, $P_t(z)$. We often refer to the economy-wide forecast ${}_tFP_t$ as the (posterior) average opinion, thus adopting the term coined by Keynes. ${}_tFP_t$ is given by

$${}_tFP_t = \frac{1}{N} \sum_{z=1}^{N} {}_tF_z P_t \tag{2}$$

The quantity demanded in market z, $y_t^d(z)$, is assumed to be governed by

$$y_t^d(z) = \beta [M_t - P_t(z)] + u_t^d(z) + v_t^d \tag{3}$$

---

[8] Also, our interpretations do not necessarily have the concurrence of any individual author in whole or in part.

where β is the demand parameter; $u_t^d(z)$ is a relative demand shock, $u_t^d(z) \sim N(0, \sigma_{u^d}^2)$ and $(1/N) \sum_{z=1}^N u_t^d(z) = 0$; v_t^d is a velocity shock, $v_t^d = \rho v_{t-1}^d + \epsilon_t$, $|\rho| < 1$, and $\epsilon_t \sim N(0, \sigma_\epsilon^2)$; M_t is a money supply, assumed nonstochastic and fixed by the monetary authority; all variables are expressed in logarithms, and $y_t^d(z)$ is measured relative to the natural rate of output.[9]

We can now obtain solutions for $P_t(z)$ and P_t. Equating $y_t^s(z)$ in (1) and $y_t^d(z)$ in (3) yields

$$P_t(z) = \frac{1}{\alpha + \beta} [\beta M_t + \alpha_t F_z P_t + u_t(z) + v_t^d - v_t^s] \qquad (4)$$

where $u_t(z) = u_t^d(z) - u_t^s(z)$; $u_t \sim N(0, \sigma_u^2)$, $\sigma_u^2 = \sigma_{u^s}^2 + \sigma_{u^d}^2$; $u_t^d(z)$, $u_t^s(z)$, v_t^d, and v_t^s are assumed to be serially uncorrelated and uncorrelated with each other at all lags.

Averaging $P_t(z)$ in (4) across markets yields

$$P_t = \frac{1}{\alpha + \beta} [\beta M_t + \alpha_t F P_t + v_t^d - v_t^s] \qquad (5)$$

1.2.2. A guide to the problems considered in this book

We have already noted that one of the fundamental difficulties in providing an operational meaning for the REH is the absence of a definition and specification of "the objective probability distribution of outcomes." By "the objective" distribution, Muth and others meant the distribution of endogenous variables implied by the particular model being analyzed by the economist. At the very least this must mean in this context that the probability distributions of $P_t(z)$ and P_t are given by (4) and (5).

Phelps (Chapter 2) questions the plausibility of the assumption of perceived unanimity of beliefs in the situation in which the monetary authority undertakes an antiinflationary policy by changing the behavior of the money supply. He investigates the effects of the announced restrictive monetary policy when every agent believes in the central bank's new policy but does not necessarily know or believe that other agents know or believe in the announcement.

Phelps uses a price-setting model rather than a Walrasian auction market. In such a framework, the price preset on an island z does not contain information on the relative demand disturbance. Thus, the forecast of P_t

---

[9] Also, random variables $u_t^s(z)$, v_t^s, ϵ_t, and $u_t^d(z)$ are assumed to be uncorrelated serially and with each other.

on every island, $_{t-1}F_zP_t$, is based on the same information set $I_{t-1}=\{P_{t-1},P_{t-2},\ldots,M_{t-1},M_{t-2},\ldots\}$. In order to adapt the price-taking model set up in the previous section to the informational assumptions in the Phelps analysis, we assume that

$$_tF_zP_t=(1-\theta_t^{(z)})\,_{t-1}F_zP_t+\theta_t^{(z)}P_t(z) \tag{6}$$

where $\theta_t^{(z)}\in(0,1)$ and $_{t-1}F_zP_t$ is the prior average forecast of P_t in z based on I_{t-1}.[10]

Using (6) in (4), we obtain

$$P_t(z)=a_1^{(z)}M_t+a_2^{(z)}\,_{t-1}F_zP_t+a_3^{(z)}[u_t(z)+v_t^d-v_t^s] \tag{7}$$

where $a_1^{(z)}=\beta/[\beta+\alpha(1-\theta_t^{(z)})]$, $a_2^{(z)}=\alpha(1-\theta_t^{(z)})/[\beta+\alpha(1-\theta_t^{(z)})]$, and $a_3^{(z)}=a_1^{(z)}/\beta$. Aggregating (7) over z, we obtain

$$P_t=a_1M_t+a_2\,_{t-1}FP_t+a_3[v_t^d-v_t^s] \tag{8}$$

where $a_i=(1/N)\sum_{z=1}^N a_i^{(z)}$ $(i=1,2,3)$. Note that $a_1+a_2=1$.

In order to focus solely on the problem of the "beliefs of others," Phelps makes a number of standard rational expectations assumptions. He assumes that $a_i^{(z)}=a_i$ for all z and $i=1,2,3$ and that all agents know these coefficients. He also supposes that the behavior of P_t is known by all agents to be correctly specified in (8). In contrast to the situation under rational expectations, he supposes that individual agents do not know $_{t-1}FP_t$. With these assumptions he formulates *model theoretic expectations* in place of rational expectations. A model theoretic forecast based on (8) can be formally written as

$$_{t-1}FP_t=a_1\,_{t-1}FM_t+a_2\,_{t-1}F^2P_t+a_3\,\rho v_{t-1}^d \tag{9}$$

where $_{t-1}F^2=_{t-1}F_{t-1}F$ and $_{t-1}F$ is assumed to be a linear operator.

Now suppose that at the end of the period $t-1$ the central bank announces that it will stabilize M_t at some constant value M. If individual agents do not know or believe that other agents know or believe in the announced new policy, they will try to guess the average opinion $_{t-1}FM_t$.[11]

---

[10] The property in (6) has been proposed by Frydman (1982b). It can be thought of as a representation of homogeneity of individual forecasts. Moreover, Frydman shows that (6) can be justified as optimal forecasts based on subjective distributions held by individual agents.

[11] It should be noted that if one does *not* presume that the assumption of perceived or actual unanimity of beliefs necessarily holds, model theoretic expectations seem to correspond more closely to Muth's original statement of the REH than to the usual formulation of rational expectations.

Phelps shows that repeated application of the model theoretic expectations in (9) will lead to the infinite regress problem emphasized by Keynes in his "beauty contest" example.

The expression for the resulting price level, P_t, is given by

$$P_t = a_1 M_t + a_1 \sum_{i=1}^{\infty} a_2^i {}_{t-1} F^i M_t + \frac{a_3}{a_1} \rho v_{t-1}^d + a_3 (\epsilon_t - v_t^s) \tag{10}$$

It also follows that forecast errors for model theoretic expectations depend on the errors of the forecasts of the average forecast of other agents. Because in the decentralized economy individual agents may not be able to ascertain the forecasts of others, those forecast errors might persist for a long period of time. The length of this period will matter for the magnitude of output losses resulting from a disinflation program.

In contrast to (10), the standard rational expectations result that the announced change in policy will have "neutral" effects can be written as

$$P_t = M_t + \frac{a_3}{a_1} \rho v_{t-1}^d + a_3 (\epsilon_t - v_t^s) \tag{11}$$

Thus, the standard rational expectations conclusions follow only if every agent believes in the government announcement and believes that other agents know and believe in the announcement, and if in fact the government carries out the announced policy.[12] Stated differently, an instantaneous transition to the new rational expectations equilibrium requires a perceived and actual unanimity of beliefs. Such consensus of perceptions cannot generally be achieved by individual agents acting alone in decentralized markets. Thus, institutions and social norms external to markets may play important roles in the success of antiinflationary policy.

Model theoretic forecasts and expectations of others' expectations also play central roles in Di Tata's analysis (Chapter 3) of transitional effects of changes in monetary policy based on the feedback rule. Using a version of the Lucas (1973) model with an explicit stochastic framework, Di Tata is able to address additional issues not considered by Phelps.

Di Tata's analysis of the moments of output and price level during the transition from one rule to another shows that the variance of output increases. Using this result, he argues that a transition from the activist policy of the feedback type (which has been pursued for a long time) to

[12] In a different model, a stronger conclusion (viz., that the convergence to the rational expectations equilibrium will not, in general, take place) has been derived by Frydman (1982a) in his analysis of learning in a decentralized market.

Friedman's fixed-money-growth rule may substantially increase output fluctuations.[13] Like all other results in Di Tata's chapter, this conclusion is based on the assumption that individual agents misperceive the expectations of other agents during a period of transition from one policy rule to another. Di Tata also shows that this misperception can provide an explanation for the serial correlation of output from its natural level.

Further aspects of the transitional effects of changes in the policy rule on output and price level can be analyzed by considering their sources. Using the model formulated in the previous section, we can derive an expression for the perceived relative price effect on output (aggregated over markets z). Using model theoretic expectations in (8) and (9) and simplifying the analysis by assuming that $_{t-1}F^2P_t = {_{t-1}}F^3P_t = \ldots$, we obtain the following expression:

$$P_t - {_{t-1}}FP_t = a_1(M_t - {_{t-1}}F^2M_t) + a_1^2({_{t-1}}F^2M_t - {_{t-1}}FM_t) + a_3(\epsilon_t - v_t^s)$$

(12)

Expression (12) makes it clear that the confusion between relative price movements and general price movements derives from two effects: first, the familiar island effect, represented by $a_3(\epsilon_t - v_t^s)$, arising from the inability of individual agents to separate aggregate and relative demand and supply shocks; second, the effect represented by $a_1(M_t - {_{t-1}}F^2M_t) + a_1^2({_{t-1}}F^2M_t - {_{t-1}}FM_t)$, arising from misperceptions by individual agents of the average of expectations held by other agents.[14] However, the confusion of individual agents between relative and absolute price movements in this model differs fundamentally from the confusion in the Lucas model. Under rational expectations, agents can form "the objective" conditional expectations of unobserved P_t on the observed $P_t(z)$. In contrast, in this model, even if agents know the distribution of shocks, they cannot form such conditional expectations, because they cannot ascertain $_{t-1}FP_t$ and $_{t-1}F^2P_t$ on the basis of information available to them in decentralized markets. Thus, the forecast errors can persist here for a long period of time.

Phelps and Di Tata analyze a transition from one rational expectations equilibrium to another. Evans (Chapter 4) considers a related problem of convergence to the rational expectations equilibrium from the situation in which agents use some initial, arbitrary forecast function, which might, in particular, be the rational forecast function for the preceding policy regime. Like Phelps and Di Tata, Evans also assumes that every

---

[13] It should be noted that this argument does not imply that a transition from erratic monetary policy to a fixed rule policy is not desirable.

[14] Note that under rational expectations the latter effect vanishes.

agent knows the true values of the parameters of the model. This assumption allows a separation of the problem of the inherent expectational stability of the rational expectations equilibrium from the problems of learning the parameters by individual agents.

As in Phelps's analysis, Evans assumes that individual agents calculate forecasts using the model and an assumption about the expectations held by other agents. In the context of the present model, Evans assumes that a version of (9) holds in which it is additionally assumed that $_{t-1}FM_t = M_t$ (i.e., agents know and believe in the announced new policy), so that

$$_{t-1}FP_t = a_1 M_t + a_2 {}_{t-1}F^2 P_t + a_3 \rho v_{t-1}^d \qquad (13)$$

Evans argues that the standard rational expectations solution $_{t-1}FP_t = {}_{t-1}\bar{F}P_t \equiv M_t + (a_3/a_1)\rho v_{t-1}^d$ does not follow solely from individual rationality and knowledge of the model, because this requires the additional assumption that $_{t-1}F^2 P_t = {}_{t-1}\bar{F}P_t$ or, equivalently, $_{t-1}F^2 P_t = {}_{t-1}FP_t$. The rational expectations solution is thus an expectational equilibrium in which agents hold the expectations they are conjectured to hold by other agents.

The question then arises as to the stability of this equilibrium. In order to describe Evans's approach to this question, let us suppose that initially *all* agents contemplate using a particular forecast function denoted by $_{t-1}F^{(0)}P_t$. Evans assumes that every agent knows or imputes to other agents the use of the same forecast, $_{t-1}F^{(0)}P_t$, as his own.[15,16] Therefore, an individual agent can improve his forecasts by revising his forecast function. The revised forecast function can be obtained by applying model theoretic expectations in (13) with $_{t-1}F^2 P_t = {}_{t-1}F^{(0)}P_t$ to obtain a new forecast. If every agent revises his forecast function in this manner, the revised average opinion, $_{t-1}F^{(1)}P_t$, can be written as

$$_{t-1}F^{(1)}P_t = a_1 M_t + a_2 {}_{t-1}F^{(0)}P_t + a_3 \rho v_{t-1}^d \qquad (14)$$

Repeating this procedure N times yields

$$_{t-1}F^{(N)}P_t = (a_1 M_t + a_3 \rho v_{t-1}^d) \sum_{i=0}^{N} a_2^i + a_2^N {}_{t-1}F^{(0)}P_t \qquad (15)$$

Letting N go to infinity gives

---

[15] For a criticism of this unanimity-of-beliefs assumption, see the comment by Calvo following Chapter 4.

[16] Note that we describe here a hypothetical conjectural revision process for forecast functions. All of the revisions take place at time $t-1$. Evans remarks that this process could also be interpreted to take place in real time. Under such an interpretation, the question of learning the forecast functions used by other agents inevitably arises. See Chapter 4 for further discussion of this point and other possible interpretations of this revision process.

$$_{t-1}F^{(N)}P_t \rightarrow {}_{t-1}\bar{F}P_t = M_t + \frac{a_3}{a_1}\rho v_{t-1}^d \tag{16}$$

where $_{t-1}\bar{F}P_t$ is the rational forecast of the prior mean of P_t.

Note that the convergence to $_{t-1}\bar{F}P_t$ takes place for any arbitrary initial forecast function $_{t-1}F^{(0)}P_t$. In Evans's terminology, the rational expectations equilibrium is globally *stable* in this model. Evans gives examples of both stable and unstable equilibria in a variety of macroeconomic models involving expectations of sales and output as well as prices.

An interesting aspect of Evans's approach is that expectational stability is not necessarily related to the stationarity or nonstationarity of the behavior of endogenous variables under either "rational" or static expectations.

Finally, as in the analyses of Phelps and Di Tata, Evans points out that even with a known change in policy, the transition to the new equilibrium will not generally be instantaneous. Even in the stable model analyzed here it is quite possible that, beginning with an initial forecast function $_{t-1}F^{(0)}P_t$ appropriate, say, to the preceding policy regime, agents will not immediately move to the limit of the revision process, because they may not believe that other agents will do so. It pays to be one step ahead of the average opinion, but no more. If a rational expectations solution is expectationally unstable, there are more fundamental problems. The attempts by agents to ascertain the average opinion of other agents might even lead to a permanent state of disequilibrium in models that do not possess a stable equilibrium.

Phelps, Di Tata, and Evans concentrate their analyses on the problem of expectations of others' expectations under the assumption that individual agents know the true values of the parameters of the model. Their analyses emphasize the point that individual rationality and knowledge of the model do not necessarily imply that individual agents will form equilibrium forecasts. Moreover, in the analyses of Phelps and Di Tata, model theoretic expectations – which embody the assumption that individually rational agents can and will use the model in forming their forecasts – lead to an infinite regress problem. This infinite regress problem is usually circumvented by the assumption that every agent forms his expectations according to the equilibrium forecast function under the presumption that other agents also use their equilibrium forecast functions. Thus, the assumption of the rational expectations equilibrium entails the *collective consistency* of individual plans. It is important to emphasize that such collective consistency of plans is not sufficient to provide the economic justification for the relevance of the notion of the rational expectations equilibrium in the analysis of decentralized markets. The traditional neoclassical analysis of individual behavior is not based on the collective consistency of plans, but on the assumption of *individual rationality*. Thus, in order to reconcile the neoclassical approach with the notion of the rational expectations equilibrium, one is required to connect the postulated equilibrium behavior with the rational behavior of individual agents. This connection between rational expectations and individual rationality in decentralized competitive markets is investigated by Frydman in Chapter 5.

The crucial feature of Frydman's approach is the postulate that information available to individual agents includes *only information they can acquire according to the model* in the process of making individual decisions and observing market outcomes.[17] This postulate requires that the REH be *internally consistent* with other informational assumptions of the model.

In order to carry out an analysis of internal consistency in the Lucas (1975) business cycle model, Frydman assumes that individual agents can somehow observe the rational expectations equilibrium prices.[18] As is well known, the dynamics of the Lucas business cycle model crucially depend on the assumption that individual agents cannot observe aggregate money supply and capital stocks. Frydman argues that this assumption implies that individual agents cannot infer some of the parameters of the rational forecast functions even on the basis of equilibrium observations. Therefore, the REH conflicts with the assumption of decentralization of information on money and capital stocks in the Lucas model.

In order to investigate further the informational requirements of the rational expectations equilibrium, Frydman extends the model formulated in the previous section to allow for differences in supply parameters. He demonstrates that the parameters of the rational expectations equilibrium forecast functions of an individual agent depend on the supply parameters of other agents. This result is not surprising, because the equilibrium price function depends in this model on all of the supply parameters. However, an important implication of this result is that in order to base the rational expectations equilibrium on individual behavior, one would have to require that every individual agent know the

[17] This postulate was already emphasized by Hayek (1948a). It also plays an important role in the approach of Phelps et al. (1970). It should be noted that the distinction between "the situation as perceived by individual suppliers... and the aggregate situation as seen by an outside observer" (Lucas, 1973, p. 133) lies at the very foundation of the Lucas approach to modeling business cycle behavior.

[18] It will become clear shortly why this analysis has to be interpreted as purely hypothetical.

behavioral parameters of the other agents.[19] The imposition of this requirement not only would have no "operational meaning" in the decentralized economy but also would undermine the fundamental notion that decentralized markets economize on the information required by agents in making their economic decisions.

There is another serious problem in the definition of the rational expectations equilibrium. It is clear that markets can be in the rational expectations equilibrium if and only if individual agents form their expectations according to the equilibrium forecast functions. Thus, the assumption of rational expectations cannot be given an "operational meaning" by assuming that markets are in the rational expectations equilibrium.[20] The hypothesis that agents use equilibrium forecast functions has no "operational meaning" unless and until it is shown that it is possible for the agents to learn the parameters of those functions and converge to equilibrium.

In the spirit of the REH, Frydman investigates the possibility of "rational learning," that is, learning on the basis of the correct specification of the structure of the model. He demonstrates that such learning will require that individual agents know the average forecast function used by other agents. Because individual agents cannot ascertain the average opinion in decentralized markets, Frydman concludes that individual agents cannot learn the parameters of the rational forecast functions on the basis of information available to them and the correct specification of the model.

An implication of this analysis is that individual agents cannot use regression techniques to form standard "optimal" (i.e., minimum mean square error) forecasts.

The conclusion that individual agents cannot form optimal forecasts on the basis of the correctly specified models raises the question of learning on the basis of misspecified models. Frydman investigates least-squares forecasting on the basis of misspecified models and shows that if all other agents use any specific least-squares forecast function, an individual agent will be led to use a different forecast function. Thus, the average forecast function is fundamentally indeterminate in this model; that is, the parameters and variables in this function cannot be ascertained by individual agents acting in isolation or by an "outside observer." This result provides a rationale in the context of the model for

---

[19] The usual presumption that one can conduct the rational expectations analysis "as if" every agent knows the parameters of the equilibrium price function is discussed in Section 5.3 of Chapter 5.

[20] For an explicit statement of such a justification of rational expectations, see Lucas (1975).

the analyses of Phelps and Di Tata, who assumed that individual agents cannot ascertain the average opinion. It also implies that autoregressive behavior of output and prices can be explained by an appeal to learning, without the introduction of price sluggishness, serial correlation of exogenous shocks, costs of adjustment, or wage contracts.

Frydman concludes that the assumption of rational expectations is simply ad hoc, as it cannot be justified by an appeal to the postulate that individual agents process "optimally" the information available to them. Consequently, there is an important distinction between the basic optimality postulate in economics and the REH. Furthermore, the notion of decentralization as formalized in the rational expectations models appears difficult to reconcile with the assumption of the rational expectations equilibrium.

The inability to specify optimal forecasting rules for individual agents has prompted a search for nonoptimal rules that will lead to convergence. Bray (Chapter 6) demonstrates convergence to the rational expectations equilibrium for a particular rule in the context of a simplified version of the Sargent and Wallace (1975) model.

Bray's analysis can be illustrated in a modified version of our model. Assuming that M_t is equal to a constant for all t, say M, and that $\rho \equiv 0$, we can write (8) as

$$P_t = b_1 M + b_2 {}_{t-1}FP_t + a_3 \eta_t \tag{17}$$

where we assume that η_t are independent identically distributed (i.i.d.) random variables with zero mean and finite variance and $0 < b_1 + b_2 < 1$.[21]

Bray postulates that the forecast function for the next period's price is the average of past prices; that is,

$$_{t-1}FP_t = \frac{1}{t} \sum_{i=0}^{t-1} P_i \tag{18}$$

She demonstrates that $_{t-1}FP_1$ converges almost surely to the rational expectations equilibrium forecast function, $\bar{F}P_t$, in this model; $_{t-1}\bar{F}P_t$ is given by

$$_{t-1}\bar{F}P_t = \frac{b_1 M}{1 - b_2} \quad \text{for all } t \tag{19}$$

It should be noted that Bray's ingenious result relies on the assumption that all agents will collectively adhere to the individually nonoptimal and

---

[21] In Bray's model the rational forecast function depends on *unknown* parameters. To preserve this property here and obtain convergence, we assume that $b_1 + b_2 < 1$.

biased forecasts postulated in (18).[22] Such collective adherence to individually nonoptimal forecast rules conflicts with the assumption of individual rationality and the traditional conception of individual behavior in decentralized markets.

Bray's model is characterized by an absence of any stochastic exogenous variables that are not i.i.d. disturbances. In Chapter 7, Frydman introduces a modification of the model that allows for the more general stochastic properties of exogenous variables. To illustrate his result, suppose that $\rho \neq 0$ (i.e., v_t^d is autocorrelated). Then we can write (17) as

$$P_t = b_1 M + b_2 \,_{t-1}FP_t + a_3 \rho v_{t-1}^d + a_2 \eta_t \qquad (20)$$

where from (3) and (8), $\eta_t = \epsilon_t - v_t^s$.

Assuming that $_{t-1}FP_t$ is given by Bray's forecast rule, Frydman proves that

$$_{t-1}FP_t = \frac{1}{t} \sum_{i=0}^{t-1} P_i \xrightarrow[\text{almost} \atop \text{surely}]{} \frac{b_1 M}{1 - b_2} \qquad (21)$$

However, in contrast to Bray's model, the rational expectations forecast function in the model in (20) is given by

$$_{t-1}\bar{F}P_t = \frac{b_1 M}{1 - b_2} + \frac{a_3 \rho}{1 - b_2} v_{t-1}^d \qquad (22)$$

Given that the agents use only the mean of past values of prices in their forecasts, it is not surprising that the forecast rule in (18) does not lead to convergence to the rational expectations equilibrium in the model allowing for non-i.i.d. exogenous variables.[23]

Furthermore, note that if $_{t-1}FP_t = E(P_t)$, then (20) implies that $E(P_t) = b_1 M/(1 - b_2)$. In view of this result and (21), Frydman defines an alternative weaker notion of equilibrium, called the *unconditional expectational equilibrium*. This equilibrium is characterized by the equality of the forecast function, $_{t-1}\bar{F}P_t$, and $E(P_t)$. It can be interpreted as a notion of aggregate equilibrium, in the sense that the average (across agents)

---

[22] Bray herself discusses this important qualification of her result. This point has also been discussed by Frydman (1982*a*).

[23] We also note that the rational forecast function in Bray's model contains just one reduced-form parameter: $b_1 M/(1 - b_2)$. The literature does not contain any results on convergence of least-squares forecasts when the rational forecast function contains more than one unknown reduced-form parameter. In another analysis of convergence, Bray (1982) reduced, by assumption, the number of unknown parameters of the rational forecast function from two to one.

forecast $_{t-1}\tilde{F}P_t$ is on the average (over time) correct.[24, 25] More intuitively, this forecasting procedure supposes that agents are trying to forecast only the means of the endogenous variables, rather than their particular realizations. The equilibrium average forecast is unbiased, but not, in general, rational in the sense of Muth.

The simple forecast rule proposed by Bray does not lead to convergence to the rational expectations equilibrium in a more general model analyzed by Frydman in Chapter 7. Nevertheless, in both models the sequence of prices converges to the unique limiting prices. It is, however, possible that although the specific learning process leads to convergence, limiting prices are not unique. This is the problem addressed by Kirman in Chapter 8.

Kirman conducts his analysis in a simple duopoly model. He assumes that every duopolist does not know the parameters of his demand function and prices set by the other duopolist.[26] He also assumes that every duopolist treats a price set by the other duopolist as a random disturbance term in his demand function and tries to learn the parameters of this function using the least-squares procedure.

The main result of Kirman's analysis is that there exists a set of limiting prices, set by duopolists, such that any pair of prices in this set is a limit point of the least-squares learning process. Furthermore, for a particular pair of limiting prices there exist initial prices set by the duopolists at the beginning of the learning process that lead to convergence to those limiting prices.

Another important characteristic of Kirman's results is that in the limit duopolists will not generally learn the true values of the parameters of their demand functions.[27] Yet, despite the fact that in the limit demand

[24] The lack of explicit reference to individual forecasting behavior and rationality is clearly the major deficiency of this equilibrium concept.

[25] This equilibrium notion can be used as a procedure for solving out for expectational variables in the macroeconomic models. In Chapter 7, Frydman discusses briefly its implications for the short-run effectiveness of monetary policy based on the feedback rule and an interpretation of the standard test of the rational expectations hypothesis.

[26] Kirman notes that the assumption that every agent does not know prices set by the other agent is not plausible in the duopoly situation. However, his results remain unchanged in the case of monopolistic competition with a large number of agents. In such a case, the assumption that every agent is ignorant of prices set by at least a subset of other agents is much more plausible.

[27] Note that Kirman (1975) showed that if only one parameter of the demand functions is unknown by duopolists, a reasonable learning process leads to convergence to Cournot equilibrium. The problem in Kirman's Chapter 8 in

functions are misspecified, duopolists will not be able to reject or modify misspecified models on the basis of information available to them. Agents are trapped in what Kirman calls "misinformed equilibrium," in which no agent has any reason to modify his behavior, and *every agent makes* ex ante *maximizing decisions on the basis of his perceived model.* Furthermore, these decisions are "self-fulfilling" in the sense that they also remain optimal *ex post* after the agents observe the resulting market outcomes.

Kirman's example in which there exists a whole class of outcomes of the learning process that are equilibria from the individual-optimality point of view suggests that the study of learning is not just an appendage to the elegant abstraction of the equilibrium analysis.[28] Which equilibria are empirically observed, if any, may well depend on the learning process and the set of initial conditions. As already emphasized by Hayek (1948a, p. 46), "the significant point here is that it is these apparently subsidiary hypotheses or assumptions that people do learn from experience, and about how they acquire knowledge, which constitute the empirical content of our propositions about what happens in the *real world*" (emphasis added).

The analysis in the chapters discussed thus far implies that it might be difficult to reconcile rational expectations with the basic individual-optimality assumption in economics. Moreover, convergence to the *strong form* of rational expectations equilibrium (i.e., equilibrium in the sense of Muth and Lucas) seems problematic.

Recognizing these difficulties in establishing the theoretical foundations of rational expectations, Townsend (Chapter 9) suggests that rational expectations models should be constructed and analyzed from the point of view of their ability to generate testable implications and their conformity with the observed time-series behavior of endogenous variables. Motivated by these considerations, Townsend proposes a reformulation of the standard notion of rational expectations equilibrium. His reformulation allows not only modeling of the behavior of endogenous variables but also modeling of the movements of average opinion. Thus, Townsend's approach attempts to integrate the problem of expectations of others' expectations, considered by other authors in this book, with the traditional approach in the rational expectations literature.

this book arises because there are two unknown parameters. Thus, it seems that there is a formal connection between Kirman's results and the analysis of Bray (Chapter 6) and Frydman (Chapter 7). See footnote 23 for further discussion of this point.

[28] However, see the comment by Green following Chapter 8 for a criticism of myopic optimization rules used by Kirman.

Townsend conducts his analysis in his own version of the Muth (1961) model. We shall now outline his approach in a version of the Lucas (1973) model formulated in the previous section. Thus, suppose that the behavior of the price level is given by expression (8), rewritten here with $M_t = M$ for all t:

$$P_t = a_1 M + a_2 \,_{t-1}FP_t + a_3 v_t^d - a_3 v_t^s \tag{23}$$

Applying model theoretic expectations in (23) yields

$$_{t-1}F_{(i)} P_t = a_1 M + a_2 \,_{t-1}F_{(i)} \,_{t-1}FP_t + a_3 \,_{t-1}F_{(i)} v_t^d \tag{24}$$

where $F_{(i)}$ denotes a forecast held by agent i.[29]

Averaging (24) across all agents yields

$$_{t-1}FP_t = a_1 M + a_2 \,_{t-1}F^2 P_t + a_3 \,_{t-1}Fv_t^d \tag{25}$$

Thus, the average opinion of P_t of the first order, $_{t-1}FP_t$, depends on the average opinion of the second order of P_t, $_{t-1}F^2 P_t$, and the average opinion of the first order of v_t^d, $_{t-1}Fv_t^d$.

Applying model theoretic expectations recursively in (24) and (25) and plugging the resulting expression for $_{t-1}FP_t$ into (25) can be shown to yield[30]

$$P_t = M + a_3 \sum_{j=1}^{\infty} a_2^j F^j v_t^d + a_3 v_t^d - a_3 v_t^s \tag{26}$$

Following Townsend, define a new set of variables $\phi_t = \{\phi_{0t}, \phi_{1t}, \phi_{2t}, \dots\}$. Let $\phi_{0t} = v_t^d$, and let the prior mean held by an agent i on ϕ_{0t} be denoted by $m_{0t}(i)$. Furthermore, define $\phi_{1t} = (1/N) \sum_{i=1}^{N} m_{0t}(i)$, and let the prior mean held by agent i on ϕ_{1t} be $m_{1t}(i)$. Continuing in this manner, the entire vector $m_t(i) = \{m_{0t}(i), m_{1t}(i), m_{2t}(i), \dots\}$ can be defined. Townsend assumes that beliefs held by individual agents can be characterized by the infinite dimensional normal distribution with mean vector $m_t(i)$ and covariance matrix Σ_t. It should be noted that he also suggests procedures for truncating the infinite regress.

The crucial assumption made by Townsend is that although the vector of prior means differs across agents, the covariance matrix Σ_t of beliefs is the same.[31,32] This assumption allows a specification of individual

[29] We follow Townsend here in assuming that individual agents are trying to forecast the contemporaneous value of v_t^d.

[30] Note the similarities and differences between expression (26) and expression (10) derived in our analysis of Phelps's Chapter 2.

[31] The assumption that Σ_t is the same across agents seems to preclude a plausible interpretation of Townsend's approach from the point of view of individual behavior. The assumption of unanimity of views on Σ_t, which is the covariance

forecasts and movements of average forecasts over time. The individual forecast of an agent i can be written from (26) as[33]

$$_{t-1}F_{(i)}P_t = M + a_3 \sum_{j=0}^{\infty} a_2^j m_{jt}(i) \qquad (27)$$

Using (27), every agent can formulate his output decision according to (1).[34] The resulting equilibrium price can be computed from (23) and (27), and it is given by

$$P_t = M + a_3 \sum_{j=0}^{\infty} a_2^j \phi_{jt} - a_3 v_t^s \qquad (28)$$

Expressions (27) and (28), together with the equations to be discussed shortly describing the movement of the parameters ϕ_{jt} over time, define the rational expectations equilibrium. This equilibrium notion allows for agents' forecasts of average opinions of all orders. It is important to note that this equilibrium notion presupposes that all agents take the parameters a_2 and a_3 as given or "known" to them.[35]

Finally, to specify the movements of average opinions of all orders over time, Townsend supposes that $m_t(i)$ and Σ_t are updated using Bayesian procedures. The common knowledge and unanimity on Σ_t provide individual agents with the knowledge of updating rules used by other agents. Taking those rules as given, individual agents update their decisions over time, and the economic model moves from one rational expectations equilibrium to another.

It should also be noted that Townsend defines learning and convergence in a different way than do the other authors in this book. By "learning" he does not mean learning the parameters, but acquisition of

matrix of *individual* beliefs, is even stronger than unanimity of views on the behavior of endogenous variables required in the standard REH approach. Note, however, that Townsend is aware of this problem and proposes the reinterpretation of his models as descriptive models of behavior of observed time series.

[32] More complicated specifications of the distributions of beliefs are also explored by Townsend. However, all of them rely on similar assumptions.

[33] Thus, despite the difficulties outlined in footnote 31, Townsend's approach still relies on some notion of individual behavior.

[34] Note that for simplicity we describe here Townsend's approach in the homogeneous information case, that is, after the assumption in (6) has been imposed. Townsend's approach is also applicable to the complete "island" model with relative demand shocks playing an explicit role; see Section 9.7.

[35] As in the case of the standard rational expectations approach, the difficulties of agents in learning the parameters will be present here as well.

information over time on the realizations of exogenous shocks. Furthermore, "convergence" does not refer to convergence to the rational expectations equilibrium, because this equilibrium is *assumed* to hold in
every time period. By "convergence," Townsend means convergence of
Σ_t to some steady-state matrix $\bar{\Sigma}$. In fact, he demonstrates that the limiting matrix $\bar{\Sigma}$ will not in general be equal to the null matrix; that is, convergence to the strong form of rational expectations will not take place in
the model. Nevertheless, convergence to some steady-state matrix plays
an important role in Townsend's approach. It allows the generation of
stationary behavior of endogenous variables and thus is required for use
of standard statistical techniques in the implementation of his approach
in *descriptive modeling* of *time-series* behavior. Townsend's analysis of
models with various informational assumptions shows that, *in principle,*
interesting dynamic behavior can be generated using his approach. However, as Townsend (1981, p. 31) emphasized in an earlier study, "the
theory may well be satisfactory in explaining certain stylized facts of the
data . . . and yet be rejected outright in a formal statistical test of the null
hypothesis." [36]

This book closes with a discussion by Leijonhufvud (Chapter 10) of
the Keynesian, monetarist, and rational expectations approaches to
macroeconomics. He begins with an examination of the treatment of
expectations in macroeconomic models. He distinguishes between "well-
behaved" expectations, linked in a stable manner to observable variables, and "ill-behaved" expectations, which are not only incorrect but
also inconsistent across agents.

This distinction is subsequently used in an analysis of the short-term
and long-term expectations of the price level. The key point in this part
of the analysis is that the behavior of expectations should not be analyzed
within the context of the particular economist's model; rather, it should
be based on examination of existing monetary institutions. In fact, a useful and workable model linking expectations of the price level to the
observable variables can be formulated only if monetary policy and institutions are sufficiently stable.

Recognizing insurmountable difficulties faced by agents in forming
price level expectations under the current "random-walk monetary
regime," Leijonhufvud argues for a constitutional constraint on monetary policy. However, in addition to the usual focus on the credibility
problem, Leijonhufvud emphasizes the role of a monetary constitution in alleviating the average opinion problem. As he put it, "some

---

[36] Such testing of Townsend's approach is a task for future research.

social institutions exist because they rationally solve the conjectural interdependence that cannot be left simply to the rational expectations of individual agents." [37]

After presenting an argument that a monetary constitution will make the long-term price level expectations well-behaved, Leijonhufvud points out that the behavior of the money stock, if exogenous and observed, cannot explain island-type problems of forecasting the general price and wage levels; rather, this forecasting problem is primarily attributable to the endogenous variation in bank credit, if unobserved: the Wicksellian wedge between the market and natural rates. This leads him to question the plausibility of the explanations of business cycles that rely on exogenous monetary impulses causing the agents' inability to disentangle the real and nominal disturbances.

In place of those explanations of the cycle, Leijonhufvud urges a "disequilibrium Keynes-Wicksell" theory of the cycle in which the absence of forward markets leads to the difficulties in coordinating intertemporal decisions, that is, investment and saving. Exogenous real shocks, such as technical innovations, political events abroad, and the lack of intertemporal coordination, drive the cycle.

An interesting aspect of this part of the analysis is that it is conducted in the context of the constitutional monetary regime guaranteeing the long-term stability of the price level. The belief that prices will return to the constitutionally mandated level is one of the reasons why the upswing in the cycle will peak.

The last part of Chapter 10 compares various theories of business cycles from the point of view of information available to agents and their expectations formation. Leijonhufvud identifies a key distinguishing feature of the Keynes-Wicksell disequilibrium cycle theory: that "the expectations of entrepreneurs taken collectively are inconsistent with those held in the financial markets." Because the unanimity-of-beliefs postulate is a crucial element in the rational expectations method, Leijonhufvud concludes that the "rational expectations equilibrium" approach to business cycle theory is incompatible with the Keynes-Wicksell approach.

1.3.   Review and reflections

When Muth was pondering in the early 1960s the fluctuations of farm prices and the force of expectations on their behavior, he hit on what

---

[37] See the analyses of Phelps (Chapter 2) and Frydman (1982a) for a related argument on the connections between social institutions and the average opinion problem.

may have seemed a pragmatic and crafty solution to a hitherto intractable conundrum: Why not suppose that the farmers' expectations are "essentially the same as the predictions of the relevant economic theory"? Muth believed that this supposition adequately captured the idea that "information is scarce, and the economic system generally does not waste it" (Muth, 1961, p. 316), and hence he dubbed it the rational expectations hypothesis (REH).

But this audacious proposal ran against logical and epistemological barriers. Although expectations were assumed to depend on the structure of the relevant economic model, the notion of the relevant model was left undefined. It has subsequently been presumed, either implicitly in the theoretical models or explicitly in the econometric applications, that the relevant model used by the representative or average agent is the same as the particular model being analyzed by the economist – which is what Muth did, although he warned against doing it! Econometric methods were called on to deliver the estimates of the thus-defined relevant model. But unless the actors in the economy have always lived in an epistemological garden of Eden, where the economist's model of endogenous variables has been the one and only relevant model and where each actor has never embraced another model, has never embraced the hypotheses that others have, and has never entertained the possibility that the others might forecast the exogenous factors differently, the estimation of the model is bound to be contaminated by the misestimations of the real-life actors (via their resulting supply–demand behavior). The analyst's estimation will not yield pristine estimates of the model – of the parameters as they would appear if the actors themselves always knew them. Real-time history provides no opportunity for a "tâtonnement" (of estimations) of commonly embraced and known-to-be-embraced models – a process vastly beyond any Walrasian tâtonnement involving only a sequence of (known and foreseen) prices.

Ultimately it seems that the vulgarizations of an idea either immortalize it or destroy it. It is one of the great confusions of the 1970s that the REH, as practiced by analysts, has come to be viewed as tantamount to the postulate of utility maximization with regard to the *interpretation of information*. If it is axiomatic that the household maximizes utility, according to the newest textbooks, then it follows that households process information "rationally" – meaning optimally. But this is a play on words. By "rationality," Muth meant calculation according to the specified model, the model used by the analyst – *not* the shrewd optimizing predictive behavior of an agent *necessarily* uncertain of the right model to describe the system at each moment of real time when the other agents are equally floundering about for a better (let alone the best) model.

The suggestion of the vulgar rational expectations theory – that mere intelligence by the actors will succeed in avoiding disequilibrium situations (situations of incorrect expectations) no matter what the situation or the policy rule explicitly adopted by the government – is not sustainable. It is a false and invalid rendering of what could and should have been the original Muthian contribution: the idea that the agents being modeled may themselves use models in forming their expectations.

One of our themes, then, a theme sounded here in a macroesque (rather than Marshallian) context, is the general impossibility of "rationality," as distinct from private (or individual) optimality, in expectations. The "hypothesis" of rational expectations is like the "hypothesis" of the knowability of God. There is an epistemological, or methodological, difficulty standing in the way of that hypothesis before problems of statistical inference from data are even sighted (much less surmounted). This theme serves as a sort of underlying "ground bass" for this book as a whole.

The more distinctive note sounded by this book, however, is its look into the *consequences* of the inapplicability of the REH. This book could as well have borne the title *Beyond Rational Expectations*. Are the effects and costs of adopting the hypothesis of rational expectations, despite its unsuitability, comparable to the effects and costs that might be anticipated from proceeding with the postulate of utility maximization, despite its unrealism?

The various findings here indicate a critical problem for the rational expectations method. We are quite prepared to stipulate, for the sake of argument at any rate, that the *unrealism* of the rational expectations hypothesis is a theoretical *virtue*. Never mind that the hypothesis is closer in spirit to a planned economy than to a decentralized market economy. The critical *fault* of the hypothesis is not its unrealism but rather its lack of *robustness*. Once we recognize the apparently insurmountable difficulties faced by decentralized agents in learning the parameters or knowing the behavior of some of the exogenous variables, it is natural to experiment with hypotheses of *optimal* expectations formation by agents, each one using only the information and knowledge implied by the model to be available to him. But once the theoretical door is opened to one or more hypotheses of *optimality* in the expectations formation of the individual agents, the implied behavior of the (otherwise identical) model is often found to be wrenched into directions far from the behavior implied by the rational expectations hypothesis. In short, a Pandora's box of disequilibrium behavior is opened up.

This is not to suggest, however, that there exists in the world a general tendency toward permanent and wholesale disequilibrium – toward a situation in which individual expectations of all or nearly all variables, such as the average money wage and the real rate of interest, to mention two variables prominently figuring in some disequilibrium theories of employment fluctuations, are systematically misforecast in the same direction indefinitely. With respect to expectations of some variables in some situations, we believe that there may be a rapid reequilibration – a rapid dissolving of the disequilibrium effects of the initial disturbance, such as a change in policy. Still, such a reequilibration scenario is qualitatively different from the REH implication of continuous equilibrium (in the expected-value sense), and the period of disequilibrium may be quantitatively of immense importance! Moreover, the reequilibration process may depend for its success on the power of institutions and norms *external to the market* (i.e., conventional theories, traditions, business practices, consensus over government policy, etc.).

It is perhaps striking that the issues raised in this book touch on social, or moral, philosophy. Possibly a latent motive behind the widespread (though hardly unanimous) advocacy of the rational expectations method is the passionate conviction held by some that policy analysis – which is what most economists are ultimately interested in doing or enabling – ought not to be carried out with models in which there are implied errors in expectations about the effects of the studied policy proposal; the belief is that it would be immoral of the government to adopt a policy that might produce some benefits through misexpectations of its effect. But this seems wrongheaded: First, there is nothing to prevent the government from announcing its own forecast of the effect of its policy. Second, whether or not it does that, it will not want to obtain its parameter estimates from a model made untrustworthy by the unsuitable imposition of the hypothesis that agents have enjoyed rational expectations over the sample period. Finally, where is there a true model that the government could act on with the conviction that it is true and believed by the public?

The proposal to use the rational expectations method in policy analysis raises another moral question. It has usually been considered a strength of liberal democracy that it is open to a competition of ideas and tolerates always a pluralism of beliefs. This has generally been believed to hasten adaptation to structural change in the economy and society generally. In contrast, the rational expectations program of policy analysis logically requires the authority of a single model. Hence, thoroughgoing implementation of the rational expectations method in policy making would entail the official promotion, or "establishment," of one model over the others. Moreover, to the extent that pluralism persists, it would be dangerous to impute to the population a monistic set of beliefs when in fact there is none. A great many policy undertakings met their downfall, it seems, precisely because it was not appreciated that much of the population had less than perfect confidence that the government had found the true model.

It must strike many readers as strange, as it does us, that the insurgency of rational expectations arrives decades after modernism has conquered all before it. What is it to be a modern if not to have been made to feel, through modern art and drama, the uncertain and tenuous relation of self to the external world? It is difficult to imagine how, amidst such an atomistic outlook, the rational expectations of agents viewing the world through the common prism of a shared model could have gained wide acceptance. Yet it is a significant step. It recognizes that the agents modeled may themselves form models of their surrounding world, and hence it points toward a macrotheoretical foundation for microeconomic and therefore macroeconomic behavior.

References

Arrow, Kenneth J., and Mordecai Kurz (1969). "Optimal Public Investment Policy and Controllability with Fixed Savings Ratio." *Journal of Economic Theory,* 1:141-77.

Bray, Margaret (1982). "Learning, Estimation and Stability of Rational Expectations." *Journal of Economic Theory,* 26:318-39.

Cagan, Phillip (1956). "The Monetary Dynamics of Hyperinflation." In: *Studies in the Quantity Theory of Money,* edited by Milton Friedman, pp. 25-120. University of Chicago Press.

Di Tata, Juan C. (1982). *Essays on Expectations, Money, and Economic Activity.* Ph.D. dissertation, Columbia University.

Fischer, Stanley (1977). "Long-Term Contracts, Rational Expectations, and the Optimal Money Supply Rule." *Journal of Political Economy,* 85:191-205.

Friedman, Milton (1956). *A Theory of the Consumption Function.* Princeton University Press.

  (1961). "The Lag in Effect of Monetary Policy," *Journal of Political Economy,* 69:447-66.

Frydman, Roman (1981). "Sluggish Price Adjustments and the Effectiveness of Monetary Policy Under Rational Expectations." *Journal of Money, Credit and Banking,* February, pp. 94-102.

  (1982a). "Towards an Understanding of Market Processes: Individual Expectations, Learning and Convergence to Rational Expectations Equilibrium." *American Economic Review,* 72:652-68.

  (1982b). "Subjective Forecasts and Output-Inflation Relationship." Unpublished mimeograph, Dept. of Economics, New York University.

Hall, Robert E. (1967). *Essays in the Theory of Wealth,* Ph.D. dissertation, Massachusetts Institute of Technology.

Hansen, Lars P., and Thomas J. Sargent (1981). "Formulating and Estimating Dynamic Linear Rational Expectations Models." In: *Rational Expectations and Econometric Practice,* edited by Robert E. Lucas, Jr., and Thomas J. Sargent, pp. 91-126. University of Minnesota Press.

Hayek, Friedrich A. (1948*a*). *Individualism and Economic Order,* Chapter 2. University of Chicago Press.

(1948*b*). *Individualism and Economic Order,* Chapter 4. University of Chicago Press.

Keynes, John Maynard (1921). *A Treatise on Probability.* London: Macmillan.

(1936). *The General Theory of Employment, Interest and Money.* New York: Harcourt Brace & World.

(1937). "The General Theory of Employment." *Quarterly Journal of Economics,* 51: 209–23.

Kirman, Alan P. (1975). "Learning by Firms about Demand Conditions." In: *Adaptive Economic Models,* edited by Richard H. Day and Theodore Groves, pp. 137–56. New York: Academic Press.

Knight, Frank H. (1921). *Risk, Uncertainty and Profit.* Boston: Houghton Mifflin.

Lucas, Robert E., Jr. (1966). "Optimal Investment with Rational Expectations." Mimeograph; reprinted 1981 in: *Rational Expectations and Econometric Practice,* edited by Robert E. Lucas, Jr., and Thomas J. Sargent, pp. 55–66. University of Minnesota Press.

(1972). "Expectations and the Neutrality of Money." *Journal of Economic Theory,* 4:103–24.

(1973). "Some International Evidence on Output-Inflation Tradeoffs." *American Economic Review,* 63:326–34.

(1975). "An Equilibrium Model of the Business Cycle." *Journal of Political Economy,* 83:1113–44.

(1976). "Econometric Policy Evaluation: A Critique." In *Phillips Curve and Labor Markets,* edited by Karl Brunner and Allan H. Meltzer, pp. 19–46. Amsterdam: North Holland.

Lucas, Robert E., Jr., and Thomas J. Sargent (editors) (1981). *Rational Expectations and Econometric Practice.* University of Minnesota Press.

Muth, John F. (1960). "Optimal Properties of Exponentially Weighted Forecasts." *Journal of the American Statistical Association,* 55:299–306.

(1961). "Rational Expectations and the Theory of Price Movements." *Econometrica,* July, pp. 315–35.

Nerlove, Mark (1958). *The Dynamics of Supply: Estimation of Farmers' Response to Price.* Baltimore: Johns Hopkins University Press.

Phelps, Edmund S. (1965). *Fiscal Neutrality Toward Economic Growth.* New York: McGraw-Hill.

(1968). "Money Wage Dynamics and Labor Market Equilibrium." *Journal of Political Economy,* August, pp. 678–711.

(1969). "The New Microeconomics in Inflation and Employment Theory." *American Economic Review,* 59:147–60.

(1970). "Introduction." In: *Microeconomic Foundations of Employment and Inflation Theory,* Edmund S. Phelps et al., pp. 1–23. New York: Norton.

Phelps, Edmund S., and John B. Taylor (1977). "Stabilizing Properties of Monetary Policy under Rational Expectations." *Journal of Political Economy,* February, pp. 163–90.

Phelps, Edmund S., et al. (1970). *Microeconomic Foundations of Employment and Inflation Theory.* New York: Norton.

Sargent, Thomas J., and Neil Wallace (1975). "'Rational Expectations,' the Optimal Monetary Instrument, and the Optimal Money Supply Rule." *Journal of Political Economy,* 83:241–54.

Townsend, Robert M. (1981). "Forecasting the Forecasts of Others: Formulation and

Analysis of Equilibrium Time Series Models.'' Unpublished mimeograph, Carnegie-Mellon University (to be published in *Journal of Political Economy*, 83).

Uzawa, H. (1966). ''An Optimum Fiscal Policy in an Aggregate Model of Economic Growth.'' In: *The Theory and Design of Economic Development*, edited by Irma Adelman and Eric Thorbecke, pp. 113–39. Baltimore: Johns Hopkins University Press.

Weiss, Laurence (1982). ''Information Aggregation and Policy.'' *Review of Economic Studies*, 49:31–42.

CHAPTER 2

The trouble with "rational expectations" and the problem of inflation stabilization

EDMUND S. PHELPS

The hypothesis of rational expectations, as ordinarily defined, makes a crucial assumption that is in some circumstances difficult or impossible to justify. The essence of rational expectations – rational in the sense of Muth – is that, according to the hypothesis, each agent uses the modeler's own model to make the forecasts of the endogenous variables, like prices and income, that (together with his exogenous parameter estimates) determine his actions. Of course, a market model makes the behavior of an endogenous variable, such as the money price level, a function of certain actions taken by the totality of individual agents, such as the aggregate output supplied to the goods market. Therefore, to forecast the endogenous variables as predicted by the model, each agent must forecast the other agents' forecasts of the endogenous variables and their forecasts of the exogenous parameters. It is at this point that a difficulty may arise: The individual agent cannot generally know what the other agents expect the weather, cultural fashions, and social policy to be; so how will he decide, or estimate, these expectations held by the others (if indeed they hold any)?

The rational expectations hypothesis meets this difficulty with the implicit assumption that, in fact, each agent supposes the other agents to have the same expectations about the various exogenous parameters that

The idea of model theoretic expectations without perfect foresight about the public's average opinion, developed here, I first worked out in lectures at C.E.M.A. in Buenos Aires during March of 1980. Conversations with staff and students there are gratefully acknowledged. Subsequently, Juan Di Tata, a Columbia University graduate student, independently came up with the same idea. Because he hails from Buenos Aires, I thought of titling this chapter "The Buenos Aires Problem in 'Rational' Expectations." Then Roman Frydman, of New York University, showed me his developments of a similar theme. My conversations with them provided the stimulus for this chapter. Now it is more accurately the Manhattan problem, and our efforts to meet the problem the Manhattan project. The present version was first presented in Phelps (1980). I learned on that occasion that Robert Townsend (1978) produced a similar formulation of nth-degree expectations.

he has. The notion of "rational" expectations is stretched to the point where each agent imputes to others not just his "economic" model of the endogenous economic variables but also his meteorological, cultural, and political forecasts of the exogenous variables. This approach has a certain beauty and simplicity to recommend it: The agents' expectations of the endogenous variables will display "perfect foresight" in the expected-value sense if (and only if) their expectations of the exogenous variables are in some sense correct – and the former will display "perfect conditional foresight" in any case.

But in the theory of macroeconomic disturbances – slump, inflation, and recoveries from them – to which the rational expectations hypothesis has frequently been applied, it is difficult to justify the premise that each agent presumes his expectations to be universal – as if some Jungian collective unconscious existed to bring expectations into an understood agreement. There is no nationwide expectation of Reagan's economic policy *the existence of which is public knowledge.*[1]

This chapter sets itself the task of replacing rational expectations with a more general theory in which agents may believe that others' expectations differ from their own. The new concept, model theoretic expectations, is then applied to the problem of achieving disinflation without recession.

We deal here with a familiar problem. The central bank, tired of the inflation, announces that it is embarking on a new program of disinflation. Accordingly, it explains that it will be reducing the future money supply in relation to the present trend. But it does not wish to reduce the present money supply for two reasons: If the announced program has the desired effect on price expectations, interest rates will drop, and thus the quantity of money demanded at the normal levels of employment and production will rise; so an increase of the present money supply is appro-

---

[1] It is argued by Frydman et al. (1980) that there may fail to exist a "best theory" of government policy for average opinion to gravitate toward, owing to the game-theoretic conjectural interdependence between the government and the public. The possibility of an impasse, a disequilibrium, of *unpredictable* duration is discussed by Phelps (1979). Keynes, in his 1937 article, seems to have anticipated the same point. He writes: "By 'uncertain' knowledge, let me explain, I do not mean merely to distinguish what is known for certain from what is only probable. The game of roulette is not subject, in this sense, to uncertainty.... The sense in which I am using the term is that in which the prospect of a European war is uncertain,...or the position of wealth-owners in the social system in 1970. About these matters there is no scientific basis on which to form any capable probability whatever. We simply do not know. Nevertheless, the necessity for action and for decision compels us as practical men to do our best to overlook this awkward fact" (pp. 113–14).

priate to prevent a slump. And if the program has the desired effect on future wage expectations, recently set wage rates will remain as they are (they will not have to catch up again in the familiar leapfrog process), and less recent wage rates will catch up to them only as their turns come; so if wage rates being reset in the present are going to be induced to catch up with the most recent (and highest) wage rates, they will actually need the encouragement of a booming labor market, and hence an increase of the present money supply.[2]

The bank's dilemma is somewhat like the problem of nuclear deterrence through the threat of retaliation. If inflation expectations do not drop as desired, and so actual inflation does not subside as planned, then there is little point in the bank carrying out the intention to reduce the future money supply (once the future has arrived) – unless by doing so it enhances the credibility of the disinflation plan of the next central bank president.

The firms, whose conjectures and consequent actions will determine the future price level, know all this. They know that if the disinflationary program "works," the central bank will crown its success by decelerating the future money supply as announced; and if disinflation somehow fails to materialize, the response of the central bank will be problematic – there is a chance that the bank will slow the money supply anyway. What, then, will the future price level do? And what will firms expect it to do?

Let us focus on the essentials of our expectational problem: The actual future price level will depend on the firms' expectations of the future money supply and their expectations of the future price level; other determinants are impounded ceteris paribus or mutatis mutandis, as appropriate. We adopt a model in which the future price level is an average of the prices set by many equally small firms, and each firm's price is a linear-homogeneous function of that firm's expectation of this average price and its expectation of the (future) money supply.[3] Writing $F_i x$ for the forecast of x by the ith firm, we have, for every i,

$$p_i = a_1 F_i p + a_2 F_i m \quad (0 < a_1, \ a_2 < 1; \ a_1 + a_2 = 1) \tag{1}$$

where

$$p = \frac{1}{N} \sum_{i=1}^{N} p_i \tag{2}$$

---

[2] See Phelps (1979) for a recent summary of disinflation economics.

[3] See Phelps and Winter (1970). The "ingenious forecast operator" (Barro) made its debut in Phelps (1978a). Presumably it appeared earlier in the mathematical sociology literature.

and N is the number of firms. It does not appear to matter whether we take the right-hand side of equation (1) to be a linear approximation in the relevant neighborhood or whether instead we take the model to be linear-logarithmic (in which case p and m are the logarithms of the price level and money supply).

Now we suppose, entirely in the spirit of the basic idea of rational expectations, that each firm's expectation of the endogenous variable, here the average price, is *model theoretic*; that is, each firm employs the model of the modeler to calculate the conditional expectation of the average price – the expectation conditional on the firm's forecast of the average expectation of the money supply and the average price held by the other firms:

$$p_i = a_1 F_i \left[a_1 \frac{1}{N} \sum_j F_j p + a_2 \frac{1}{N} \sum_j F_j m \right] + a_2 F_i m \qquad (3)$$

Then the average price satisfies

$$p = a_1 \frac{1}{N} \sum_i F_i \left[a_1 \frac{1}{N} \sum_j F_j p + a_2 \frac{1}{N} \sum_j F_j m \right] + a_2 \frac{1}{N} \sum_i F_i m \qquad (4)$$

Let us now suppose, in addition, that the firms have identical expectations, although there remains the irony that no firm knows this. This means that $F_i x = F_j x$ for all i and j and for every x forecast. Suppose, moreover, that each firm forecasts the sum of the parts by summing its forecasts of the parts; that is, $F_i(x+y) = F_i x + F_i y$. Finally, let Fx, where no subscript appears, denote the average forecast of x; let $F^2 x$ denote the average forecast of the forecast of x, that is $F^2 x$ means $F(Fx)$; let $F^3 x$ denote $F(F^2 x)$; and so on. In this notation, and with the foregoing assumption of homogeneous expectations (unbeknown to the expectors), equation (4) becomes

$$p = a_1^2 F^2 p + a_1 a_2 F^2 m + a_2 Fm \qquad (5)$$

Because the price setters ask themselves what the other price setters expect the price level will be, the average of the prices they set will depend on their expectations of the others' expectations of m and p.

The hypothesis of model theoretic expectations can be expanded to include the assumption that each firm believes – correctly so, according to the model theoretic hypothesis – that the other firms likewise make their forecasts in the model theoretic way: Each firm supposes that the other firms use the same model that it does to form their conditional forecasts of the price, given their expectation of the money supply. Then,

$$p = a_1 F[a_1^2 F^2 p + a_1 a_2 F^2 m + a_2 Fm] + a_2 Fm \qquad (6)$$

whence

$$p = a_1^3 F^3 p + a_1^2 a_2 F^3 m + a_1 a_2 F^2 m + a_2 F m \tag{7}$$

In this third stage of model theoretic expectations, the firm credits the other firms with the cleverness of having reached stage 2, embodied in equation (5). Keynes likened this sort of phenomenon

to those newspaper competitions in which the competitors have to pick out the six prettiest faces from a hundred photographs, the prize being awarded to the competitor whose choice most nearly corresponds to the average preferences of the competitors as a whole; so that each competitor has to pick, not those faces which he himself finds prettiest, but those which he thinks likeliest to catch the fancy of the competitors, all of whom are looking at the problem from the same point of view. It is not just a case of choosing those which, to the best of one's judgment, are really the prettiest, nor even those which average opinion genuinely thinks the prettiest. We have reached the third degree where we devote our intelligences to anticipating what average opinion expects the average opinion to be. And there are some, I believe, who practice the fourth, fifth and higher degrees.[4]

Perhaps Keynes was having a little joke on us when he spoke of those higher degrees. One gets a vertiginous feeling, the eyes dull, and the face goes slack at the fourth stage. Still, one remains curious about those higher degrees. Suppose that each firm, after long training, is able to attain the nth stage of model theoretic consciousness. By repeated use of our linear forecast operator, and elementary induction, we obtain

$$p = a_1^n F^n p + a_1^{n-1} a_2 F^n m + a_1^{n-2} a_2 F^{n-1} m + \cdots + a_2 F m \tag{8}$$

If we let n go infinity, we then have

$$p = a_2 \sum_{i=1}^{\infty} a_1^{i-1} F^i m \tag{9}$$

The reader can hardly avoid noticing that if $F^i m$ is a constant, the same for all i, then, because $a_2 = 1 - a_1$, p is implied to be equal to that constant. This is a celestial version of the familiar "quantity theorem" about the proportionality in equilibrium between money supply and price level.

This model has a significant implication for the central bank's task of reducing inflation, and perhaps one of considerable practical importance. (Observing that it is obvious – by now! – does not render it unimportant.) The point is that in order to reduce the price level (in relation to the accustomed trend), it is not sufficient that the central bank persuade each agent to reduce his private expectation of the money supply (in relation to the past trend) by the warranted amount. The prevalence of this expectation must be public knowledge – an accepted fact.

Suppose that each agent reduces his own expectation of the money supply by the warranted amount while, for whatever reason, he does not reduce by the same amount his expectation of what the average opinion

[4] Keynes (1936, p. 158).

about the money supply is, what the average opinion expects the average opinion to be, and so on (to whatever stage is thought to be relevant). Then, according to even the primitive stage-2 theory expressed in equation (5), the average price will not fall by as much as the firms' private expectations of the money supply reduction – assuming, as must be unobjectionable, that they do not expect that the average forecast of the price level has fallen by more than the amount aimed at by the central bank (an inexplicable expectation of expected deflation when only disinflation is being sought). And according to the ultimate version of the model theoretic hypothesis in equation (9), the same result follows without any qualification: The average price falls by an amount that is intermediate between the fall in the private expectation of the money supply and those "expectations of expectations" summed up in the equation.

It follows, if my assumptions are accepted, that the difficulty that disinflationary policy has to overcome in order to achieve the desired reduction of the average price level is not simply one of "credibility." It is also necessary that the policy enjoy commonly recognized credence. Disinflation is high theater, which is fully successful only if the members of the audience feel that the others have likewise "suspended their disbelief."

Before specializing the model a little, for the sake of some interesting additional results on inflation stabilization, we ought to take note of some other general results. I mentioned in the introduction that once the agents in the economy entertain hypotheses of a difference between others' expectations and their own, because they recognize that the others may be estimating certain parameters of the model differently, then the implication of "perfect foresight" is lost. There may then be an error in the average forecast of the average price – a disequilibrium in my terminology (founded by the European equilibrium theorists of the 1930s). To calculate the error in the present model, we may rewrite equation (1) as

$$p = a_1 Fp + a_2 Fm$$

to obtain

$$p - Fp = a_2(Fm - Fp) \quad \text{and} \quad p - Fp = (1 - a_2)^{-1} a_2(Fm - p) \tag{1'}$$

And equation (8) can be rewritten as

$$p = a_1^n F^n p + a_2 \sum_2^n a_1^{i-1}(F^i m - Fm) + (1 - a_1^n)Fm \tag{8'}$$

This brings out the role of the errors in the forecasts of the forecasts of the money supply in "inflating" the price level; these forecast errors are the driving force making a wedge between p and Fm. If we subtract Fp from both sides of (8′), we obtain

$$p - Fp = a_1^n(F^n p - Fp) + a_2 \sum_{i=2}^{n} a_1^{i-1}(F^i m - Fm) + (1 - a_1^n)(Fm - Fp) \tag{8″}$$

Using (1′) to substitute for $Fm - Fp$ then results in the conclusion

$$p - Fp = \left[a_2 \sum_{i=2}^{n} a_1^{i-1}(F^i m - Fm) + a_1^n(F^n p - Fp) \right] \cdot A(n) \tag{10}$$

where $A(n) \equiv a_2^{-1}(1 - a_1^n)$.

Is it the case, then, that when a new disinflationary intention is proclaimed by the central bank (with all earnestness), "anything can happen," because there is no telling what forecasts people will make of the other people's forecasts, *their* forecasts of others' forecasts, and so on ad infinitum (and maybe ad nauseam)? Keynes seems to have thought that the social world did indeed suffer such a tendency toward recurrent episodes of disequilibrium (and the feeling that disorder has become the normal state of affairs was a theme of some near contemporaries such as Katherine Anne Porter and Robert Rauchenberg). But perhaps there exist mechanisms or habits governing the formation of expectations that, if they prevail widely enough in a society, will serve to bring expectations of expectations in line with the reality of expectations, or the other way around.

The distinctive feature of rational expectations in its original, very strong version is that each agent projects his views onto the others:

$$F_i Fp = F_i p, \; F_i F^2 p = F_i Fp, \; F_i F^3 p = F_i F^2 p, \ldots$$

$$F_i Fm = F_i m, \; F_i F^2 m = F_i Fm, \; F_i F^3 m = F_i F^2 m, \ldots$$

Then, believing that they have the same views as he and knowing that they have the same behavioral function (and knowing that this is common knowledge), he reasons that the other agents will choose the same p as he. Hence, $F_i p = p_i$. By equation (1), therefore, $F_i p = F_i m$, and hence, by equation (5), $p = F_i m$. The agents thus turn out to be correct about their forecasts of price, and forecasts of forecasts.

In my presentation at the recent conference for Abba Lerner, I noticed how remarkably powerful such a hypothesis of symmetry is.[5] For suppose that each firm is uncertain that the central bank will in fact carry out its stated intention to reduce the money supply even in the event that prices fall by less than the planned amount. At first blush this less than

---

[5] Phelps (1979).

perfect credibility possessed by the central bank would seem to jeopardize the prospects of the new disinflationary program. For will not the firms now reduce their prices relative to the accustomed trend by less than the amount desired by the bank – because there is a chance that the bank will not carry out its money supply reduction in that event? But on the hypothesis of symmetry under discussion, the answer is no. Because there is a chance that the central bank *will* cut back the money supply relative to trend, each firm will at first reckon on reducing to *some* extent, however small, its own price. But then it will impute to the other firms this same small price reduction, and so, in round two of its analysis, it will decide to reduce its price some more [because a_1 is positive in equation (1)]. The end result is that each firm will be led to reduce its price by the whole amount sought by the central bank; only in that conjectural equilibrium will each firm not find itself in the contradictory position of wanting its price to be less than the average.

Such expectations might be called superrational, or "rational in the first degree." This chapter has taken the attitude that they are not very compelling. Yet a weakened version of this symmetry is perhaps not without interest. Consider the hypothesis of second-degree rationality: "Sure, I believe that on this thorny question my belief differs from average opinion; I am not always representative in all matters, you know. But when it comes to average opinion about average opinion, I have no real beliefs. For working purposes I assume that, on average, the others expect their views to be the average opinion." Suppose, then, that

$$\cdots + F_i F^n x = F_i F^{n-1} x = \cdots = F_i F^2 x = F_i F x \tag{11}$$

for every i and for every x ($=m, p$). Then, reasoning along the aforementioned lines, each firm must conclude that every other firm will suppose that its prices will be matched by the rest of the firms. Hence, $F_i F p = F_i p$ for every i. For the ith firm, therefore, we have [using model theoretic equation (3)],

$$F_i p = a_1 F_i F p + a_2 F_i F m \quad \text{and} \quad F_i F p = F_i p \tag{12}$$

whence

$$F_i p = F_i F m \tag{13}$$

"So I believe that they will set average price in proportion to their average opinion about the money supply" – so each agent will say to himself. And because, in reality, the agents are all alike, $F p = F^2 m$. This leads to

$$p = a_1 F^2 m + a_2 F m \tag{14}$$

on averaging (1) over the behaviorally similar and like-minded firms, and

$$p - Fp = a_2 (Fm - F^2 m)$$

If firms generally overestimate the forecast of money, they will overforecast price.

Now each agent, if he is an economist, and certainly if he has read my paper for the Lerner conference, will grasp the remarkable implication of his belief that on average the opinion of the others is that their opinion is shared by the rest. If they think that, they must think that the average price will be driven down (relative to trend) to the level the central bank desired (because each firm would want to undercut the others' average price otherwise), and, correspondingly, they must think that the central bank will proceed with certainty with the planned cutback of the money supply (relative to trend). Therefore, each firm's $F_i m$ and $F_i p$ being down (relative to trend) by the amount intended by the central bank, each firm will be impelled – whatever it would have expected had their expectations been its decision to make – to reduce its own price (relative to trend) by the same amount.

Let me paraphrase the argument so that there will be less chance it will not be understood. The firms are believed to be led by an iterative-conjectural process to expect the average price and the money supply to fall (relative to trend) by the amount desired by the bank, and so they are all believed to have decided to reduce their respective prices by that same amount; consequently, each firm feels impelled to reduce its own price by that same amount too. It is a case of rumor, fear and the madness of crowds (the title of a book in my library by the psychologist J. P. Chaplin) – but, in this case, all to a happy end. I suppose that a formal demonstration of this proposition is now unnecessary, and a close reading of it would be tedious.

In this chapter I have suggested that even though the agents acting in the economy use a common model and know they do, there are circumstances in which they will not presume that they are estimating (or, better, guessing) the parameters of that model identically. I have taken as an example of such a circumstance the announcement of a new disinflationary program by the central bank. In that situation, I have argued, there is no very strong argument for thinking that the new program of the central bank will enjoy the credibility and the presumed credence that are necessary for prompt disinflation without any intervening trial period of insufficient disinflation and deficient employment (as the central bank tries to persuade price setters of its determination to reduce the inflation).

Some will conclude that our situation is hopeless but not serious: We can pretend that resolute disinflation will not cause temporary unemployment, and maybe the temporary unemployment will vanish before the disinflationary resoluteness does; so let us lash ourselves (as inextricably as we can) to the mast of the gold standard, and the devil take the hindmost.

Nevertheless, I have held out some hope: Maybe there will prevail a widespread tendency to suppose that "they" take their views to be shared – that the average estimate of average opinion is equal to the actual average opinion. Then it is unnecessary for the success of a disinflationary policy that I suppose that they think as I do; I am driven to think as I suppose they do. They have overwhelming numbers; so if I think that they see eye to eye with the central bank and that the bank will justify their confidence, then I am induced to go along with my perception of the probable behavior of the group.

If the leaders of a country's economic policy are determined to embark on a program of disinflation, then they ought (in order to avoid temporary unemployment or eventual retrenchment of the program, or both) to devise a way to convey the idea that expectation of disinflation should be presumed, that it should be taken to be a fact. The need is for a "signal" that everyone can and will assume to be interpreted by the others in a like-minded way. If the mere announcement of the new disinflationary policy by the central bank constitutes such a *public* signal, then well and good! Unfortunately, historical researches have increasingly suggested that more visible and palpable signals are needed to do the trick. The German hyperinflation was ended in 1923 when the government fired tens of thousands of postal workers[6] – a useful symbol. A good utilitarian might suggest that imprisonment of the current head of the central bank would be a great deal cheaper! In any case, there seems to be a need for a symbol, a catalyst, that will precipitate the expectation on the part of all persons that a certain desired expectation has become general, shared. We need a *sociology* of inflation stabilization!

References

Di Tata, J. C. (1980). "Expectations of Others' Expectations and the Transitional Non-Neutrality of Fully Believed Systematic Monetary Policy." Draft of Ph.D. dissertation, Columbia University, p. 45.

Fellner, W. (1978). "The Core of the Controversy about Reducing Inflation: An Introductory Analysis." In: *Contemporary Economic Problems,* edited by W. J. Fellner, Washington, D. C.: American Enterprise Institute.

Frydman, R. (1980). "Unanimity of Opinions and Convergence to Rational Expectations." Working paper, Department of Economics, New York University, p. 20.

Frydman, R., G. O'Driscoll, and A. Schotter (1980). "Rational Expectations of Government Policy: An Application of Newcomb's Problem." Working paper, Department of Economics, New York University, p. 17.

[6] Sargent (1980).

Keynes, J. M. (1936). *The General Theory of Employment, Interest and Money*. London: Macmillan.
  (1937). "The General Theory of Employment." *Quarterly Journal of Economics,* 51:209-23.
Muth, J. F. (1961). "Rational Expectations and the Theory of Price Movements." *Econometrica,* 29:315-35.
Phelps, E. S. (1978*a*). "Disinflation without Recession: Adaptive Guideposts and Monetary Policy." *Weltwirtschaftliches Archiv,* 114:783-809.
  (1978*b*). "Commodity-Supply Shock and Full-Employment Monetary Policy." *Journal of Money, Credit and Banking,* 10:206-20.
  (1979). "Obstacles to Curtailing Inflation." In: *Essays in Post-Keynesian Inflation,* edited by J. H. Gapinsk and C. E. Rockwood, pp. 179-93. Cambridge, Mass.: Ballinger.
  (1980). "The Trouble with 'Rational Expectations' and the Problem of Inflation Stabilization." Presented at the Vargas Institute conference, World Inflation and Inflation in Brazil, Rio de Janeiro, December 15-16, 1980.
Phelps, E. S., and S. G. Winter, Jr. (1970). "Optimal Price Policy under Atomistic Competition." In: *Microeconomic Foundations of Employment and Inflation Theory,* edited by E. S. Phelps et al., pp. 309-37. New York: Norton.
Sargent, T. J. (1980). "The End of Four Big Inflations." Presented at the Vargas Institute conference, World Inflation and Inflation in Brazil, Rio de Janeiro, December 15-16, 1980.
Townsend, R. (1978). "Market Anticipations, Rational Expectations and Bayesian Analysis." *International Economic Review*; 19:481-94.

Comment

PHILLIP CAGAN

Phelps's chapter can be summarized by considering the problem of how much of his presentation I should summarize for you before taking up my own comments. It is not necessary for me to summarize it if you have read it, because it is elegant in its simplicity. Can I expect that most of you have read it? Probably not, if you expected me, given the limitations on your time, to summarize it for you. Would you expect me to summarize it? Only if you thought that I expected you *not* to read it, which would be the case if I expected you to believe that I expected you to conclude that I did not expect you to read it. But should I expect you to believe that? One has the feeling that this recursive morass is convergent to something; yet we cannot count on the conditions for convergence always being satisfied. A certain symmetry of expectations, as Phelps points out, may be sufficient but is not guaranteed. I want to argue further that most economic agents seek *confirmation* of their expectations before they act.

Phelps's chapter and some of the other chapters in this book with their intricate models very elegantly demonstrate the important proposition that we cannot count on expectations leading market behavior to a definite position. I find this congenial to my expectations about short-run outcomes, even though the economy somehow reaches appropriate long-run positions. I shall devote my comments to why I believe these results are consistent with the market behavior we observe.

As expectations are now modeled, the economic application pertains most closely to farming, where planting decisions are made well ahead of sales and the harvest is thrown on a market that clears through price adjustments. We know that farmers make planting mistakes that are not entirely due to changes in demand and the weather. To a considerable extent they are also due to misperceptions of the effect of everyone adjusting plantings in response to favorable or unfavorable prices for the previous crop. Evidence of such misperceptions is given by the hog and cattle cycles, in which low prices lead to low supply and the low supply leads in turn to high prices and to increased supply and so on. It is also relevant that farmers everywhere exert pressure on governments to prevent price declines, because of the industry's extreme susceptibility to overproduction.

In most other industries the problem of forecasting price is largely avoided. The price does not deviate much from unit costs in the short run, and inventories and order queues absorb most of the fluctuations in demand. It is true that firms must rely on expectations in planning new capacity, and they frequently make mistakes – witness the overproduction of computer chip capacity a few years ago – but by and large firms can confirm who is building what and can keep abreast of the prospects for industry capacity.

Because expectations are notoriously subject to error, no one in his right mind relies on them if he can avoid it; confirmation is constantly sought. Economic as well as most other behavior relies on confirmation of expectations before committing money and resources, unless it is impossible to do so, as in gambling, mineral prospecting, and R&D. Confirmation requires coordination of adjustments among firms and industries, and this produces step-by-step adjustments. This is the basic reason, I believe, why macro adjustments in the economy are so slow.

Let me illustrate by considering the major macro adjustment treated in the literature – the real balance effect of a sudden reduction in the money supply. Suppose that Robinson Crusoe and his man Friday have been divested by an antitrust decree. After affirmative action and other influences from the mainland, we find the following situation: Crusoe manufactures baskets that he sells to Friday. Friday in turn uses the baskets to collect fruit, part of which he sells to Crusoe. Friday also manufactures nets that Crusoe purchases for fishing, and part of the catch is sold to Friday. To handle all these transactions, they at one time collected sea shells to use as money and a store of value, and a benign equilibrium of constant nominal and real prices settled over their island.

Then one day a storm destroys half of the sea shells in the possession of both Crusoe and Friday. They are quite aware that either they must devote resources to acquiring more sea shells or nominal prices will have to fall by one-half (ignoring wealth effects). But Crusoe cannot cut the price of his fish in half unless Friday reduces the price of his nets by one-half. And Friday cannot cut the price of his fruit in half unless Crusoe reduces the price of his baskets by one-half. And neither of them will cut the price of his manufactured product by one-half unless the cost of his sustenance – the fish and fruit – is also cut by one-half. We have a problem of coordination. No one will start reducing prices based only on expectations of a new hypothetical equilibrium. There is no overpowering incentive to go first. The real balance effect involves an important externality, in that each firm's price change contributes very little to the overall change in the price level on which the real balance effect depends.

In one of Phelps's examples, firms perceive an exogenous reduction in nominal aggregate demand, and each knows that, with a less than proportional fall in all prices, the decline in real demand calls for some reduction in its profit margin. Every firm expects that others know this and initially plans a partial reduction in prices in response to the decline in real demand. However, only that part of the reduction in nominal demand that exceeds the general decline in prices entails a decline in real demand. Each firm therefore initially plans a reduction in price below the general price decline in order to respond to the decline in real demand. Because every other firm is expected to do the same, all prices are expected to decline to the point where, in fact, no decline in real demand occurs, which leads all firms to reduce prices proportionately to the exogenous decline in nominal aggregate demand. This full price response occurs because each firm plans to make some partial price response to an expected decline in real demand and expects all other firms to have the same expectations and response.

But will firms act on expectations of how other firms respond to expectations? If confirmation is needed before price decisions are implemented, the firms in Phelps's example will behave differently and will not immediately reach the equilibrium described in his example. (Phelps also doubts that they will.)

To be sure, instantaneous confirmation could be achieved if all prices were reduced simultaneously, but there is no mechanism for this except through an economy-wide agreement, which is called "collusion" and has been outlawed, no doubt for a good reason. And while Crusoe and Friday might nevertheless get together, as Adam Smith says, for a little merriment and collusion, we can hardly imagine five million cutthroat U.S. competitive businesses and labor unions doing so. Hence, changes in the money stock do not produce instantaneously complete real balance effects. Without a complete real balance effect, a decrease in the money supply reduces *real* demands and supplies, and because expectations of full-employment equilibrium are not confirmed, the process of adjustment involves both price and output effects and therefore is protracted.

In my interpretation, therefore, if expectations lack confirmation, they cannot provide the basis for a coordinated adjustment of real balances via price changes. And confirmation without simultaneity is attained only by a slow trial-and-error process. Furthermore, although market clearing with freely falling prices would achieve the needed adjustment of all prices, such flexibility of prices does not help to distinguish permanent changes from transitory changes. For various reasons discussed in the literature, markets have developed methods of filtering transitory changes through the use of inventories and price contracts – both implicit and explicit. It is an unavoidable by-product of this filtering that simultaneous or even rapid changes in all prices to attain full-employment equilibria via real balance effects, though they exist in theory, are virtually impossible to attain in one step and can be approached only through a different dynamic process that works slowly.

I am not saying that expectations play no role in the economy. They do in many markets, particularly those for assets, and primarily in the short run. There is no reason not to model such expectations in the rational mode. Although rational expectations may sometimes be adaptive, at most times they are more forward-looking. But when purchases and sales take place without confirmation of expectations, as on commodity or financial exchanges, there are difficulties. We frequently observe the phenomenon of overshooting in such markets, which seems to me to be evidence of the very difficulty of forecasting average opinion that chapters in this book also point to. We observe the gold and foreign-exchange markets, for example, frequently groping for an equilibrium level after some new information or situation develops. The traders do not know where the new equilibrium will be, and they are not sure where others think it will be. It is remarkable that, except in rare pathological cases (such as the "tulip" crazes), these markets converge to an equilibrium band fairly quickly. The reason is that overshooting soon acquires a self-fulfilling and scary dynamic of its own, from which many traders soon run for cover and thereby produce a reversal; the reversal identifies, for the given information, a clear limit to average opinion. With a series of reversals displaying convergence, market activity settles down to some equilibrium band.

Other than assuming adaptive expectations where appropriate, however, we are presumptious to think we can model expectations in their more sophisticated forms. Expectations models differ fundamentally from the usual economic maximizing behavior, to which economic agents gravitate because it is the only behavior that is rational and that characterizes the survivors. Maximizing behavior requires that economic agents can in fact find the maximum position on their own. If that position is affected by the expectations of others, I do not see that maximizing behavior under such circumstances, even with Bayesian learning, is any longer well defined. There is simply no telling what other humans are up to if their behavior is not confined to simple maximizing rules.

Economics has traditionally separated itself from the other social sciences by modeling economic agents in an environment that is differentiated from human caprice by mechanical optimizing rules and the central tendencies of a large number of independent actors. Expectations of natural events cause no problem. But expectations of a higher order – expectations of others' expectations – force economics away from this traditional safe haven. Where such expectations are important to an area of study, we shall find ourselves – God forbid! – in the same barrel with sociology and political science. To avoid that, I expect that we shall with good sense eventually shunt those areas aside and confine our musings to the classical issues that are not highly dependent on higher-order expectations.

CHAPTER 3

Expectations of others' expectations and the transitional nonneutrality of fully believed systematic monetary policy

JUAN CARLOS DI TATA

One of the most striking results of the rational expectations literature is the proposition that systematic monetary policy has no effect on the probability distribution of output, unless the monetary authority possesses an informational advantage over the public. In the absence of such superior information, systematic variations in the money supply will be completely anticipated, and the Phillips curve will become vertical, even in the short run, as suggested by Lucas (1972), Sargent and Wallace (1975), and Barro (1976).

Some of the assumptions underlying the rational expectations paradigm have been challenged in recent macroeconomic research. One strand of the literature, represented mainly by Fischer and Phelps and Taylor, has reintroduced stickiness of wages and prices to revitalize the effect of systematic monetary policy on short-run output behavior. The theory is that frequent or rapid transmission of price and wage decisions is too costly to warrant responses by many firms in the time within which the central bank can react to economic disturbances (Fischer, 1977; Phelps and Taylor, 1977).

A different approach has been followed by those emphasizing credibility and uncertainties about temporary versus permanent changes in economic conditions. John Taylor (1975) constructed a model in which the agents already know the "true" model of the economy, with the single exception of the value of one parameter in the equation describing the money supply rule. He showed that the monetary authority will be able to influence output in the transitional period during which the agents are gradually discovering the true value of the aforementioned parameter.

This chapter could not have been written without the invaluable help of Edmund S. Phelps, my thesis advisor. He was the first to develop similar ideas, and he stimulated me to write on this topic. I have also benefited from the comments of Guillermo Calvo and members of the money-macro workshop at Columbia University. A discussion with Roman Frydman is also acknowledged. Views expressed herein do not necessarily reflect those of the International Monetary Fund.

Policy effectiveness can arise in this context for two reasons. First, the public may have prior beliefs about policy that differ from the true policy being followed by the monetary authority. In this situation, disclosure of honest intentions on the part of the central bank does not assure immediate credibility.

A second reason capable of revitalizing monetary effectiveness is policy deception. The public does not have prior beliefs about policy, but the dishonest government creates these beliefs by convincing people that it will do one thing, when actually it does something different.

The purpose of this chapter is to consider a new and different source of transitional nonneutrality of systematic monetary policy. The discussion will place some of the implicit assumptions made in the modern "rational expectations" literature in a fresh and new perspective and will arrive at some reservations against these assumptions. Moreover, a more general modeling of expectations formation will be introduced. The kind of expectations formation modeled here might be designated by the term *model interlinked expectations*: "model" because the assumption will be maintained that market participants form their expectations according to the model of the economy, and "interlinked" bcause we want to stress the fact that rational individuals will start developing expectations of others' expectations of the relevant variables once they realize that the public's average opinion affects the behavioral pattern of the variable being forecasted.

The source of transitional nonneutrality considered here is completely different from the one that has been emphasized by Taylor. As a matter of fact, this chapter assumes that there is neither a lack of credibility on the part of rational agents nor any policy deception on the part of the government. It will be postulated, primarily for analytical convenience, that a new government announces the rule that it is going to follow and sticks to it and that each and every agent believes completely in the announcement.

An essential element in the argument is that although everybody is assumed to share actually the same beliefs about the new policy (100 percent credibility), each and every agent is supposed to form expectations of the public's average opinion that differ from his own. The latter seems to be an assumption that it is quite reasonable for the economic analyst to entertain in a world where the acquisition of information about others' beliefs is costly.

Three features of the model will emerge from the discussion:

1. The effectiveness of fully believed systematic monetary policy to affect the probability distribution of output during periods in which each rational agent assumes that his complete credibility on the new policy is not shared by average opinion

2. The isolation of a pure expectational source of serial correlation in output behavior
3. The obstacles that even fully believed monetary authorities face in attempting to reduce inflation to the optimum level

3.1. Rational expectations and beliefs about others' expectations

Implicit in the rational expectations literature is the suggestion that people can form expectations of relevant variables "individually," without explicitly considering the role played by expectations held by other people on the behavior of the relevant variable under consideration! Omission of the other agents' expectations can be justified only by postulating that, in truth, each agent imputes to everyone else his own expectations: Each market participant presumes that everyone else is forming expectations by employing the same model of the economy that he is using in his own forecasting process and that everyone else assigns to the monetary rule the same degree of credibility that he is assigning to it. Once we entertain the possibility that each rational agent assumes the other market participants to be using a model of the economy different from his own, not sharing his own beliefs about the monetary rule, then the previously mentioned "rational expectations" implicit assumption is no longer tenable, and expectations of average opinion must be explicitly considered when modeling expectations formation.

When forecasting the price level, each rational agent will have to form expectations of the economy-wide average opinion about the price level, as well as expectations of the economy-wide average opinion about the economy-wide average belief about the price level, and so forth. In so doing, each agent will have to form his own beliefs about the model of the economy being employed by the other agents. Keynes himself anticipated this phenomenon of expectations of expectations, and he provided an ingenious related example (Keynes, 1936).

Imagine a real-world economy characterized by a past history of dishonest governments that have not been honoring their announcements about the shifts in policy being instituted. Let us now assume that a new government with a different background takes office and announces a new permanent change in policy. An interesting question arises: Will complete credibility on the part of each and every agent in the determination of the new policymakers to honestly pursue their announcement be enough to secure that the change in policy will have no effects on output, so that prices and wages will adjust completely to the new monetary circumstances? The "rational expectations school" answer to this question would be a definite yes. If a change in policy is completely believed, then there is no reason to expect anything more than changes in purely nominal terms, without any effects on quantities. However, this chapter will show that the rational expectations answer to the former question is no longer valid if the representative agent incorrectly believes that average opinion assigns less than 100 percent credibility to the policy shift. Because collecting information concerning the beliefs held by a numerous group of people is enormously costly in terms of time and effort, we can easily argue that agent i cannot assume with certainty that his own beliefs are shared by everyone else.

As a matter of fact, the aforementioned "others' credibility" approach to the problem is just one of the two possible interpretations. The other one has been suggested to me by Guillermo Calvo (personal communication), and I find it quite appealing. Let us assume away the problem of "others' credence." Let us also assume that each and every agent in the economy has received and processed the information announcing the policy shift. For each market participant, there still remains the problem of guessing whether or not all the other market participants also received and processed the message sent by the government. Some proportion of the public might not have been listening and may be acting on old information. Then market participants will be misperceiving average opinion if they believe that some nonnegligible proportion of the public is still forming expectations according to the old monetary rule.[1]

In the following pages this argument will be developed formally, and the monetary nonneutrality will be isolated mathematically.

3.2.   The model

The structure of the economy will be assumed to be described by the equations

$$y_t^s = a_0 + a_1(p_t - {}_{t-1}^{*}p_t) + e_t \tag{1}$$

---

[1] The only way I can imagine in which this problem can be circumvented is by assuming the existence of some external institution to which the market participants report their beliefs. This institution could compute average opinion and disseminate this information back to the market participants. As Frydman suggests, however, "the possibility of creating such an institution is particularly remote on the economy-wide level. This means that the assumption that the information on the average opinion can be collected is not plausible in macroeconomic models" (Frydman, 1982). Even if we were willing to postulate the unlikely existence of such an institution, rational agents would still face the problem of knowing if all the other market participants were making use of the information on average opinion disseminated by this institution. On the other hand, it is reasonable to assume that market participants will not have this information at their disposal within the first period after the shift in policy.

$$y_t^d = m_t - p_t + v_t \tag{2}$$

where y_t, p_t, and m_t represent the natural logarithms of output, the price level, and the money supply, respectively; v_t and e_t are normally distributed serially uncorrelated stochastic terms with mean zero and variances σ_v^2 and σ_e^2; v_t represents shocks to velocity, and e_t is a shock to the aggregate supply schedule. They are distributed independently of each other. The variable $_{t-1}^* p_t$ represents the psychological expectation being held by the public as of the end of period $t-1$; a_0 and a_1 are two constants, a_0 representing the "natural" level of output.

The aggregate supply function (1) is of the Lucas (1973) type. Output is a direct function of the difference between the current price level and people's prior expectation of the current price level. Unexpected increases in the price level trigger output responses, because suppliers, being unable to separate relative from general price movements, mistakenly interpret that their relative prices have gone up. The Lucas supply function is used for the sake of the argument, but the validity of our results does not depend on it. The aggregate demand function (2) is a simple velocity equation.

The monetary authorities are supposed to be attempting to stabilize the economy by "leaning against" the shocks to velocity. They reduce the money supply when velocity goes up and increase the money supply when velocity goes down, according to the following reaction function:

$$m_t = m_0 - g_0 v_{t-1} \tag{3}$$

where $m_0 > 0$ may be interpreted as the "average" money supply, and $g_0 > 0$ is a constant representing the reaction coefficient. It will be assumed that by looking at equation (2), the monetary authorities are able to identify *ex post* the velocity disturbance v_t, so that there is no difficulty for the central bank in following a rule such as (3). The information about v_t is provided to the market participants at the end of period t. The monetary authorities are therefore reacting countercyclically only to disturbances that have already been perceived by the public.

Let us assume that rule (3) has been followed by the central bank for quite some time and that the economy is in a long-run steady-state rational expectations equilibrium. Suppose that at the end of period t_{0-1} a new government takes office and announces that starting in period t_0 it will adopt a new monetary rule of the form[2]

$$m_t = m_1 - g_1 v_{t-1} \tag{4}$$

[2] The incorporation of a disturbance to the money supply process will not alter the main conclusions of this chapter in any sense.

Equation (4) differs from (3) in the "average" money supply ($m_1 \neq m_0$) and in the degree of feedback ($g_1 \neq g_0$). The announcement made by the monetary authorities enters in the information set used by market participants at the end of period t_{0-1} to calculate their expectations of the price level to prevail at period t_0.

3.3.   Results under the assumption of Muthian rationality

We are interested here in summarizing the results under the assumption that people form expectations rationally in the Muthian sense (Muth, 1961).

The operational definition of rational expectations postulates that market participants know the model of the economy and that each agent's psychological expectation of the log of the price level to prevail at t, held as of the end of period $t-1$, is equal to the mathematical expectation of p_t calculated using the model and all the information assumed to be available as of the end of period $t-1$. Imposing this requirement,

$$_{t-1}^{*}p_t = E_{t-1}p_t$$

Equating (1) to (2) (market clearing condition) and using (4) to substitute for m_t, we obtain

$$a_0 + (1+a_1)p_t - a_1 E_{t-1}p_t - m_1 + g_1 v_{t-1} = v_t - e_t \tag{5}$$

Taking the conditional expectation of (5) as of the end of period $t-1$ and rearranging terms, we get

$$E_{t-1}p_t = m_1 - g_1 v_{t-1} - a_0 \tag{6}$$

Substituting (6) back into (5), we obtain the following expression for p_t:

$$p_t = m_1 - g_1 v_{t-1} + \frac{v_t - e_t}{1 + a_1} - a_0 \tag{7}$$

Then the final expression for output is

$$y_t = a_0 + a_1 \left(m_1 - g_1 v_{t-1} + \frac{v_t - e_t}{1 + a_1} - a_0 - m_1 + g_1 v_{t-1} + a_0 \right) + e_t$$

$$= a_0 + \frac{a_1}{1 + a_1} v_t + \frac{e_t}{1 + a_1} \tag{8}$$

The variance of output is

$$\mathrm{var}(y_t) = \frac{a_1^2 \sigma_v^2 + \sigma_e^2}{(1 + a_1)^2} \tag{9}$$

The mean of the price level can be determined as

$$Ep_t = m_1 - a_0 \quad (t \geqslant t_0) \tag{10}$$

and its variance is

$$\text{var}(p_t) = \left[\frac{1}{(1+a_1)^2} + g_1^2 \right] \sigma_v^2 + \frac{\sigma_e^2}{(1+a_1)^2} \quad (t \geqslant t_0) \tag{11}$$

Muthian rationality ensures that the shift in policy has no transitional effects on the distribution of output: $Ey_{t(t \geqslant t_0)} = Ey_{t_0 - 1}$; var $y_{t(t \geqslant t_0)} =$ var $y_{t_0 - 1}$. On the other hand, feedback control has no effect on output, neither in the steady-state position in which the economy was before the shift in policy nor in the new rational expectations equilibrium that the economy achieves immediately after the change in the monetary rule.

The shift in policy will make a permanent difference only for the distribution of the price level. The mean of the price level will increase or decrease depending on whether $m_1 > m_0$ or $m_1 < m_0$, and its variance will be greater if $g_1 > g_0$ and smaller if $g_1 < g_0$.

3.4.   Results under the hypothesis that people form incorrect expectations of average opinion

From equation (5), but avoiding the assumption of Muthian rationality, we have the following expression for the price level to prevail at time t:

$$p_t = \frac{a_1 \,_{t-1}^*p_t + m_t - a_0 + v_t - e_t}{1 + a_1} \tag{12}$$

where $_{t-1}^*p_t$ is the economy-wide average psychological expectation of the price level to prevail at time t, held as of the end of period $t-1$.

According to our idea of model interlinked expectations, and in the spirit of the rational expectations approach, we assume that each and every agent uses the model of the economy to form his conditional expectation of the price level to prevail at time t.

Let $F_{t-1}^i p_t$ represent the model interlinked forecast of p_t held by agent i, conditional on all information available as of the end of period $t-1$.[3] We shall assume that $F^i(ax) = aF^i x$ and $F^i(x+y) = F^i x + F^i y$ for every x, y forecast, where a is a constant. Then, taking the conditional model interlinked forecast of (12), we have

$$F_{t-1}^i p_t = \frac{a_1 F_{t-1}^i (_{t-1}^*p_t) + F_{t-1}^i m_t - a_0}{1 + a_1} \tag{13}$$

Suppose also that there is a very large number of market participants

---

[3] The forecast operator was first introduced in the economics literature by Phelps (1978). It was subsequently used elsewhere by the same author (Phelps, 1980).

who make use of the same information set and, moreover, that all the market participants have identical expectations (although each of them believes that his expectation is different from average opinion). This means that

$$F_{t-1}^i({}_{t-1}^*p_t) = F_{t-1}^j({}_{t-1}^*p_t); \quad F_{t-1}^i m_t = F_{t-1}^j m_t;$$

$$F_{t-1}^i p_t = F_{t-1}^j p_t \quad \text{for all } i \text{ and } j$$

Taking into account the former assumption of identical expectations, we eliminate the superscripts in (13) and obtain

$$F_{t-1}p_t = \frac{a_1 F_{t-1}({}_{t-1}^*p_t) + F_{t-1}m_t - a_0}{1+a_1} \tag{14}$$

where $F_{t-1}p_t$, $F_{t-1}({}_{t-1}^*p_t)$, and $F_{t-1}m_t$ denote the conditional average forecast of the price level, the average forecast of the psychological average forecast of the price level, and the average forecast of the money supply, respectively.

Let us now assume that each agent in this economy believes that the others are forming expectations according to the model interlinked hypothesis; that is, each market participant believes that all the other market participants are also forming expectations of average opinion and are using the model of the economy to make their own forecasts. Imposing this requirement,

$$F_{t-1}({}_{t-1}^*p_t) = F_{t-1}(F_{t-1}p_t) = F_{t-1}^2 p_t$$

where $F_{t-1}^2 p_t$ denotes the average forecast of the average model interlinked forecast of the price level. Then, (14) becomes

$$F_{t-1}p_t = \frac{a_1 F_{t-1}^2 p_t + F_{t-1}m_t - a_0}{1+a_1} \tag{15}$$

Taking the conditional forecast of (15), we obtain

$$F_{t-1}^2 p_t = \frac{a_1 F_{t-1}(F_{t-1}^2 p_t) + F_{t-1}^2 m_t - a_0}{1+a_1}$$

Then,

$$F_{t-1}^2 p_t = \frac{a_1 F_{t-1}^3 p_t + F_{t-1}^2 m_t - a_0}{1+a_1} \tag{16}$$

We have reached the third stage of model interlinked expectations. We could go on and on calculating expectations of higher degrees by following an identical procedure.

To simplify the argument, we shall postulate that each and every agent believes that his forecast of the average opinion about the price level is shared, on average, by the other market participants. The latter means that

$$F^2_{t-1} p_t = F^3_{t-1} p_t \qquad (17)$$

where $F^3_{t-1} p_t$ represents the average expectation of the average opinion about the average forecast of the price level. Substituting from (17) into (16) and rearranging terms, $F^2_{t-1} p_t$ can be determined to be

$$F^2_{t-1} p_t = F^2_{t-1} m_t - a_0 \qquad (18)$$

Going back to (15) and substituting the right-hand side of (18) for $F^2_{t-1} p_t$, we obtain the following solution for the average forecast of the price level:

$$F_{t-1} p_t = \frac{a_1 F^2_{t-1} m_t + F_{t-1} m_t - a_0(1 + a_1)}{1 + a_1} \qquad (19)$$

Expression (19) shows that the average expectation of the price level depends not only on the public's forecast of the money supply but also on people's average belief about the others' expectations of the money supply.

Using expressions (12) and (19) to substitute for p_t and $_{t-1}^* p_t$ in equation (1), we obtain

$$y_t = a_0 + a_1 \left[\frac{(m_t - F_{t-1} m_t) + a_1(m_t - F^2_{t-1} m_t)}{1 + a_1} \right] + \frac{a_1}{1 + a_1} v_t + \frac{e_t}{1 + a_1}$$

This expression for output shows clearly that even when a change in the money supply is completely believed ($m_t = F_{t-1} m_t$), such a change will have nonneutral effects on output if people do not believe that it is completely believed (i.e., if $F^2_{t-1} m_t \neq F_{t-1} m_t$).

Let us now analyze the effects of our shift in policy when each market participant forms incorrect expectations of the average forecast of the money supply. The analysis will be carried out under the following assumptions:

1. Each agent is uncertain about the average expectation of the money supply because he finds it too costly to collect information about the economy-wide average opinion.
2. The new monetary policy is completely anticipated by each and every market participant. Everyone therefore forms expectations of the money supply according to rule (4). Each agent, however, misperceives average opinion because he guesses incorrectly that some proportion of the public either did not receive the central bank's message and is still acting on the old information provided by rule (3) or does not assign full

credibility to the authorities' announcement. The latter "others' credence" approach to the problem seems to be particularly relevant in two cases. First, suppose that the government maintains $g_1 = g_0$ but announces an "average" money supply $m_1 < m_0$. Then each agent may wrongly predict that some nonnegligible percentage of the population believes that the central bank is trying to generate overemployment by making people forecast that it will supply $m_1 < m_0$ when, actually, it intends to maintain the same "average" money supply. Second, suppose that the bank maintains the same average money supply $(m_1 = m_0)$ but announces that it will abandon its former countercyclical policy in order to adopt a Friedmanian rule without feedback $(g_1 = 0; g_0 > 0)$. Then, although each agent may believe in the firmness of the bank's intentions, he may also guess incorrectly that some proportion of the public forecasts that the monetary authorities will not give up monetary activism completely (because, presumably, the bank is not confident of having convinced the market participants to adjust their expectations according to its announcement).

3. At the end of each period, people receive new information about the price level and the shock to velocity during the period; e_t (the disturbance to the aggregate supply schedule) remains unobserved. However, the distribution of e_t is assumed to be known by everyone.

According to the stated assumptions, we shall postulate that each and every agent forecasts average opinion about the money supply by assuming that the average market participant is uncertain about the government's intentions and therefore assigns probability θ to the new rule (4) and probability $1 - \theta$ to the previously expected monetary rule. Under our alternative interpretation, $1 - \theta$ could be understood as representing the proportion of the total population that each agent wrongly believes to be still acting on old information.[4] Then,

$$F^2_{t_0-1} m_{t_0} = \theta(m_1 - g_1 v_{t_0-1}) + (1 - \theta)(m_0 - g_0 v_{t_0-1})$$

$$F^2_{t_0} m_{t_0+1} = \theta(m_1 - g_1 v_{t_0}) + (1 - \theta)[\theta(m_1 - g_1 v_{t_0}) + (1 - \theta)(m_0 - g_0 v_{t_0})]$$

$$= \theta \sum_{i=0}^{1} (1 - \theta)^i (m_1 - g_1 v_{t_0}) + (1 - \theta)^2 (m_0 - g_0 v_{t_0})$$

Generalizing for $s \geq 0$,

[4] In this latter case, it is more reasonable to postulate that agents will form expectations of the average forecast of the money supply by giving weights of θ and $1 - \theta$ to rule (4) and *rule (3)* (not to the previously expected rule), respectively.

$$F^2_{t_{0+s-1}} m_{t_{0+s}} = \theta \sum_{i=0}^{s} (1-\theta)^i (m_1 - g_1 v_{t_{0+s-1}}) + (1-\theta)^{s+1} (m_0 - g_0 v_{t_{0+s-1}}) \tag{20}$$

Expression (20) implies that each agent will only gradually adjust his beliefs about the others' forecasts of the parameters of the monetary rule (each agent predicts that the average market participant is transitionally uncertain about whether the shift in policy is temporary or permanent).[5]

It would not be reasonable to assume that the value of θ is constant over time. We must take into account that at the end of each period, each agent will receive new information and will consequently revise his forecast of the probability attached by average opinion to the previously expected rule. In any case, market participants will be able to discover the *true* probability (1) assigned by average opinion to the new monetary rule only after the completion of a Bayesian learning procedure.[6] An extended model will allow for the time dependence of θ.

Even assuming that people receive information about the aggregate supply disturbance e_t and are therefore able to discover average opinion at the end of the first period after the shift in policy, there remains a further complication that could leave the economy in disequilibrium for many periods. Suppose for simplicity that $g_1 = g_0$ but $m_1 < m_0$. Then, although each rational agent can determine from the model that average opinion assigned a probability equal to 1 to the new "average" supply last period, he may also forecast that average opinion will assign a positive probability to an "average" money supply greater than m_1 *this period,* on the grounds that the others may believe that the government, being disappointed with the unemployment generated last period, will probably decide to relieve the economy by increasing the "average" money supply by some intermediate amount.

[5] Although in a different model, an assumption similar in spirit has been used by Taylor (1979). In Section 1.2 of his survey, Taylor summarizes the results of postulating uncertainty on the part of each agent after a major shift in policy (he does not deal with the problem of uncertainty about others' beliefs analyzed in this chapter). He models the effects of a new disinflationary policy that is not fully believed by postulating that, when forming their expectations, people incorporate new information about inflation as well as the previously expected rate of inflation. In an earlier study he derived similar but more rigorous results using Bayesian procedures (Taylor, 1975).

[6] Robert M. Townsend (1978) applied Bayesian techniques to analyze the process of convergence to the rational expectations equilibrium in a model that also incorporates the infinite regress problem of firms forming expectations of others' beliefs.

Our assumed mechanism of expectations updating implies that $F^2_{t_{0+s-1}} m_{t_{0+s}}$ converges to the new monetary rule (4) in the long run. The economy will therefore go through a period of transitional disequilibrium characterized by the misperception of average opinion by each rational agent. From now on, and in order to simplify the notation, we shall eliminate the subscripts of the forecast operator. Then $Fx_{t_{0+s}}$ (for $x = m, p$ and $s \geqslant 0$) will denote the forecast of $x_{t_{0+s}}$, conditional on all information assumed to be available as of the end of period t_{0+s-1}.

Going back to (19), substituting the right-hand side of (20) for $F^2 m_{t_{0+s}}$ and rule (4) for $Fm_{t_{0+s}}$ and rearranging terms, we obtain

$$Fp_{t_{0+s}} = \frac{a_1 [\theta \sum_{i=0}^{s} (1-\theta)^i (m_1 - g_1 v_{t_{0+s-1}}) + (1-\theta)^{s+1} (m_0 - g_0 v_{t_{0+s-1}})]}{1 + a_1}$$

$$+ \frac{m_1 - g_1 v_{t_{0+s-1}} - a_0 (1 + a_1)}{1 + a_1} \quad (s \geqslant 0) \tag{21}$$

Making $_{t_{0+s-1}}^{*} p_{t_{0+s}} = Fp_{t_{0+s}}$, (12) can be written as

$$p_{t_{0+s}} = \frac{a_1 Fp_{t_{0+s}} + m_{t_{0+s}} - a_0 + v_{t_{0+s}} - e_{t_{0+s}}}{1 + a_1} \tag{22}$$

Substituting for $Fp_{t_{0+s}}$ from equation (21) and for $m_{t_{0+s}}$ from equation (4), we obtain the following result for the price level to prevail at time t_{0+s}:

$$p_{t_{0+s}} = \frac{[a_1^2 \theta \sum_{i=0}^{s} (1-\theta)^i + 2a_1 + 1] m_1 + a_1^2 (1-\theta)^{s+1} m_0}{(1+a_1)^2}$$

$$+ \frac{v_{t_{0+s}} - e_{t_{0+s}}}{1 + a_1} - a_0$$

$$- \frac{[a_1^2 \theta \sum_{i=0}^{s} (1-\theta)^i + 2a_1 + 1] g_1 + a_1^2 (1-\theta)^{s+1} g_0}{(1+a_1)^2} v_{t_{0+s-1}} \quad (s \geqslant 0) \tag{23}$$

Substituting (21) and (23) back into (1) and rearranging terms, the final expression for output is

$$y_{t_{0+s}} = a_0 + \frac{a_1^2 (1-\theta)^{s+1} (m_1 - m_0)}{(1+a_1)^2} + \frac{a_1 v_{t_{0+s}} + e_{t_{0+s}}}{1 + a_1}$$

$$+ \frac{a_1^2 (1-\theta)^{s+1} (g_0 - g_1)}{(1+a_1)^2} v_{t_{0+s-1}} \quad (s \geqslant 0) \tag{24}$$

The mean value of output can be calculated as

$$Ey_{t_{0+s}} = a_0 + \frac{a_1^2 (1-\theta)^{s+1} (m_1 - m_0)}{(1+a_1)^2} \quad (s \geqslant 0) \tag{25}$$

and its variance is

$$\text{var } y_{t_0+s} = \left[\frac{a_1^2}{(1+a_1)^2} + \frac{a_1^4(1-\theta)^{2(s+1)}(g_0-g_1)^2}{(1+a_1)^4} \right] \sigma_v^2$$

$$+ \frac{1}{(1+a_1)^2} \sigma_e^2 \quad (s \geq 0) \tag{26}$$

The mean value of the price level is

$$Ep_{t_0+s} = \frac{(a_1^2\theta \sum_{i=0}^{s}(1-\theta)^i + 2a_1 + 1)m_1 + a_1^2(1-\theta)^{s+1}m_0}{(1+a_1)^2} - a_0 \quad (s \geq 0) \tag{27}$$

and its variance is

$$\text{var } p_{t_0+s} = \left[\frac{1}{(1+a_1)^2} \right.$$

$$+ \frac{\{[a_1^2\theta \sum_{i=0}^{s}(1-\theta)^i + 2a_1 + 1]g_1 + a_1^2(1-\theta)^{s+1}g_0\}^2}{(1+a_1)^4} \left. \right] \sigma_v^2$$

$$+ \frac{\sigma_e^2}{(1+a_1)^2} \quad (s \geq 0) \tag{28}$$

3.5. Comments on the results

From equation (25) it is apparent that if each agent believes that the other market participants do not believe completely in the government's announcement, the new monetary policy will have transitional effects on the mean value of output. If the new "average" money supply m_1 is lower than m_0, then the mean value of output will be lower than the natural rate, and vice versa. The less credibility each agent imputes to average opinion, the larger $1-\theta$ and the larger the reduction in the transitional mean value of output if $m_1 < m_0$. In this way, a perfectly anticipated and believed shift in policy is still able to produce effects on real economic variables that will last for the transitional period during which market participants are still correcting their forecasts of average opinion.

The reason for the output effects is that each agent's conditional expectation of the price level to prevail at time t_0+s is "contaminated" by the incorrect prediction that average opinion does not believe completely in the new average money supply. Whereas the path of the price level is determined by the actual economy-wide average expectation of it [see expression (22)], each agent incorrectly forecasts that the average expectation of the price level is different from his own expectation. The latter makes him form expectations of the price level that are biased upward (if $m_1 < m_0$) and encourages each supplier to reduce his output through the usual Lucas confusion between aggregate and relative price movements. The opposite response would result (an increase in output supply) if $m_1 > m_0$. The latter would make the mean value of output transitionally higher than the natural level.[7]

Under the assumption of Muthian rationality, each agent forecasts that his beliefs are shared by everyone else ($Fm_{t_0+s} = F^2 m_{t_0+s}$ because $\theta = 1$ for all $s \geqslant 0$). The latter assures that the shift in policy has no transitional effects on the mean value of output ($Ey_{t_0+s} = a_0$ for all $s \geqslant 0$).

On the other hand, the mean value of the price level [expression (27)] will be transitionally higher than the Muthian solution [given by (10)] if $m_1 < m_0$, and lower if $m_1 > m_0$.

In the Muthian case, the mean value of the price level immediately reflects the new average money supply m_1. On the contrary, if each market participant assumes that the other market participants do not believe completely in the new average money supply, then his expectations of others' beliefs will modify the behavior of the price level in such a way that the mean value of the latter will not fully reflect the new monetary circumstances. Uncertainty about others' beliefs, even in a world of complete price flexibility, is enough reason for the generation of certain unresponsiveness of the price level to announced changes in monetary conditions. In the long run, (27) will converge to (10), and the economy will achieve Muthian rationality.

What about the transitional effects of changes in the monetary variance? As is apparent from (26) and (9), a change in the monetary variance ($g_1 \neq g_0$) can only produce a transitional *increase* in the variance of output. A shift in the degree of feedback cannot be used by the government to obtain transitional benefits in the form of a reduction in output variance. Such a measure can only produce undesired results, even if it is fully believed from the very beginning, as in our case.[8]

---

[7] These deviations of the mean value of output from the natural level are a consequence of the lack of information about others' beliefs. The mean value of output would remain at its natural level if each agent were informed that all the other market participants shared his own full degree of credibility. This lack of information would be beneficial for the government if its objective function gave credit to expanding output above its full-information position on the grounds of existence of positive external effects (income taxation, unemployment compensation, etc.). According to Barro (1976), expansions of output above the natural rate are not justified if the policymaker's objective function is based on minimizing the gap between actual and full-information output.

[8] This conclusion is in conformity with footnote 46 in Barro's study (1976, p. 25). Although he does not deal explicitly with the transitional effects of changes in the monetary variance, he mentions that "presumably, the variance of actual about full information output is minimized when perceptions about σ_m^2 are

Imagine an economy that has suffered a negative shock to velocity in period t_{0+s-1}. Suppose that $g_0 > g_1$. Given that the new rule is also leaning against velocity shocks, people will expect an increase in the money supply for period t_{0+s}. However, if each agent assumes that the others are still expecting a degree of feedback stronger than g_1, then each agent's expectations of the price level to prevail at time t_{0+s} will be biased upward. The reason for this bias is that each agent's conditional expectation of the price level to prevail at time t_{0+s} will again be contaminated by the incorrect belief that average opinion expects a larger increase in the money supply. Whereas the path of the price level is determined by the actual economy-wide average expectation of it [see (22)], each agent believes that the economy-wide average expectation of the price level is different from his own expectation. This leads suppliers to reduce their output in period t_{0+s} through the usual Lucas confusion between aggregate and relative price movements. The opposite response would result (an increase in output supply) if $g_1 > g_0$. Under Muthian rationality, $\theta = 1$, and the shift in policy does not generate any transitional effects on the variance of output.

Our result that the change in monetary variance can produce only a transitional increase in the variance of output has some implications for the debate about the adoption of an activist rule or a Friedmanian $x\%$ rule. Suppose that the criterion for monetary policy is Barro's criterion of minimizing the expected squared gap between output and full-information output. Let us now assume that our economy has been subject to substantial feedback for a long time and that $m_1 = m_0$. What would be the consequences of abandoning our activist rule in order to adopt a Friedmanian rule without feedback? The conclusion is as follows: If we depart from a long-run Muthian expectational position characterized by each agent's complete credibility in an activist rule that the government has followed for a long period of time (and the certainty that others' credibility is also complete), then an announced shift to a nonactivist rule can only have disruptive transitional effects, even if the new monetary policy is completely anticipated from the very beginning. The reason is, again, the uncertainty on the part of each individual about the other agents' credibility.

Given the fact that announced activist rules that have been pursued for a long time can do no harm under rational expectations, then it can be argued in a "weak" sense that a shift to a nonactivist rule is not advisable. If such a shift is decided, it may well be the case that the monetary

correct." In our case, again, uncertainty about others' beliefs is the reason behind the increase in the output variance that results after the announced change in the feedback coefficient.

authorities will feel impelled in the future to provide feedback again, in order to smooth out the output fluctuations that the abandonment of feedback created in the first place.[9]

On the other hand, uncertainty about others' beliefs makes the variance of the price level [right-hand side of (28)] transitionally lower than the Muthian solution [given by (11)] if $g_1 > g_0$, and higher if $g_1 < g_0$. In the Muthian case, the variance of the price level immediately reflects the new monetary variance generated by the change from g_0 to g_1.

3.6.   Serial correlation in output

It has long been recognized that forecast errors cannot be serially correlated in rational expectations models that exhibit complete price and wage flexibility and that the theory must appeal to some other mechanism (long-lived wage contracts) to explain the observed persistence in output behavior.

Our example, although rudimentary, is at least able to isolate a possible expectational source of positive serial correlation in output. Let us assume for simplicity that $m_1 \neq m_0$ but $g_1 = g_0$. Then the key error-orthogonality property of rational expectations models is lost because

$$E[(p_{t_0+s} - F_{t_0+s-1} p_{t_0+s})(p_{t_0+s-j} - F_{t_0+s-j-1} p_{t_0+s-j})] > 0$$

for $s \geq 0$ and $1 \leq j \geq s$ during the transitional period in which the agents are still revising their forecasts of the probability that average opinion assigns to the previously expected "average" money supply and their beliefs about the probability that average opinion believes that average opinion assigns to the previously expected "average" money supply, and so forth. Therefore, even a model that assumes that everyone anticipates the new policy is still able to explain serial persistence in output on pure expectational grounds.

If we provide the market participants with all the information necessary to revise all their expectations of higher degrees *completely* at the end of the first period after the shift in policy, then the serial correlation in output will disappear. However, serial persistence triggered by a

---

[9] We might even imagine a situation in which the transitional increase in the variance of output leads each agent to expect with some positive probability that the government, being disappointed with the results of the shift in policy, will try to smooth out output fluctuations by adopting feedback again. These anticipations will make things worse if the government maintains its Friedmanian policy, because they will increase even more the variance of output about its full-information level.

completely anticipated shift in monetary policy will reappear in a model incorporating an accelerator effect, as in the equilibrium business cycle model of Lucas (1975).

3.7.   Expectations of expectations and the disinflation issue

The credibility problem faced by any central bank attempting to reduce the rate of inflation has been extensively discussed in the literature (Taylor, 1975, 1979; Fellner, 1978).[10] In Taylor's words: "The information problem which economic agents face is whether the change [he is referring to a reduction in the growth rate of the money supply] is a permanent one, or whether the central bank will soon give up on its resolve" (Taylor, 1979, p. 10).

Let us assume away Taylor's problem by maintaining our former assumption that all the market participants find the new rate of money growth fully credible. Is this requirement enough to ensure that the government will be able to achieve its disinflationary objective without causing a temporary slump in the process?

It is apparent that our former arguments can be easily extended to account for the problem of reducing inflation. The same simple model can be modified in order to analyze the effects of a shift in the rate of money growth. Assuming for simplicity that the demand for real cash balances is independent of the money rate of interest (the "old" quantity theory of money), the only two necessary modifications are the introduction of systematic growth in the money supply equation and the subtraction of the lagged price level from p_t and $F_{t-1} p_t$ in the aggregate supply function. An immediate conclusion is that the expected rate of inflation will remain transitionally higher than the new rate of money growth if each agent assumes that average opinion is assigning some probability to the resumption of the former monetary policy by the central bank. There will therefore emerge a transitional reduction in output that will last until each agent is completely convinced that the other market participants also fully believe in the permanence of the new lower rate of monetary growth, and so on.

If the government's purpose is to achieve a rapid adjustment of inflationary expectations, it should give strong and credible signals of its disinflationary purposes. The latter will shorten the adaptation process by convincing people to adjust their own forecasts as well as their forecasts of average opinion about monetary growth accordingly.

[10] A game-theoretic approach to the problem can be found in Phelps (1979).

3.8.   Conclusions

The purpose of this chapter has been to discuss the monetary nonneutrality that emerges after an anticipated major shift in policy once we abandon some of the implicit assumptions of the rational expectations school paradigm. This task has been carried out by assuming that although each and every agent shares the same opinion about the money supply (full credibility in the new rule), each agent imputes to everyone else an opinion that is different from his own. The cost of acquiring information about the others' beliefs has been invoked as the source of the assumed expectational difference.

Under the aforementioned assumptions, it has been shown that the rational expectations short-run neutrality condition is no longer tenable. Therefore, after a major shift in policy, *perceived* unanimity of beliefs seems crucial for the Muthian rational expectations paradigm. This school implicitly assumes that each rational agent believes that his model of the economy is also being used by the others in their forecasting processes and that his beliefs about the exogenous variables are also held unanimously.

Our results suggest that Muthian rationality may be achieved only in the long run, after the completion of a transitional period in which each agent revises his beliefs about average opinion and his beliefs about average opinion about average opinion, and so on. During this transition, agents will not form expectations rationally in the Muthian sense, and the shift in policy will have effects on output. Suppliers' mistaken opinions about others' beliefs will lead them to form incorrect forecasts of the aggregate price level and will promote output effects through the usual Lucas mechanism.

It has also been argued that full credibility in the newly announced rate of monetary growth is not a sufficient condition for the attainment of disinflation without recession in a model exhibiting complete price and wage flexibility. If agents misperceive average opinion about the rate of monetary growth, there will emerge a transitional period of unemployment. We have also isolated a possible pure expectational source of output persistence under conditions of full credibility.

This chapter has assumed that each and every agent believes that the other market participants use a model similar to his own to form expectations of the price level but that they do not share his own views about the parameters of the money supply equation. The more general case in which each market participant believes that some proportion of the public uses a model of the economy that is different from his own (although it may actually be the same) was not included in the analysis. If professional economists are still discussing the effectiveness of systematic monetary policy, it is quite reasonable to presume that some people may form expectations or may believe that some proportion of the population forms expectations according to a model of the economy that implies short-run monetary effectiveness (as in the models of Fischer or Phelps and Taylor). If that is the case, systematic changes in the money supply will have short-run effects on real variables.

References

Barro, R. J. (1976). "Rational Expectations and the Role of Monetary Policy." *Journal of Monetary Economics,* 2:1–33.

Fellner, W. (1978). "The Core of the Controversy about Reducing Inflation: An Introductory Analysis." In: *Contemporary Economic Problems,* edited by W. Fellner. Washington, D.C.: American Enterprise Institute.

Fischer, S. (1977). "Long-Term Contracts, Rational Expectations, and the Optimal Money Supply Rule." *Journal of Political Economy,* 85:191–206.

Frydman, R. (1982). "Towards an Understanding of Market Processes: Individual Expectations, Market Behavior and Convergence to Rational Expectations Equilibrium." *American Economic Review,* 72:652–68.

Keynes, J. M. (1936). *The General Theory of Employment, Interest and Money.* New York: Harcourt Brace & World, p. 156.

Lucas, R. E. (1972). "Expectations and the Neutrality of Money." *Journal of Economic Theory,* 4:103–24.

(1973). "Some International Evidence on Output–Inflation Trade-offs." *American Economic Review,* 63:326–34.

(1975). "An Equilibrium Model of the Business Cycle." *Journal of Political Economy,* 83:1113–44.

Muth, J. F. (1961). "Rational Expectations and the Theory of Price Movements." *Econometrica,* 29:315–35.

Phelps, E. S. (1978). "Disinflation without Recession: Adaptive Guideposts and Monetary Policy." *Weltwirtschaftliches Archiv,* 114:783–809.

(1979). "Obstacles to Curtailing Inflation." In: *Essays in Post-Keynesian Inflation,* edited by J. H. Gapinski and C. E. Rockwood, pp. 179–93. Cambridge, Mass.: Ballinger.

(1980). "The Trouble with 'Rational Expectations' and the Problem of Inflation Stabilization." Presented at the Vargas Institute conference, World Inflation and Inflation in Brazil, Rio de Janeiro, December 15–18, 1980, p. 16.

Phelps, E. S., and J. B. Taylor (1977). "Stabilizing Powers of Monetary Policy under Rational Expectations." *Journal of Political Economy,* February, pp. 163–90.

Sargent, T. J., and N. Wallace (1975). "Rational Expectations, the Optimal Monetary Instrument, and the Optimal Money Supply Rule." *Journal of Political Economy,* 83:241–54.

Taylor, J. B. (1975). "Monetary Policy during a Transition to Rational Expectations." *Journal of Political Economy,* 83:1009–22.

(1979). "Recent Developments in the Theory of Stabilization Policy." Presented at the Federal Reserve Bank of St. Louis and the Center for the Study of American Business Conference on "Stabilization Policy: Lessons from the 1970's and Implications for the 1980's." St. Louis, Missouri, October 1979, p. 41.

66   **Comment by C. Bull**

Townsend, R. M. (1978). "Market Anticipations, Rational Expectations, and Bayesian Analysis." *International Economic Review,* 19:481–94.

Comment

CLIVE BULL

Di Tata's chapter can be interpreted in two ways: namely, as an analysis of a macroeconomic policy problem or as an illustration of a problem with rational expectations models. If one were to interpret the chapter strictly as an analysis of macroeconomic policy, one would have to conclude that it is of little importance. I feel sure that if we all knew the "true" model and we all found the proposed monetary policy credible, we would certainly be able to find a way to fix up any problem stemming from a lack of perceived unanimity of beliefs. Indeed, a simple opinion poll that asked if you believed that the central bank intended to pursue its new policy would do in this case.[1] Obviously, the real-world problem is to find a disinflationary policy for an economy in which people do not find proclaimed monetary policies credible and do not share a common, let alone true, model of the economy.

Although the specific policy analysis presented in the chapter is of little interest, it does provide some insight, ironically, into the problems of generating credibility in a monetary policy. Consider the Federal Reserve's proclaimed policy of decelerating the growth of the money stock. Although I believe that the board of governors is willing to incur large political costs to maintain this policy, I nevertheless believe that a long enough period of high interest rates will create sufficient political pressure to deflect the Fed from its policy. If, furthermore, my model of the economy also says that the average opinion held about the success of the monetary policy by a group of individuals known collectively as Wall Street affects the level of interest rates, then my view of the credibility of the Fed's policy will depend on my view of Wall Street's beliefs. Replace the Fed, Wall Street, and interest rates by, respectively, Bank of England, T.U.C., and union wage claims and you have a British example. The moral being, of course, that to sell your policy to the public you must convince them that groups they regard as powerful have already bought it. Appealing over the heads of these groups to the people will not work unless you can simultaneously persuade them that traditionally powerful

[1] Note that, as Frydman (1982) has pointed out, an opinion poll will not solve the average opinion problem where the average opinion concerns an endogenous variable. Here it concerns an exogenous variable, namely, the intentions of the central bank.

groups are no longer so strong as to be able to deflect you from your policy. Given the track record of politicians, this latter condition seems sure to fail.

The more interesting interpretation of Di Tata's chapter is as an illustration of the importance of average opinion and its vagaries for macroeconomic behavior in a rational expectations model. Perhaps the most interesting issue in this area is the ability of individuals in an economy to learn their way into a rational expectations equilibrium. Di Tata, however, focuses on different issues that arise once the true model of the economy has been learned.[2]

Although it is clear that Di Tata and others in this book view average opinion and its behavior as highly significant for macroeconomic behavior, it is perhaps worthwhile looking at one of the necessary conditions for this to be true. In particular, for average opinion to have any role to play, it is crucial that the aggregate output function have the property that current production depend significantly on current predictions of next period's price level (i.e., that it have the form of the Lucas supply function). Thus, if one thinks that predictions of future price levels have little impact on current output decisions, one would not expect the behavior of average opinion to have a significant effect on aggregate output. But how reasonable is the form of the Lucas supply function? This comment is not the proper place to go into this question, though it should be noted that it is far from clear that the Lucas supply function can be derived rigorously from the Lucas and Rapping (1969) model in the usual rational expectations island-paradigm context.[3]

To put the importance of the Lucas supply function for the fruitfulness of theoretical work on the average opinion in some perspective, let us assume, arguendo, that there is no Lucas-and-Rapping-based support for the supply function. In order to keep average opinion at the center of the stage, a supply function that looked like the Lucas supply function would have to be generated. If we ask where this might come from at the micro level, then we must reply with some argument to the effect that most industries have output functions similar in form to the Lucas supply function. But this form is precisely the form taken in markets subject to "cobwebs." Perhaps this should not be surprising, as it is the setting in which Muth first developed his concept of rational expectations (Muth, 1961).

[2] With a changing monetary policy rule he cannot escape the convergence issue entirely. As his focus is on other issues, he quite reasonably deals with convergence by fiat, forcing, exogenously, individuals' priors over the average opinion to converge to the new policy rule.

[3] See Bull and Frydman (1983) for an elaboration of this point.

It seems, then, that the importance of average opinion, if the Lucas and Rapping model fails to support the Lucas supply function, depends on the prevalence of cobweb-type output functions within the economy. Unfortunately, cobwebs are regarded as something of a rarity in economics, outside some parts of the agricultural sector. After all, cobwebs are generally thought to occur only where substantial irreversible (at low cost) commitments to future sales are made, where inventories are very costly to hold, and where the product is sold on an auction market. It seems unlikely that a significant number of industries in the economy would fulfill these requirements.

Although the foregoing discussion looks rather pessimistic as far as the significance of work on average opinion is concerned, I think there is still a large area, investment, where it is of primary importance. Firm- or industry-specific physical capital formation is the principal way in which agents in the economy commit themselves to future output. This results in investment expenditure being highly sensitive to expectations. To the extent that fluctuations in these expectations, through their effects on investment expenditure, affect actual rates of return on investment, it is clear that average opinion and guesses about average opinion will play a crucial role in the evolution of the capital stock and so output. Moreover, the bond and equity markets allow these expectations formation processes to work themselves out very quickly. So one must consider not only the complicated interaction between expectations and investment but also the role that financial markets play in aggregating and homogenizing expectations. Naturally this is not a new view; Wicksell and Keynes spring to mind immediately. But perhaps with the development of the concept of average opinion and the rapid development of our knowledge about both learning and the information content of prices, we can at last explore this view rigorously and with a realistic hope for success.

References

Bull, C. D., and R. Frydman (1983). "The Derivation and Interpretation of the Lucas Supply Function." *Journal of Money, Credit and Banking,* February, pp. 82–94.

Frydman, R. (1982). "Towards an Understanding of Market Processes: Individual Expectations, Market Behavior and Convergence to Rational Expectations Equilibrium." *American Economic Review,* 72:652–68.

Lucas, R. E., and L. Rapping (1969). "Real Wages, Employment and Inflation." *Journal of Political Economy,* 77:721–54.

Muth, J. F. (1961). "Rational Expectations and the Theory of Price Movements." *Econometrica,* 29:315–35.

CHAPTER 4

The stability of rational expectations in macroeconomic models

GEORGE EVANS

The assumption of rational expectations developed by Muth (1961) has been widely employed in theoretical macroeconomic models. The question of the stability of such rational expectations solutions has been considered from several perspectives, some of which have been discussed by Shiller (1978). An important problem is that agents may not know the true values of key parameters, or, more fundamentally, they may not know the true structure, so that they cannot form (strong-form) rational expectations. Taylor (1975) and Friedman (1979) looked at macroeconomic models in which agents were trying to learn the values of certain parameters and considered whether or not expectations would eventually converge to rational expectations. In microeconomic contexts, the problem of learning about parameters using Bayesian techniques in models with rational expectations has been considered by Cyert and DeGroot (1974) and Townsend (1978). Bray (1982) has used a Bayesian process to examine learning in an asset market. More general learning rules have been considered by Blume and Easley (1982) in a general equilibrium context in which different agents observe different signals.

There is, however, a fundamental problem of stability that is present even if the true structure of the economy is completely known. It will be shown that the conventional rational expectations solution can be thought of as an expectations equilibrium. If expectations start out of equilibrium, it will not usually be individually rational for agents to move immediately to the collective rational expectations solution. A

This chapter is a much revised version of Part 3 of my doctoral dissertation "Three Essays on the Variance of Inflation, Expectations and Macroeconomic Stability" (University of California, Berkeley, 1980). I am grateful to Richard Sutch, James Pierce, George Akerlof, Olivier Blanchard, Roger Craine, Steve Goldman, Robert Harris, Brian Loasby, and Pauline Andrews for comments and suggestions at previous stages. I am indebted to Roman Frydman for pointing out a flaw in an earlier proof of Proposition 5. I have also benefited from many comments received at seminars when earlier versions of this chapter were presented. I am, of course, responsible for any remaining errors. Mrs. Shirley Hewitt provided able computing assistance.

revision process begins, and we can consider whether or not convergence occurs. A simple technique for examining expectational stability was applied by DeCanio (1979) to the analysis of a single market, and it is one of the techniques used by Bray to analyze a sequence of asset markets. This chapter extends the technique of DeCanio to define expectational stability for general models and then applies the concept to several macroeconomic examples.

It may be helpful to relate the approach taken here to the work of others presented in this book. It is important conceptually to separate the problem of imperfect knowledge of the model by agents from the problem of "regressive expectations," that is, from the complications that arise from considering the expectations each agent holds of other agents' expectations. These difficulties may be faced separately or in conjunction. The first problem can be considered in isolation provided that expectations do not help determine the motion of the system. However, even when expectations do influence outcomes, the problem of learning can still be isolated if we restrict ourselves to expectational equilibria. This is the approach taken by Townsend (1978), who looks at the question whether or not agents learn the true value of a parameter when they are following Nash equilibrium decision rules. The equilibrium approach to learning is further developed by Townsend in Chapter 9.

If disequilibria are permitted, then the problem of learning about parameters becomes confounded with the problem of expectations of expectations. There are both positive and negative results. Bray (Chapter 6) shows for the Sargent-Wallace (1975) model that if agents are boundedly rational, so that they ignore the expectations-of-expectations problem, then their estimates of a key parameter will converge to its true value almost surely. On the other hand, Frydman (Chapter 5) shows for a similar model that when agents take seriously the problem of others' expectations it is impossible for them to learn relevant parameters. Essentially the model becomes underidentified.

The approach taken in this chapter is to concentrate on the expectations-of-expectations problem in preference to the problem of learning about the models.[1] Even when the true model is known, individually rational agents must take into account the expectations of others when forming their expectations and making their decisions. Indeed, we could go further and allow agents to form expectations of other agents' expectations of other agents' expectations, and so on into higher degrees. This is the development pursued by Phelps (Chapter 2). In the closely related

---

[1] However, as will be discussed in Section 4.1.3, one possible interpretation of the revision process examined in this chapter is that it describes a process of learning about reduced-form parameters.

procedure adopted here, we start with an arbitrary out-of-equilibrium expectation-generating function and calculate the expectations that individually rational agents will hold if they take the expectations of others as given and generated by this initial expectation mechanism. This leads to a new expectation function that can be sequentially updated by individual rationality, and we can look at whether or not the process converges to a rational expectations solution. This process has several possible interpretations that are discussed in Section 4.1.3. By approaching the problem is this way it is hoped that something can be learned about the inherent stability of rational expectations equilibria that does not depend on the extent of ignorance of agents about the model.

The plan of this chapter is as follows. In Section 4.1.1 a general reduced-form stochastic process is considered that makes allowance for nonlinearities in the structure and for expectations of future variables. A rational expectations solution is defined, and in Section 4.1.2 it is shown that this solution can typically be viewed as a Nash equilibrium. In Section 4.1.3, expectational stability is defined. Despite the level of generality in Section 4.1, some useful results are obtained. In Section 4.2 the stability test is applied to several macroeconomic models, including some in which expected sales and expected future output play important roles. Examples of both stable and unstable models are given. Conclusions are drawn in Section 4.3.

4.1. Equilibrium and stability of rational expectations

4.1.1. General framework and definition of rational expectations

We consider a stochastic process with the reduced form

$$x_t = F(x_{t-1}, \ldots, x_{t-1-l}; {}_{t-1}x^*_{t+m}, \ldots, {}_{t-1}x^*_{t+1}, {}_{t-1}x^*_t; v_t) \tag{1}$$

where x_t is a $p \times 1$ vector of the state variables at time t, v_t is an unobserved disturbance vector, which we shall assume is identically and independently distributed over time, and ${}_{t-1}x^*_{t+i}$, for $i = 0, 1, \ldots, m$, is the psychological expectation of x_{t+i} formed at $t-1$ on the basis of the information set Ω_{t-1}.[2] Typically we shall assume $\Omega_{t-1} = \{x_{t-i}, i \geqslant 1\}$. F is assumed known, and x_t may include exogenous variables that do not depend on the ${}_{t-1}x^*_{t+i}$.

This formulation is quite general, applicable to market models and to

---

[2] We leave open the precise meaning of "psychological expectation." In many contexts it is most naturally defined as an average of the predictions of the agents in the economy. In the cases considered in this chapter, an assumption of homogeneity of expectations across agents avoids complications.

macroeconomic models of various types. There is still quite a lot that can be said about rational expectations in this context. We start by showing that the system (1) can be rewritten more compactly. Let $k = \max(m, l)$. Define the following vectors:

$$y_t = \begin{bmatrix} x_t \\ \vdots \\ x_{t-k} \end{bmatrix} \quad \text{and} \quad {}_{t-1}y^*_{t+m} = \begin{bmatrix} {}_{t-1}x^*_{t+m} \\ \vdots \\ {}_{t-1}x^*_{t+m-k} \end{bmatrix} \tag{2}$$

Note that y_t and ${}_{t-1}y^*_{t+m}$ are both vectors of length $(k+1)p$. In the case of $l > m$ the variable ${}_{t-1}y^*_{t+m}$ involves expectations of past variables. Given our information assumption, it is natural to define ${}_{t-1}x^*_s = x_s$ for $s \leqslant t-1$.

Proposition 1
The system (1) can be written equivalently, using the variables defined in (2), as

$$y_t = f(y_{t-1}, {}_{t-1}y^*_{t+m}, v_t) \tag{3}$$

by suitable choice of f. If F is C^n (i.e., if F has n continuous derivatives), then f is C^n.

Proof
Using (2), we define

$$\bar{F}(y_{t-1}, {}_{t-1}y^*_{t+m}, v_t) = F(x_{t-1}, \ldots, x_{t-1-l}; {}_{t-1}x^*_{t+m}, \ldots, {}_{t-1}x^*_t; v_t)$$

and

$$e_j(y_{t-1}, {}_{t-1}y^*_{t+m}, v_t) = x_{t-j} \quad \text{for } j = 1, \ldots, k$$

Setting

$$f = \begin{bmatrix} \bar{F} \\ e_1 \\ \vdots \\ e_k \end{bmatrix}$$

it can be seen that (1) and (3) are equivalent. Because the e_j are continuously differentiable of all orders (i.e., e_j is C^∞), we have that f is C^n whenever F is C^n.

Proposition 1 allows us to proceed with the system (3). We now consider the determination of ${}_{t-1}y^*_{t+m}$, that is, the m-period ahead forecasts of y_t formed at the end of period $t-1$. An arbitrary expectation-generating mechanism constructs $_{t-1}y^*_{t+m}$ using the information set Ω_{t-1}. It is often convenient to take $\Omega_{t-1} = \{y_{t-1}\}$, and this can be justified as follows. We assume that $\Omega_{t-1} = \{x_{t-1}, \ldots, x_{t-1-r}\}$, that is, that information sufficiently old is unavailable or discarded (alternatively we can assume that the expectation-generating mechanism ignores information older than $t-1-r$). Now writing (3) with $k = \max(l, m, r)$ we have that Ω_{t-1} is a subset of y_{t-1}. Using this convention, we can write an arbitrary expectation-generating mechanism as

$$_{t-1}y^*_{t+m} = \pi(y_{t-1}) \tag{4}$$

Conventional "adaptive expectations" mechanisms are simply intuitively appealing forms of π in (4).[3] For example, we might have $_{t-1}x^*_{t+i} = \Sigma\lambda_j x_{t-j}$ with fixed weights λ_j. A particularly simple case would be the static expectations $_{t-1}x^*_{t+i} = x_{t-1}$; that is, future variables are expected to be whatever they have most recently been observed to be.

We now define rational expectations in a way that is consistent with Muth (1961) and the recent macroeconomic literature. Given some expectation mechanism π, we define

$$\phi(y_{t-1}, v_t) = f[y_{t-1}, \pi(y_{t-1}), v_t] \tag{5}$$

and call ϕ the realization function. Under π, the economy evolves according to $y_t = \phi(y_{t-1}, v_t)$, so that ϕ can be used to predict y_t when π as well as f is known.

We must also consider predictions of future variables. Define, for $s \geq 2$ integer,

$$\phi^s(y_{t-1}, v_t, \ldots, v_{t+s-1}) = \phi[\phi^{s-1}(y_{t-1}, v_t, \ldots, v_{t+s-2}), v_{t+s-1}] \tag{6}$$

and

$$\phi^1(y_{t-1}, v_t) = \phi(y_{t-1}, v_t)$$

It follows that

$$y_{t+m} = \phi^{m+1}(y_{t-1}, v_t, \ldots, v_{t+m}) \tag{7}$$

so that, if π and f are known, ϕ^{m+1} can be used to predict y_{t+m}.

We say that $\bar{\pi}(y_{t-1})$ is a (collectively) rational-expectation-generating process, or RE, if

$$\bar{\pi}(y_{t-1}) = E[\bar{\phi}^{m+1}(y_{t-1}, v_t, \ldots, v_{t+m}) \mid \Omega_{t-1}] \tag{8}$$

where E is the mathematical expectation operator, and where $\bar{\phi}$ satisfies

---

[3] We have difficulties with some forms of adaptive expectations that take weighted averages of an infinite sequence of past values of a variable. However, such mechanisms might plausibly be thought of as approximations to more realistic mechanisms using a finite amount of past history.

$$\bar{\phi}(y_{t-1}, v_t) = f[y_{t-1}, \bar{\pi}(y_{t-1}), v_t] \tag{9}$$

The stochastic process $y_t = \bar{\phi}(y_{t-1}, v_t)$ described by the expectation-generating process (8) and the realization process (9) is called an REE, or rational expectations equilibrium. Of course, a given model (3) may fail to have an REE, or it may have a multiplicity of REEs. For an interesting example of multiple equilibria, see Taylor (1977).

In the case in which $m = 0$, so that expectations of future variables are not involved, (8) and (9) can be combined to yield a definition of a rational-expectation-generating process as a function $\bar{\pi}(y_{t-1})$ satisfying

$$\bar{\pi}(y_{t-1}) = E[f(y_{t-1}, \bar{\pi}(y_{t-1}), v_t) \mid \Omega_{t-1}] \tag{10}$$

4.1.2. Rational expectations, Nash equilibria, and consistency of expectations

The definition of rational expectations given in (8) was referred to as a collective rational expectation in order to emphasize a possible divergence between these expectations and those that might appear more rational to individual agents. The expectations appearing in (3), $_{t-1}y_{t+m}^*$, should usually be thought of as an average of the expectations held by many different agents in the economy. If an individual agent firmly believed that the average expectation differed from the (collective) rational expectation defined implicitly by (8) and (9), assuming (for convenience) uniqueness, then it would not typically be rational for that agent to hold these expectations. That is, when account is taken of the large number of agents in the economy, individually rational actions and expectations for different agents become interdependent. This point can be most clearly made by reformulating the model (3) in a game theoretic context and exhibiting the REE as a Nash equilibrium. The connection between REE and Nash equilibria in a particular market model was established by Townsend (1978). This section demonstrates that this correspondence holds generally.

Combining (3) and (4), our model of the economy is

$$y_t = f(y_{t-1}, \pi(y_{t-1}), v_t) \tag{11}$$

where $\pi(y_{t-1})$ represents the average psychological expectation of y_{t+m}. We must take account of the fact that there are many agents in the economy, and they may have differing expectations. Furthermore, we recognize that expectations can matter (i.e., can affect the evolution of the economy) only if they affect the actions of these agents. Thus, f should be regarded as implicitly incorporating the dependence of these actions on expectations.

Bearing these points in mind, we say that the model (11) possesses an underlying framework in which it is embedded if the following conditions are met. Let $\pi_i(y_{t-1})$, for $i=1,\ldots,L$, represent the psychological expectation of y_{t+m} held by agent i, as a function of y_{t-1}. We assume that the optimal strategy for agent i to follow depends only on y_{t-1} and on the true expected future course of the economy. Letting g_i stand for this dependence (assumed single-valued), we thus assume that the actual strategy of agent i is given by

$$a_i(y_{t-1}) = g_i[y_{t-1}, \pi_i(y_{t-1})] \quad \text{for } i=1,\ldots,L \tag{12}$$

where $a_i(y_{t-1})$, the strategy function of agent i, maps y_{t-1} to a vector of actions parametrized by real numbers. Equation (12) gives the true optimal strategy for agent i if $\pi_i(y_{t-1})$ is the true mathematical expected value of y_{t+m} given Ω_{t-1} and given the actual strategies of other agents.

The evolution of the economy is described by

$$y_t = \tilde{f}[y_{t-1}, \{a_j(y_{t-1})\}, v_t] \tag{13}$$

where $\{a_j(y_{t-1})\} = [a_1(y_{t-1}),\ldots,a_L(y_{t-1})]$ and $\tilde{f}$ is such that

$$f[y_{t-1}, \pi(y_{t-1}), v_t] = \tilde{f}(y_{t-1}, \{g_j[y_{t-1}, \pi(y_{t-1})]\}, v_t) \tag{14}$$

for every $\pi(y_{t-1})$. Equation (14) says that the model (11) can be thought of as arising from the underlying framework (12) and (13) in the sense that it describes the evolution of y_t that would obtain if each agent held the same expectation $\pi(y_{t-1})$ and followed what they believed to be their optimal strategy corresponding to the expectation.

We shall want to pursue the interdependence of the π_i. However, at this stage we can already see the connection between rational expectations and Nash equilibria. When the model (11) is embedded in the underlying framework (12)–(14), we say that an REE obtains if $\pi_j(y_{t-1}) = \bar{\pi}(y_{t-1})$ for $j=1,\ldots,L$, where $\bar{\pi}(y_{t-1})$ is given by (8) and (9). We say that the set of strategy functions $a_j(y_{t-1})$ constitutes a Nash equilibrium if each is optimal given the others. This can be expressed in the following way. Let

$$\tilde{\phi}^1(\{a_j\})(y_{t-1}, v_t) = \tilde{f}[y_{t-1}, \{a_j(y_{t-1})\}, v_t] \tag{15}$$

and for $s \geqslant 2$ integer, define

$$\tilde{\phi}^s(\{a_j\})(y_{t-1}, v_t, \ldots, v_{t+s-1})$$
$$= \tilde{\phi}^1(\{a_j\})[\tilde{\phi}^{s-1}(\{a_j\})(y_{t-1}, v_t, \ldots, v_{t+s-2}), v_{t+s-1}]$$

Equation (15) is the realization function that applies when agents follow the specified strategies. Here, $\{a_j\} = (a_1,\ldots,a_L)$. Then, from (12) and the immediately following definition, it can be seen that a Nash equilibrium obtains if and only if

$$a_i(y_{t-1}) = g_i(y_{t-1}, E[\tilde{\phi}^{m+1}(\{a_j\})(y_{t-1}, v_t, \ldots, v_{t+m}) \mid \Omega_{t-1}]) \qquad (16)$$

for $i = 1, \ldots, L$.

Proposition 2

Suppose the model (11) is embedded in the underlying structure (12)–(14). Then every REE is a Nash equilibrium. If the g_i (which map expectations into strategies) are one-to-one for each y_{t-1}, then the converse holds.

Proof

Assume that an REE obtains, so that $\pi_i(y_{t-1}) = \bar{\pi}(y_{t-1})$. By (12) and (16), a Nash equilibrium is established if we can show that $\bar{\pi}(y_{t-1})$ is the true expected value of y_{t+m} given the actual set of strategies. The latter is

$$E[\tilde{\phi}^{m+1}(\{a_j\})(y_{t-1}, v_t, \ldots, v_{t+m}) \mid \Omega_{t-1}]$$

where

$$\tilde{\phi}^1(\{a_j\})(y_{t-1}, v_t) = \tilde{f}(y_{t-1}, \{g_j[y_{t-1}, \bar{\pi}(y_{t-1})]\}, v_t)$$
$$= f[y_{t-1}, \bar{\pi}(y_{t-1}), v_t] \quad \text{[by (14)]}$$
$$= \bar{\phi}(y_{t-1}, v_t)$$

Arguing by induction on the power of $\tilde{\phi}$, we have

$$E[\tilde{\phi}^{m+1}(\{a_j\})(y_{t-1}, v_t, \ldots, v_{t+m}) \mid \Omega_{t-1}]$$
$$= E[\bar{\phi}^{m+1}(y_{t-1}, v_t, \ldots, v_{t+m}) \mid \Omega_{t-1}]$$
$$= \bar{\pi}(y_{t-1}) \quad \text{[by (8)]}$$

To show the converse, suppose that (16) holds. By (12) and the assumption that the g_i are one-to-one, we have

$$\pi_i(y_{t-1}) = E[\tilde{\phi}^{m+1}(\{a_j\})(y_{t-1}, v_t, \ldots, v_{t+m}) \mid \Omega_{t-1}]$$

Because $\pi_i(y_{t-1})$ does not depend on i, we can write $\pi_i(y_{t-1}) = \pi(y_{t-1})$. Following the same line of argument as before, we can show that

$$\tilde{\phi}(\{a_j\})(y_{t-1}, v_t) = \phi(y_{t-1}, v_t) = f[y_{t-1}, \pi(y_{t-1}), v_t]$$

so that

$$\pi_i(y_{t-1}) = \pi(y_{t-1}) = E[\phi^{m+1}(y_{t-1}, v_t, \ldots, v_{t+m}) \mid \Omega_{t-1}]$$

But this is just the definition of $\bar{\pi}(y_{t-1})$ given in (8) and (9), so that we have an REE. This establishes the proposition.

We now pursue the question of expectations one level deeper. Because from (13) it is clear that the current and future values of y depend on the current and future strategies of all agents, it is clear that each agent's expectation $\pi_i(y_{t-1})$ should depend on the strategies followed by other agents and hence on their expectations. We thus augment the model by introducing conjectures of expectations held by other agents. This will be helpful in analyzing out of equilibrium behavior, as in Section 4.1.3.

Let $\pi_{j(i)}(y_{t-1})$, for $j=1,\ldots,L$, but $j\neq i$, represent the conjectured expectation-formation mechanism that agent j is assumed to hold by agent i. Let

$$a_{j(i)}(y_{t-1}) = g_j[y_{t-1}, \pi_{j(i)}(y_{t-1})] \quad \text{for } j \neq i \tag{17}$$

be the corresponding conjectured strategy, which agent j is assumed to follow by agent i, where each agent is assumed to follow the optimal strategy corresponding to the assumed expectation. We are implicitly assuming that the g_j are part of the known structure.

We make the assumption of individual rationality, which we now define. Let

$$\tilde{\phi}^1(\{a_{j(i)}\})(y_{t-1}, v_t) = \tilde{f}[y_{t-1}, \{a_{j(i)}(y_{t-1})\}, v_t] \tag{18}$$

with powers of $\tilde{\phi}(\{a_{j(i)}\})$ defined in the usual way. Equation (18) is a conjectured realization function, specifying the value of y_t that will arise under the strategies that i conjectures to be followed by other agents. Here $\{a_{j(i)}\} = (a_{1(i)},\ldots,a_{L(i)})$, and an apparent problem with (18) is that we have not defined $a_{j(i)}$ for $j=i$. For (18) to be well defined, we must therefore assume that the effect of any single agent's strategy on y_t is negligible, an assumption we shall call *individual negligibility*. We can now define *individual rationality* as the assumption that

$$\pi_i(y_{t-1}) = E[\tilde{\phi}^{m+1}(\{a_{j(i)}\})(y_{t-1}, v_t,\ldots, v_{t+m}) \mid \Omega_{t-1}] \tag{19}$$

In other words, each individual is assumed to form his expectations of y_{t+m} as the mathematical expected value given the available information and given the assumed expectations (with corresponding strategies) held by others.

The complete underlying structure (12)–(14) and (17)–(19) exhibits the crucial interdependence of expectations and the possible divergence between individual rationality and collective rationality. Suppose that for each agent i we are given a set $\{\pi_{j(i)}\}$ of assumed expectations held by other agents. Using (17)–(19), the individual rational expectations for each agent can be calculated. The corresponding strategies are found using (12), and the evolution of the economy is determined by (13). Every different set of conjectured expectations may lead to different individual rational expectations and actions and to a different path for the economy.

The interdependence and corresponding indeterminacy of individual rational expectations and strategies are fundamental. One way to view the matter is that individuals are implicitly involved in a game, which we assume to be noncooperative. (We have not specified the entire payoff matrix, because for our purposes it is sufficient to know the optimal strategy for a given expected value of y_{t+m}.) Just as in general there is no best strategy for an agent in a game, so there is no single rational expectation and corresponding best strategy for an agent in our economy. In particular, suppose that an individual agent confidently believes that all other agents are forming expectations according to some fixed adaptive process. Then that agent's individual rational expectation will not (usually) be the collective rational expectation $\bar{\pi}(y_{t-1})$ specified in (8), but rather some other specific calculable expectation.

It is true that if an agent believes that other agents hold a collective rational expectation $\bar{\pi}(y_{t-1})$, then it will be individually rational for that agent to hold $\bar{\pi}(y_{t-1})$. Furthermore, any other given set of conjectured expectations will be inconsistent in the sense that at least some agents will not have the expectations they are conjectured to have by other agents. A requirement of such expectational consistency guarantees, and thus seems to underlie, a rational expectations equilibrium.

Let us say that expectations are consistent if $\pi_{j(i)}(y_{t-1}) = \pi_j(y_{t-1})$ for $i, j = 1, \ldots, L$ and $i \neq j$. We say that conjectured rationality obtains if $\pi_{j(i)}(y_{t-1}) = \bar{\pi}(y_{t-1})$ for $i, j = 1, \ldots, L$ and $i \neq j$, where $\bar{\pi}(y_{t-1})$ satisfies (8) and (9). The following proposition, together with Proposition 2, relates the concepts of expectational consistency, conjectured rationality, rational expectations, and Nash equilibria.

Proposition 3

Suppose that the model (11) is embedded in the complete underlying structure (12)–(14) and (17)–(19) in which individual rationality holds and the assumption of individual negligibility is met.

(a) If for some agent i, $\pi_{j(i)}(y_{t-1}) = \bar{\pi}(y_{t-1})$ for $j = 1, \ldots, L$ and $j \neq i$, where $\bar{\pi}(y_{t-1})$ is rational, then $\pi_i(y_{t-1}) = \bar{\pi}(y_{t-1})$.

(b) Expectations are consistent if and only if conjectured rationality obtains.

(c) If expectations are consistent, then an REE obtains.

Proof

To show (a), substitute (17) into (18) and use the assumption of conjectured rationality. The conjectured realization function of agent i is thus given by

$$\tilde{\phi}^1(\{a_{j(i)}\})(y_{t-1}, v_t) = \tilde{f}(y_{t-1}, \{g_j[y_{t-1}, \bar{\pi}(y_{t-1})]\}, v_t)$$

$$= f[y_{t-1}, \bar{\pi}(y_{t-1}), v_t] \quad [\text{using (14)}]$$

$$= \bar{\phi}(y_{t-1}, v_t)$$

Applying the definition of individual rationality, (19), it then follows that $\pi_i(y_{t-1}) = \bar{\pi}(y_{t-1})$.

The converse of (b) now follows from (a). The forward direction follows from (c), because $\pi_{j(i)}(y_{t-1}) = \pi_i(y_{t-1})$ for $i \neq j$ and $\pi_i(y_{t-1}) = \bar{\pi}(y_{t-1})$ imply $\pi_{j(i)}(y_{t-1}) = \bar{\pi}(y_{t-1})$. We thus turn to (c). From (12) and (17) it can be seen that consistent expectations imply consistent strategies; that is, $a_{j(i)}(y_{t-1}) = a_j(y_{t-1})$ for $i, j = 1, \ldots, L$ and $i \neq j$. Inserting this into (19), we have

$$\pi_i(y_{t-1}) = E[\tilde{\phi}^{m+1}(\{a_j\})(y_{t-1}, v_t, \ldots, v_{t+m}) \mid \Omega_{t-1}]$$

from which it follows that $\pi_i(y_{t-1})$ does not depend on i, so that we can write $\pi_i(y_{t-1}) = \pi(y_{t-1})$. But now an argument identical with that given in the proof of the converse direction of Proposition 2 establishes that $\pi(y_{t-1}) = \bar{\pi}(y_{t-1})$; that is, we have an REE.

Propositions 2 and 3 show the senses in which a rational expectations solution is an equilibrium concept. Once expectations of expectations are brought into the picture, it is clear that individual rationality and knowledge of the true model are insufficient to justify rational expectations. A requirement of collective consistency of expectations with expectations of expectations seems needed to justify the rational expectations equilibrium. We might call a consistent expectations equilibrium a complete REE. Outside of a complete REE we can expect disequilibrium adjustment to occur, and the question then arises whether or not an REE can be attained from an initial disequilibrium position. It is to this question of stability that we now turn.

4.1.3. Expectational stability

Once it is recognized that the conventional rational expectations solution defined by (8) and (9) is not a consequence simply of individual rationality, but rather is an equilibrium concept, it becomes natural to inquire into the stability of this equilibrium. Suppose that agents begin with an arbitrary set of conjectures about the expectation-formation mechanisms employed by other agents and act appropriately. Outside of a complete REE, the conjectures of at least some agents will turn out to be incorrect. Suppose that agents learn the nature of their mistakes and modify their conjectures accordingly. We can ask whether or not such a process of learning leads to an REE.

Mathematically our definition of stability can be most simply stated in terms of the discussion in Section 4.1.1. The definition of expectational stability follows and generalizes that given by DeCanio (1979) in the analysis of a market. Assuming that model (11) describes the economy, suppose we are given some initial expectation-generating mechanism $\pi_0(y_{t-1})$. This might, for example, be an expectations mechanism appropriate to a previous policy regime, but in general we allow π_0 to be arbitrary. Equation (5) describes the realization process $\phi_0(y_{t-1})$ corresponding to this expectation mechanism. Powers of ϕ_0 are defined in the usual way by (6). We now proceed recursively. Suppose that $\pi_{N-1}(y_{t-1})$ and $\phi_{N-1}(y_{t-1}, v_t)$ are defined. Then we define

$$\pi_N(y_{t-1}) = E[\phi_{N-1}^{m+1}(y_{t-1}, v_t, \ldots, v_{t+m}) \mid \Omega_{t-1}] \tag{20}$$

and

$$\phi_N(y_{t-1}, v_t) = f[y_{t-1}, \pi_N(y_{t-1}), v_t] \tag{21}$$

provided the required expectation exists. We say that $(\pi_N, \phi_N) \to (\pi, \phi)$ for a given π_0 if $\pi_N(y_{t-1})$ converges pointwise to $\pi(y_{t-1})$ and $\phi_N(y_{t-1}, v_t)$ converges pointwise to $\phi(y_{t-1}, v_t)$. If $m = 0$, note that (20) and (21) reduce to

$$\pi_N(y_{t-1}) = E\{f[y_{t-1}, \pi_{N-1}(y_{t-1}), v_t] \mid \Omega_{t-1}\} \tag{22}$$

Proposition 4
Suppose that in the system (20)–(21) we have $(\pi_N, \phi_N) \to (\bar{\pi}, \bar{\phi})$ for a given π_0. Suppose also that f is continuous and that $\phi_N^{m+1} \to \bar{\phi}^{m+1}$, where the convergence is uniform with respect to the disturbances $v_t, \ldots, v_{t+m}$. Then $(\bar{\pi}, \bar{\phi})$ is an REE of (11); that is, equations (8) and (9) are satisfied.

Proof
Taking limits of both sides of equation (21) and using the continuity of f, we immediately have (9). Letting $\xi(v_t, \ldots, v_{t+m})$ denote the joint distribution of $v_t, \ldots, v_{t+m}$, using the definition of expectation, and taking limits of both sides of (20), we have

$$\bar{\pi}(y_{t-1}) = \lim_{N \to \infty} \int \phi_{N-1}^{m+1}(y_{t-1}, v_t, \ldots, v_{t+m}) \, d\xi(v_t, \ldots, v_{t+m})$$

$$= \int \bar{\phi}^{m+1}(y_{t-1}, v_t, \ldots, v_{t+m}) \, d\xi(v_t, \ldots, v_{t+m})$$

$$= E[\bar{\phi}^{m+1}(y_{t-1}, v_t, \ldots, v_{t+m}) \mid \Omega_{t-1}]$$

where the second equality here uses the fact that the limit of the integral is the integral of the limiting function when convergence is uniform (Apostol, 1974, Theorem 9.8). Thus, (8) holds, and $(\bar{\pi}, \bar{\phi})$ is an REE.

Proposition 4 shows, provided that f is continuous and the convergence of (π_N, ϕ_N) is sufficiently strong, that the system (20)–(21) can only converge to an REE. In the case of $m = 0$, the convergence condition is that $\phi_N \to \bar{\phi}$ uniformly with respect to v_t. For $m \geqslant 1$ it can be shown that the convergence condition is met if $\phi_N \to \bar{\phi}$ uniformly with respect to all variables and if $\bar{\phi}$ is uniformly continuous.

Of course, it is perfectly possible for (π_N, ϕ_N) not to converge for a specified π_0 or for the limit to depend on the choice of π_0. We are now in a position to define the (expectational) stability of an REE. An REE $(\bar{\pi}, \bar{\phi})$, as defined in (8)–(9), of the model (11) is said to be *globally stable* if $(\pi_N, \phi_N) \to (\bar{\pi}, \bar{\phi})$ for every initial π_0. Note that if an REE is globally stable, then it must be unique.

Several interpretations of this definition of expectational stability are possible. We should perhaps begin by distinguishing it from other definitions of the stability of rational expectations that occur in the literature. First, stability in the sense here used is not the same thing as boundedness of the REE over time or stationarity of the REE stochastic process. We are instead concerned with convergence to the REE. Second, we are not principally concerned with whether or not, starting from a model of the economy that is incompletely known, agents will eventually learn the true model. We are instead concerned with the stability of the expectations themselves, and this question remains even if the true model, including all parameter values, is known by all agents.

Our definition of expectational stability can be interpreted in terms of the underlying framework given in Section 4.1.2. Suppose that initially all agents begin with some particular expectation mechanism π_0, for example some simple adaptive process, so that the economy follows the stochastic process ϕ_0. Suppose that each agent now realizes that other agents are using the expectation mechanism π_0 and as a result takes π_0 to be the conjectured expectation, that is, $\pi_{j(i)} = \pi_0$ for $i \neq j$, on the basis of which new individual rational expectations are calculated. It is then easy to see that for each agent, $\pi_i = \pi_1$. The economy would then follow the stochastic process ϕ_1, and (π_1, ϕ_1) might be called the first-order individual rational expectations path. In the next round, individually rational agents might then conjecture expectations $\pi_{j(i)} = \pi_1$ and calculate the second-order rational expectations $\pi_i = \pi_2$ leading to the path ϕ_2. Continuing in this way we can generate (π_N, ϕ_N) and ask if the process converges. Our definition of expectational stability can thus be interpreted as a learning process in which rational agents learn about the expectation mechanism employed by others and use their knowledge of the model to formulate new individual rational expectations mechanisms taking this information into account.[4]

Several specific interpretations of this revision process are possible. First, it could describe a hypothetical tâtonnement process in which a central agency conducts a survey of expectations mechanisms that is then made public, leading to a revision of expectations, made public in a new survey, and so on. The stability test determines whether or not such an iterative process will converge. Second, the revision process might be purely notional. Starting from an initial disequilibrium point, agents consider improving their forecasts using the model. Then they try to anticipate similar revisions of expectations by other agents, then the revision of the revision of others' expectations, and so on. Again, if a model is expectationally stable, such a process will converge.

Third, the revision process could describe learning in real time. In this case an apparent requirement of the foregoing interpretation is that expectations are observable or can be inferred from observable variables. Even if this is not the case, the stability process described by (20) and (21) may have a natural interpretation. If agents use the expectation mechanism π_N, this leads to the stochastic processes ϕ_N and ϕ_N^{m+1}, which can be estimated from data on y_t. ϕ_N^{m+1} may then be used by agents to calculate π_{N+1}. This account can apply even if f is unknown, provided ϕ_N^{m+1} is estimable. On this interpretation, however, expectation mechanisms are changed only after estimates of ϕ_N^{m+1} converge in probability to their true values.

The usefulness of the concept of expectational stability, here employed, obviously depends on the economic model being analyzed and the precise assumption about the information available to agents, including information about average expectations. Bray (1982) argued that it is more realistic to consider models in which parameters are unknown, learning is occurring in real time, and expectation mechanisms are altered with each data point. There is much to commend this view. However, in addition to being more difficult to analyze, such learning processes are sensitive to the precise assumptions made concerning prior knowledge of the structure, availability of the data, and the maintained hypothesis about the functional form of expectations during the learning process. The definition of expectational stability used in this chapter attempts to separate out the problem of learning about parameters from the expectations-of-

---

[4] With this interpretation, learning occurs at the same rate for all agents. This is the only natural assumption to make, given our premises of individual rationality and a common information set.

expectations problem, focusing on the latter so that we can learn something about the inherent stability of the model when subject to deviations of expectations from a collectively self-fulfilling solution.

4.2. Macroeconomic examples

4.2.1. *Linear models with expectations of current variables*

We start with a simple example: the textbook income-expenditure model. Firms try to set output, Y_t, equal to expected sales, while actual sales, S_t, depend on the sum of consumption, C_t, and investment, I_t, with the former depending on output via the consumption function. We have

$$Y_t = {}_{t-1}S_t^* + u_t$$

$$S_t = C_t + I_t$$

$$C_t = a + bY_t + \epsilon_t \quad (a > 0, \ 0 < b < 1)$$

$$I_t = I + \eta_t \quad (I > 0) \tag{23}$$

where u_t, ϵ_t, and η_t are white-noise disturbances. In terms of the framework of Section 4.1.2, the strategy that each firm must determine is its own level of output. This depends on its expected sales, which depend in turn on aggregate output.

Solving the system (23) for sales, we obtain

$$S_t = A + b_{t-1}S_t^* + v_t = A + b\pi(\Omega_{t-1}) + v_t \tag{24}$$

where $A = a + I$, $v_t = \eta_t + \epsilon_t + bu_t$, and $\pi(\Omega_{t-1})$ indicates that ${}_{t-1}S_t^*$ may depend on any variables in the information set.

Using (10), we have that a rational expectation must satisfy

$$\bar{\pi}(\Omega_{t-1}) = E[A + b\bar{\pi}(\Omega_{t-1}) + v_t \mid \Omega_{t-1}] = A + b\bar{\pi}(\Omega_{t-1})$$

Thus, the REE is given by

$$\bar{\pi}(\Omega_{t-1}) = (1-b)^{-1}A \quad \text{and} \quad S_t = (1-b)^{-1}A + v_t \tag{25}$$

with corresponding solutions for Y_t, C_t, and I_t.

Rather than calculate stability for this model directly, we shall derive stability from a more general result. We consider a specialization of model (3) in which $m = 0$ and f is linear. That is, suppose that our model is

$$y_t = k + Ay_{t-1} + B_{t-1}y_t^* + v_t \tag{26}$$

We have the following result:

Proposition 5

In the model (26), suppose that $\det(I-B) \neq 0$ and that the eigenvalues of B are all less than 1 in magnitude. Then there is a unique globally stable REE.

Proof

Applying (10), we have that a rational expectation must satisfy

$$\bar{\pi}(y_{t-1}) = k + Ay_{t-1} + B\bar{\pi}(y_{t-1}) \quad \text{or} \quad \bar{\pi}(y_{t-1}) = (I-B)^{-1}(k + Ay_{t-1})$$

provided that $I-B$ is invertible. Clearly, in this case, $\bar{\pi}$ is unique. The corresponding realization function is

$$\bar{\phi}(y_{t-1}, v_t) = (I-B)^{-1}(k + Ay_{t-1}) + v_t$$

For stability, note that from (22)

$$\pi_N(y_{t-1}) = k + Ay_{t-1} + B\pi_{N-1}(y_{t-1})$$

or

$$\pi_N(y_{t-1}) - \bar{\pi}(y_{t-1}) = B[\pi_{N-1}(y_{t-1}) - \bar{\pi}(y_{t-1})] \quad \text{for } N \geq 1$$

By repeated substitution, this can be rewritten as

$$\pi_N(y_{t-1}) = B^N[\pi_0(y_{t-1}) - \bar{\pi}(y_{t-1})] + \bar{\pi}(y_{t-1})$$

We now take limits of both sides. Provided that all eigenvalues of B are less than 1 in absolute magnitude, we can show that $\lim_{N \to \infty} B^N = 0$. This is easy to see when B is diagonalizable, so that B can be written as $B = CDC^{-1}$, where D has eigenvalues on the diagonal and zeros elsewhere. Because $B^N = CD^NC^{-1}$, it is clear that $B^N \to 0$. More generally, Schur's lemma guarantees that any square matrix B can be written as $B = URU^{-1}$, where R is upper triangular with eigenvalues on the diagonal. It is then possible to show that $R^N \to 0$. Because $B^N = UR^NU^{-1}$, we have that B^N tends to the zero matrix. From this, it follows that $\lim_{N \to \infty} \pi_N(y_{t-1}) = \bar{\pi}(y_{t-1})$. Similarly, it is easy to see that $\phi_N(y_{t-1}, v_t) \to \bar{\phi}(y_{t-1}, v_t)$. Hence, the REE $(\bar{\pi}, \bar{\phi})$ is globally stable.

Note that in Proposition 5 it need not be assumed that π_0 is linear. It is also clear that the proof holds for any information set Ω_{t-1} that includes y_{t-1}. The condition for stability is considerably simpler than that obtained by DeCanio (1979) for a market model, because (26) assumes that variables have already been stacked in accordance with Proposition 1. This will always be possible provided that lags are finite and the disturbance is white noise.

The stability of the unique REE (25) for the income–expenditure model (23) follows immediately from Proposition 5, because B is just the coefficient b and because we have assumed $0 < b < 1$. Note, however, that if $b > 1$ (a situation that might arise if I_t depended positively on Y_t), the REE would be unstable.

As another simple application, we consider a standard macroeconomic model involving aggregate demand and supply equations:

$$m_t = \delta + p_t + q_t + \epsilon_t \quad (\delta > 0)$$

$$q_t = q_n + \gamma(p_t - _{t-1}p_t^*) + \eta_t \quad (\gamma > 0) \tag{27}$$

Here p_t and q_t are the logarithms of the price level and aggregate output, and m_t is the logarithm of the money supply, assumed fixed at $m_t = m$; q_n is the natural rate of output; ϵ_t and η_t are white-noise disturbances. The first equation is a highly simplified aggregate demand relationship in which nominal output is proportional to the money supply. The second equation is an aggregate supply relationship in which output is related to unexpected inflation. The system (27) can be solved for p_t to give

$$p_t = (1+\gamma)^{-1}(m - \delta - q_n) + \gamma(1+\gamma)^{-1}{}_{t-1}p_t^* - (1+\gamma)^{-1}(\eta_t + \epsilon_t) \tag{28}$$

Because $0 < \gamma(1+\gamma)^{-1} < 1$, we have immediately from Proposition 5 that the REE is unique and globally stable. It is easy to show that $\bar{\pi} = m - \delta - q_n$, so that the REE realization functions are

$$p_t = (m - \delta - q_n) - (1+\gamma)^{-1}(\eta_t + \epsilon_t)$$

$$q_t = q_n + (1+\gamma)^{-1}\eta_t + [(1+\gamma)^{-1} - 1]\epsilon_t \tag{29}$$

The techniques used in this section can be extended to examine stability in linear models with future expectations. See Evans (1983) for details and applications to the Sargent-Wallace (1975) and Taylor (1977) models.

4.2.2. Instability in a nonlinear model with expectations of future variables

We next turn to a model that illustrates the possibility of nonconvergence to the REE taking the form of cycling: a version of the business cycle model of Goodwin (1951). This illustrates at the same time the complications that arise when we go beyond the framework of the preceding section. In Goodwin's model, a strong multiplier–accelerator interaction is constrained by nonlinearities, namely, a ceiling and a floor to investment. We consider a discrete stochastic version of Goodwin's simplest model:

$$Y_t = C_t + I_t + A + \epsilon_t$$

$$C_t = bY_t + \lambda_t$$

$$I_t = h(K_{t-1}, {}_{t-1}Y^*_{t+1}) + \eta_t$$

$$K_t = K_{t-1} + I_t \tag{30}$$

where

$$h(K_{t-1}, {}_{t-1}Y^*_{t+1}) = \begin{cases} L & \text{if } v_{t-1}Y^*_{t+1} - K_{t-1} \geqslant L \\ -M & \text{if } v_{t-1}Y^*_{t+1} - K_{t-1} \leqslant -M \\ v_{t-1}Y^*_{t+1} - K_{t-1} & \text{otherwise} \end{cases} \tag{31}$$

with $0 < b < 1$ and v, L, and $M > 0$. Y_t, C_t, I_t, and K_t are aggregate net output, consumption, investment, and the end-of-period capital stock, respectively. A represents autonomous spending, and ϵ_t, λ_t, and η_t are white-noise disturbances. The first equation of (30) says that aggregate output depends on demand. The second equation is the consumption function. The third equation specifies net investment as the nonlinear function (31) of the existing capital stock at the end of the preceding period and the rate of output expected in the subsequent period. The desired capital stock that firms wish to have at the end of period t is proportional to the rate of output expected in period $t + 1$. Thus, investment is set equal to $v_{t-1}Y^*_{t+1} - K_{t-1}$ unless it is constrained by the ceiling, L, or the floor, $-M$. One possible interpretation is that L is the net capacity of the capital goods industry and M is the maximum rate at which capital goods can be scrapped.

In Goodwin's (nonstochastic) version, expected output was determined by an adaptive mechanism, a simple example of which is ${}_{t-1}Y^*_{t+1} = Y_{t-1}$. There is a stationary-state solution $\tilde{Y} = (1-b)^{-1}A$, with $\tilde{K} = v\tilde{Y}$. Provided, however, that $v > 1 - b$ (as Goodwin assumed), the multiplier-accelerator interaction will drive aggregate output to the ceiling or floor if the initial condition is any position other than the stationary state. Thereafter, the economy goes through alternate booms and busts, the durations of which depend on the parameters involved.

We consider the REE in this model and investigate its expectational stability.[5] The analysis is simplified by changing units to normalized output, X_t, and capital stock, J_t, as follows:

---

[5] In terms of the framework of Section 4.1.2, the strategy of each firm is the level of investment it chooses. Each firm's optimal strategy depends on expected future output, which depends on the future strategies of other firms.

$$X_t = (1-b)L^{-1}(Y_t - \tilde{Y})$$
$$J_t = L^{-1}(K_t - \tilde{K}) \tag{32}$$

The reduced form for (30) can then be written as

$$X_t = g(J_{t-1},\,_{t-1}X_{t+1}^*) + u_t$$
$$J_t = J_{t-1} + g(J_{t-1},\,_{t-1}X_{t+1}^*) + \eta_t \tag{33}$$

where

$$g(J_{t-1},\,_{t-1}X_{t+1}^*) = \begin{cases} 1 & \text{if } \xi_{t-1}X_{t+1}^* - J_{t-1} \geqslant 1 \\ -d & \text{if } \xi_{t-1}X_{t+1}^* - J_{t-1} \leqslant -d \\ \xi_{t-1}X_{t+1}^* - J_{t-1} & \text{otherwise} \end{cases} \tag{34}$$

and where $\xi = v(1-b)^{-1}$, $d = M/L$, and $u_t = L^{-1}(\lambda_t + \epsilon_t)$.

The equations specifying the REE can be found by applying equations (8) and (9) with $m=1$. This can be most simply set forth as follows. Let $\theta(J_{t-1}, X_{t-1}) = {}_{t-1}X_t^*$ represent the expected value of X_t and $\pi(J_{t-1}, X_{t-1}) = {}_{t-1}X_{t+1}^*$ represent the expected value of X_{t+1}, each expectation formed at the end of $t-1$. Then an RE $(\bar{\theta}, \bar{\pi})$ must satisfy

$$\bar{\theta}(J_{t-1}, X_{t-1}) = g[J_{t-1}, \bar{\pi}(J_{t-1}, X_{t-1})] \tag{35}$$

$$\bar{\pi}(J_{t-1}, X_{t-1}) = E\{\bar{\theta}[J_{t-1} + \bar{\theta}(J_{t-1}, X_{t-1}) + \eta_t,\ \bar{\theta}(J_{t-1}, X_{t-1}) + u_t] \mid \Omega_{t-1}\} \tag{36}$$

A new problem is that (36) involves taking expectations of nonlinear functions of the disturbances. This considerably complicates the problem, and we shall not attempt the general solution. However, suppose that $\eta_t \overset{\text{i.i.d.}}{\sim} N(0, \sigma_\eta^2)$ and $u_t \overset{\text{i.i.d.}}{\sim} N(0, \sigma_u^2)$, and suppose that the variances of the disturbances, σ_η^2 and σ_u^2, are small. In that case, the right-hand side of (36) can be replaced by an approximation obtained by setting η_t and u_t equal to their expected values, giving us

$$\bar{\pi}(J_{t-1}, X_{t-1}) = \bar{\theta}[J_{t-1} + \bar{\theta}(J_{t-1}, X_{t-1}),\ \bar{\theta}(J_{t-1}, X_{t-1})] \tag{36'}$$

Equations (35) and (36') specify an exact solution for the RE of model (33) in the deterministic case (in which circumstances RE reduces to perfect foresight) and an approximate solution for the RE in the case of normal disturbances with small variances.

It is straightforward to check that the following functions solve (35) and (36'):

$$\bar{\theta}(J_{t-1}, X_{t-1}) = \begin{cases} 1 & \text{if } J_{t-1} \leqslant -1 \\ -J_{t-1} & \text{if } -1 < J_{t-1} < d \\ -d & \text{if } J_{t-1} \geqslant d \end{cases}$$

$$\bar{\pi}(J_{t-1}, X_{t-1}) = \begin{cases} 1 & \text{if } J_{t-1} \leqslant -2 \\ -(J_{t-1}+1) & \text{if } -2 < J_{t-1} \leqslant -1 \\ 0 & \text{if } -1 < J_{t-1} < d \\ -(J_{t-1}-d) & \text{if } d \leqslant J_{t-1} < 2d \\ -d & \text{if } J_{t-1} \geqslant 2d \end{cases} \tag{37}$$

The REE is given by

$$X_t = \bar{\theta}(J_{t-1}, X_{t-1}) + u_t$$
$$J_t = J_{t-1} + \bar{\theta}(J_{t-1}, X_{t-1}) + \eta_t \tag{38}$$

Most of the time will be spent near $X_t = -J_{t-1} + u_t$ and $J_t = \eta_t$, because usually the nonlinearities will not be encountered. Infrequently (because σ_η^2 and σ_u^2 are small) a large disturbance will take the economy into a business cycle along the ceiling or floor.

We now consider the question of stability. Applying definition (20)–(21) and expressing Nth-order expectations analogously to (35)–(36), we have

$$\theta_N(J_{t-1}, X_{t-1}) = g[J_{t-1}, \pi_{N-1}(J_{t-1}, X_{t-1})] \tag{39}$$

$$\pi_N(J_{t-1}, X_{t-1})$$
$$= E\{\theta_N[J_{t-1} + \theta_N(J_{t-1}, X_{t-1}) + \eta_t, \ \theta_N(J_{t-1}, X_{t-1}) + u_t] \mid \Omega_{t-1}\} \tag{40}$$

Using, again, the approximation for small σ_η^2 and σ_u^2, we replace (40) by

$$\pi_N(J_{t-1}, X_{t-1}) = \theta_N[J_{t-1} + \theta_N(J_{t-1}, X_{t-1}), \ \theta_N(J_{t-1}, X_{t-1})] \tag{40'}$$

The question is whether or not (39) and (40') converge to (37) from a given π_0. Although it is possible to show instability formally for some special cases, it is not possible to obtain a general proof. Computer calculations have consequently been used to construct (39) and (40') for a range of parameter values. Taking $\pi_0(J_{t-1}, X_{t-1}) = X_{t-1}$, instability was found for all parameter values ξ and d and for all values of the arguments J_{t-1} and X_{t-1} (other than $J_{t-1} = X_{t-1} = 0$), provided $\xi > 1$ (i.e., $v > 1 - b$). The instability takes the form of complex cycling of the values of π_N as N increases; that is, π_N might flip between maximum and minimum values with each increment of N, though the precise pattern depends on ξ and d.[6]

Intuitively, the reason for instability is as follows. With

$$\pi_0(J_{t-1}, X_{t-1}) = X_{t-1}$$

[6] If ξ is less than or equal to 1, the model is expectationally stable.

Goodwin's cyclical path over time is generated: Booms turn to busts when there is an excess of capital stock, J_{t-1}, for expected output. Under first-order rationality, the bust is anticipated and occurs at smaller levels of capital stock. There is a corresponding increase in the frequency of the business cycle. As N increases, the extent of anticipation becomes greater. Convergence, however, will not occur, because if for a given J_{t-1} and X_{t-1} a boom next period is expected to turn to a bust the following period, a higher degree of rationality will generate the bust this period; a similar result occurs if a bust is expected to turn to boom. The sequential application of individual rationality does not, in this model, lead to collective rationality. Instead, agents cycle perpetually through disequilibrium expectation functions.

4.2.3. Expectational stability and stationarity under static expectations

It may appear from the preceding examples that, in the case of linear models, there is a simple connection between expectational stability as defined in Section 4.1.3 and dynamic stability under some form of adaptive expectations in the sense, say, of stationarity of the realization function obtained under static expectations, $_{t-1}y_{t+m}^* = y_{t-1}$.

Formally, there is no such connection. From the model (26) and from Proposition 5, we can see that whereas expectational stability depends on the roots of B, stationarity under the static expectations $_{t-1}y_t^* = y_{t-1}$ depends on the roots of $A + B$. Of course, it is easy to construct expectationally stable models that are nonstationary under RE or under static expectations simply by assuming nonstationary exogenous variables, but it is not easy to find economically plausible examples of expectationally unstable models that are stationary under static expectations and stationary exogenous variables. However, the following model, which is stationary under static expectations, does exhibit (borderline) expectational instability.

We consider the model

$$s_t = a + bx_t + c(m - p_t) + \epsilon_t$$
$$x_t = {}_{t-1}s_t^*$$
$$q_t = x_t + u_t$$
$$p_t = d(x_{t-1} - x_n) + {}_{t-1}p_t^* + \eta_t \tag{41}$$

where $a, c, d > 0$, $0 < b < 1$, and ϵ_t, u_t, and η_t are white noise. All variables are expressed as logarithms. The first equation is the aggregate demand equation, which relates sales, s_t, to the underlying rate of aggregate output, x_t, and to the real money supply, expressed as the difference between the (logarithm of the) nominal money supply, m, assumed constant, and the (logarithm of the) price level, p_t. The latter effect can be thought of as either a Pigou effect or Keynes effect. The second and third equations state that firms set the underlying rate of output to equal expected sales, but that actual output, q_t, deviates from this level by white noise, due, say, to uncontrollable factors affecting production. The last equation of (41) is the supply schedule, which states that unexpected inflation depends on the underlying rate of output with a one-period lag. There are several rationales that could be given for such a lag, some of which are discussed by Okun (1975), but an important point to note is that the implied direction of causation requires the disequilibrium interpretation of aggregate supply discussed in Gordon (1981) rather than the equilibrium interpretation of Lucas (1972, 1973).

The reduced form of (41) is

$$s_t = a + c(m + dx_n) - cdx_{t-1} + b_{t-1}s_t^* - c_{t-1}p_t^* + \epsilon_t - c\eta_t$$

$$x_t = {}_{t-1}s_t^*$$

$$q_t = {}_{t-1}s_t^* + u_t$$

$$p_t = -dx_n + dx_{t-1} + {}_{t-1}p_t^* + \eta_t \tag{42}$$

If we let $y_t' = (s_t, x_t, q_t, p_t)$, then (42) can be expressed in the form (26) with B matrix:

$$B = \begin{bmatrix} b & 0 & 0 & -c \\ 1 & 0 & 0 & 0 \\ 1 & 0 & 0 & 0 \\ 0 & 0 & 0 & 1 \end{bmatrix} \tag{43}$$

Because $\det(I - B) = 0$, the conditions for Proposition 5 are not met. However, applying (10) by taking expected values of the first and last equations in (42), it is easy to show that there is a unique REE stochastic process. Writing $\pi^p = {}_{t-1}p_t^*$ and $\pi^s = {}_{t-1}s_t^*$, the full REE solution is

$$\bar{\pi}^p = \bar{p} \quad \text{where} \quad \bar{p} = m + c^{-1}[a - (1 - b)]x_n$$

$$x_t = \bar{\pi}^s = x_n$$

$$s_t = x_n + \epsilon_t - c\eta_t$$

$$q_t = x_n + u_t$$

$$p_t = \bar{p} + \eta_t \tag{44}$$

It should be noted that if at any time the underlying rate of output x_t ever differed from x_n, no rational expectations solution would exist for the price level in the following period. This fact, which is the source of $\det(I-B)=0$, explains why x_t identically equals x_n over all time on the REE path (of course, actual output may differ from x_n by white noise).

Turning now to the question of stability, note that the eigenvalues of B include a root of 1, which suggests (borderline) instability. The following argument sketches the demonstration. As pointed out in the proof of Proposition 5, the Nth-order expectations satisfy $\pi_N(y_{t-1})= k+Ay_{t-1}+B\pi_{N-1}(y_{t-1})$. Thus, in particular, we have $\pi_N^p(y_{t-1})= d(x_{t-1}-x_n)+\pi_{N-1}^p(y_{t-1})$, and it is clear that for any π_0^p, $\pi_N^p(y_{t-1})$ can reach a limit only if $x_{t-1}=x_n$. It follows that the realization processes ϕ_N can reach a limiting stochastic process only if the latter obeys $x_t=x_n$ identically, as in the REE (44). It can be shown by direct calculation, assuming $x_{t-1}=x_n$, that for any initial π_0^s, π_0^p, we have

$$\lim_{N\to\infty} \pi_N^p(y_{t-1})=\pi_0^p(y_{t-1})$$

and

$$\lim_{N\to\infty} \pi_N^s(y_{t-1})=x_n+c(1-b)^{-1}[\bar{p}-\pi_0^p(y_{t-1})]$$

Hence, the limiting realization process for x_t is

$$x_t=x_n+c(1-b)^{-1}[\bar{p}-\pi_0^p(y_{t-1})]$$

But this is consistent with $x_t=x_n$ identically only if $\pi_0^p(y_{t-1})=\bar{p}$, which is the REE for π^p. Hence, the REE (44) is unstable. Given any initial price expectation mechanism other than the RE, then (π_N, ϕ_N) will fail to converge.

Intuitively, the source of expectational instability is the fact that prices do not respond to output within the period. "Nonrational" price expectations can consequently be temporarily self-fulfilling, with the full reaction taking the form of output and sales changes. Sequential individual rationality leads the economy into a Keynesian trap that, in the succeeding period, leads to explosive prices.

Although the REE is unstable, it can easily be seen that under static expectations the realization function can be stationary. Substituting $_{t-1}p_t^*=p_{t-1}$ and $_{t-1}s_t^*=s_{t-1}$ into (42) and solving for q_t and p_t, we obtain

$$q_t = (a+cm)+bq_{t-1}-cp_{t-1}+(u_t+bu_{t-1}+\epsilon_{t-1})$$

$$p_t = dx_n+dq_{t-1}+p_{t-1}+(\eta_t+du_{t-1}) \tag{45}$$

Applying the standard test to this system of stochastic difference equations, it can be shown that (45) is stationary provided that $b + cd < 1$. Provided this condition is met, we can see that (q_t, p_t) follow a vector ARMA $(1, 1)$ process with means $(x_n, \bar{p})$.

Although this model possesses an unstable REE, it may strain economic plausibility in its assumption that prices do not at all respond to output within the period (a nonzero positive response of p_t to x_t would render the model expectationally stable). Nevertheless, the model exhibits one of the ways that a collectively rational solution can be unattainable under individual rationality, and it is interesting that a nonstationarity problem need not arise under static expectations.

4.3.   Conclusions

The Nash view of the REE presented in Section 4.1.2 shows that the REE cannot be deduced from individual rationality alone. Rather, the REE is an equilibrium that in its complete form combines individual rationality with a requirement of collective consistency of expectations. Thinking in terms of the strategies that correspond to the expectations of individual agents, the REE can be viewed as a Nash equilibrium.

It is thus important to know whether or not this equilibrium can be attained by individually rational agents if expectations start out of equilibrium. Section 4.2 provides macroeconomic examples of both stable and unstable REEs. These models illustrate the two types of nonconvergence possible, with the sequential application of rationality leading to expectational cycling in one case and to explosive paths in the other.

The stability test given in Section 4.1.3 is a useful way of assessing the realism of an REE solution in a model. If an REE is unstable, it is possible to conclude either that rational expectations are unlikely to be attained or that the model itself is in some way defective, but in either case the stability test has indicated potential difficulties. Furthermore, in cases of multiple equilibria, stability analysis can help by narrowing down the possible rest points to stable REE and, if given a historically determined initial expectation mechanism, in choosing between the equilibria.

Even in cases with a unique stable equilibrium, our analysis suggests the possible importance of out-of-equilibrium behavior. Suppose that (27) were known to be the true model of the economy, with $dm/dt = 10$ percent and a corresponding mean rate of inflation. The REE suggests that a preannounced policy of reducing dm/dt to zero would end inflation with no cost of lost output because of the immediate adaption of price expectations. Our analysis points up a difficulty with this line of reasoning, separate from and additional to the problem that (27) may not be the true model or be known to be the true model. It is quite possible that most agents will not believe that other agents will immediately fully shift their expectations to the (collectively rational) zero mean rate of inflation. For example, agents might initially believe that, on average, other agents would stop at second-order rationality calculated from the previously appropriate expectation of 10 percent. Attempting to be exactly one step ahead of the average opinion, agents would thus adopt third-order rationality. The "correct" expectation would then be the fourth order of rationality, though, of course, this could not have confidently been anticipated. If an elapse of real time is required for this process to converge to the collectively rational expectation of a zero rate,[7] such a policy will be costly in terms of forgone output.[8] In other words, even if an REE is stable and agents are individually rational it may not be sensible to assume that convergence takes place instantaneously with a known change in structure.

References

Apostol, Tom (1974). *Mathematical Analysis,* 2nd ed. Reading, Mass.: Addison-Wesley.

Blume, Lawrence, and David Easley (1982). "Learning to Be Rational." *Journal of Economic Theory,* 26:340–51.

Bray, Margaret (1982). "Learning, Estimation and the Stability of Rational Expectations Equilibria." *Journal of Economic Theory,* 26:318–39.

Cyert, R. M., and M. H. DeGroot (1974). "Rational Expectations and Bayesian Analysis." *Journal of Political Economy,* 82:521–36.

DeCanio, Stephen J. (1979). "Rational Expectations and Learning from Experience." *Quarterly Journal of Economics,* 93:47–58.

Evans, George (1983). "Expectational Stability and the Multiple Equilibria Problem in Linear Rational Expectations Models." Unpublished manuscript, Department of Economics, Stanford University.

Friedman, Benjamin M. (1979). "Optimal Expectations and the Extreme Information Assumptions of 'Rational Expectations' Macromodels." *Journal of Monetary Economics,* 5:23–41.

Goodwin, R. M. (1951). "The Nonlinear Accelerator and the Persistence of Business Cycles." *Econometrica,* 19:1–17.

Gordon, Robert J. (1981). "Output Fluctuations and Gradual Price Adjustment." *Journal of Economic Literature,* 19:493–530.

Lucas, Robert E., Jr. (1972). "Expectations and the Neutrality of Money." *Journal of Economic Theory,* 4:103–24.

[7] However, if such policy switches were repeated in an expectationally stable model, agents might eventually adopt the collective rational expectations immediately with policy changes.

[8] A connected additional problem is that the knowledge that a policy of monetary restraint might for this reason be costly could in turn undermine belief that the policy would be adhered to.

(1973). "Some International Evidence on Output–Inflation Tradeoffs." *American Economic Review,* 63:326–34.

Muth, J. F. (1961). "Rational Expectations and the Theory of Price Movements." *Econometrica,* 29:315–35.

Okun, A. M. (1975). "Inflation: Its Mechanisms and Welfare Costs." *Brookings Papers on Economic Activity,* 2:351–401.

Sargent, T. W., and N. Wallace (1975). "Rational Expectations, the Optimal Monetary Instrument, and the Optimal Money Supply Rule." *Journal of Political Economy,* 83:241–54.

Shiller, Robert J. (1978). "Rational Expectations and the Dynamic Structure of Macroeconomic Models: A Critical Review." *Journal of Monetary Economics,* 4:1–44.

Taylor, J. B. (1975). "Monetary Policy during a Transition to Rational Expectations." *Journal of Political Economy,* 83:1009–22.

(1977). "Conditions for Unique Solutions in Stochastic Macroeconomic Models with Rational Expectations." *Econometrica,* 45:1377–85.

Townsend, Robert M. (1978). "Market Anticipations, Rational Expectations, and Bayesian Analysis." *International Economic Review,* 19:481–94.

Comment

GUILLERMO A. CALVO

One could rather loosely define a rational expectations equilibrium (REE) as a situation where every agent maximizes his objective function subject to available information and budget constraints, and where no one would be induced to change his actions even if he could actually observe all the possible "runs" of the system. In much of the current macroeconomics literature an REE is further constrained by the assumption that everybody shares the same expectations function (we shall refer to this type of equilibrium as an REE*).

The first central result in Mr. Evans's nice presentation is to show that an REE* is equivalent to an REE if the latter is a Nash equilibrium of a noncooperative game and if agents are individually "negligible"; that is, a change in a single individual's strategy does not affect the relevant macro aggregates. The importance of this result, which was first proved by Townsend (1978) for a less general case, is that it provides a nontrivial way to justify the "expectational consensus" assumption underlying an REE*.

But, of course, the foregoing does not answer another important question of macroeconomists, which is whether or not there is any reason to expect that the Nash-REE equilibrium points are, in some way defined, "stable." This is the second issue Mr. Evans tackles in this chapter, but at the cost of adopting a much less general framework.

In the first place, he assumes that during the adjustment process all agents share the same expectations function. Thus, he assumes the same type of "expectational consensus" that underlies an REE*.

Second, he assumes an adjustment mechanism borrowed from DeCanio (1979), which, for the sake of clarity, I shall discuss in terms of a special case.

Let us consider a situation where equation (1) in the chapter takes the following form:

$$x_t = ax_{t-1} + bx_t^* + v_t \tag{D1}$$

where x, x^*, and v are real numbers, and a and b ($\neq 1$) are parameters. (D1) is the reduced form of the system: x_t is the outcome at time t, x_t^* is the expected value of x_t with information available at $t-1$, Ω_{t-1} (which includes x_{t-1}), and v_t is white noise.

Let $\Pi(\Omega_{t-1})$ be the common expectations of x_t based on Ω_{t-1} (i.e., x_t^*).[1] Then an REE* for model (D1) would be

$$\Pi(\Omega_{t-1}) = ax_{t-1} + b\Pi(\Omega_{t-1})$$

or

$$\Pi(\Omega_{t-1}) = \frac{a}{1-b} x_{t-1} \tag{D2}$$

Suppose now that we start with an arbitrary (but commonly agreed upon) expectations function, $\Pi_0(\Omega_{t-1})$. If (D1) and the mean of v ($=0$, by assumption) are known, then we are able to infer that

$$E[x_t/\Omega_{t-1}, \Pi_0(\Omega_{t-1})] = ax_{t-1} + b\Pi_0(\Omega_{t-1}) \tag{D3}$$

Evans defines $\Pi_1(\Omega_{t-1})$ as follows:

$$\Pi_1(\Omega_{t-1}) = E[x_t/\Omega_{t-1}, \Pi_0(\Omega_{t-1})] \tag{D4}$$

and by the same recursive method,

$$\Pi_N(\Omega_{t-1}) = E[x_t/\Omega_{t-1}, \Pi_{N-1}(\Omega_{t-1})] \tag{D5}$$

Hence,

$$\Pi_N(\Omega_{t-1}) = ax_{t-1} + b\Pi_{N-1}(\Omega_{t-1}) \tag{D6}$$

Equation (D6) defines the adjustment process studied in the chapter.

---

[1] Notice that here, as in Evans's chapter, we are, by assumption, ruling out forms like $\Pi(\Omega_{t-1}, t-1)$. Although for the present case the only REE* $\Pi(\cdot, \cdot)$ would not be a direct function of time, it should be pointed out that the stationarity assumption imposed in the chapter is by no means a general characteristic of REE* (Calvo, 1979).

The latter is said to be (globally) stable if there exists a function $\bar{\Pi}(\Omega_{t-1})$ such that

$$\lim_{N \to \infty} \Pi_N(\Omega_{t-1}) = \bar{\Pi}(\Omega_{t-1}) \quad \text{for all} \quad \Omega_{t-1} \tag{D7}$$

Clearly, if the adjustment process is stable, it converges to an REE* (this is a special case of Proposition 3 in Evans's chapter); furthermore, stability holds if and only if $|b| < 1$ (a special case of Proposition 4 in Evans's chapter).

My main problem with this adjustment process is that one has to strictly assume that agents are able to perform these calculations in their minds before any time elapses – otherwise Ω would be changing simultaneously with Π_N.

But, if so much information is available, I really wonder: Why don't agents use (D2) to immediately calculate the REE*?[2]

Let us now take it for granted that expectations are adjusted in some atemporal recursive manner; why would adjustment take the form implied by (D5)? It may seem like a good starting point, but once agents find that it fails to converge, why don't they shift to another procedure?

In sum, I feel that a much more in-depth justification will be necessary before the stability results shown in this chapter can be applied to the fundamental issue of convergence to an REE*.

References

Calvo, G. A. (1979). "On the Indeterminacy of Interest Rates and Wages with Perfect Foresight." *Journal of Economic Theory*, 19:321-37.

DeCanio, S. J. (1979). "Rational Expectations and Learning from Experience." *Quarterly Journal of Economics*, 93:47-58.

[2] Evans appears to claim that a somewhat more "dynamic" story would be consistent with this process, but he offers no formal proof.

CHAPTER 5

Individual rationality, decentralization, and the rational expectations hypothesis

ROMAN FRYDMAN

In a series of studies, Hayek (1948*b*,*c*,*d*) provided a profound analysis of market processes. He argued that "the economic problem which society faces ... is emphatically *not*" the problem of economic calculus of individual choice. "It is a problem of utilization of knowledge which is not given to anyone in its totality" (Hayek, 1948*c*, pp. 77–8). Furthermore, Hayek emphasized that the fundamental characteristic of decentralized markets is the distinction between "the objective real facts [and] data in the subjective sense as things are known to the persons whose behavior we try to explain" (1948*b*, p. 39). In a seminal study, Phelps (1970) introduced this distinction into macroeconomic theory in his well-known island parable. Subsequently, Lucas (1972, 1973, 1975) formulated his own version of the island model and introduced the rational expectations hypothesis (REH) into macroeconomic models. Lucas supposed that forecasts formed by individual agents are "optimal" in the sense of minimizing the expectation (based on the equilibrium probability distribution) of the square of the forecast error conditional on the information available to agents. Thus, the REH seemed to have provided a solution to the difficult problem of modeling individual expectations. Most important, the rational expectations solution was apparently based on the assumption that individuals behave optimally and thus was seen to be consistent with the rest of traditional economic theory.

The main objective of this chapter is a reexamination of connections between the rational expectations hypothesis, the postulate of optimality of individual behavior, and decentralization of competitive markets. In addition to the distinction between "local" and "aggregate" information, formalized in the rational expectations literature, the implications

I am grateful to Jess Benhabib, Clive Bull, Pentti Kouri, and Edmund Phelps for stimulating discussions on the subject of this chapter. I would also like to thank James Cavallo for programming assistance. I retain responsibility for any errors and opinions expressed in this chapter. Research on this chapter has been supported by the Presidential Fellowship at New York University.

of the differences in behavioral parameters characterizing individual agents are also analyzed in this chapter.

The main conclusions of the analysis can be summarized in the following two points: First, the forecasting behavior of individual agents, assumed in the rational expectations models, cannot be justified by an appeal to the assumption that individual agents process "optimally" information available to them; consequently, there is an important distinction between the basic optimality postulate in economics and the rational expectations hypothesis. Second, the notion of decentralization, as formalized in the rational expectations models, appears incompatible with the rational expectations hypothesis. The outline of the chapter is as follows:

Section 5.1 sets up a model representative of the rational expectations literature. The rational expectations equilibrium is computed and discussed. In particular, it is suggested that optimality of the individual equilibrium forecast function cannot be claimed without any reference to forecasting behavior of all agents.

Section 5.2 analyzes the possibility of learning in a representative model. The analysis utilizes an approach recently developed by Frydman (1982a). This approach is conceptually related to the famous "beauty contest" example presented by Keynes (1936, p. 156) and the analysis by Townsend (1978). In Section 5.2.1 it is demonstrated that individual agents cannot learn the relevant parameters of the equilibrium forecast function on the basis of the correct specification of the model and information available to them.[1] This conclusion in a representative model is shown to apply to models formulated by Lucas (1973), Barro (1976), and Sargent (1979, p. 379). One of the implications of this analysis is that individual agents cannot form minimum mean square error forecasts using standard regression techniques.

In Section 5.2.2, forecasting on the basis of misspecified models is discussed. It is argued that, in general, one of the key variables of the model, the average opinion defined as the average of forecasts of agents, is indeterminate. This conclusion is illustrated using an example of forecasting based on least-squares procedures. This result strengthens the conclusions of Section 5.2.1. It is also argued that convergence to the rational expectations equilibrium is not, in general, likely to take place.

Section 5.2.3 briefly discusses the implications of an analysis in Section 5.2.2 for an explanation of the autoregressive behavior of aggregate output and price level.

Section 5.3 reexamines the connection between optimality of individual

---

[1] Although the analysis is confined to classical statistical techniques, this conclusion also holds for Bayesian procedures.

behavior and the rational expectations hypothesis. The main conclusion is that the forecasting behavior postulated in the literature cannot be justified by an appeal to "optimal" processing of information by individual agents. Moreover, this behavior cannot be regarded as likely to characterize forecasting behavior of agents in decentralized markets. An argument is also presented that the rational expectations hypothesis differs in an important way from the utility maximization hypothesis.

Section 5.4 addresses the question of compatibility of decentralization and the rational expectations hypothesis. In Section 5.4.1, Lucas's model (1975) of the business cycle is analyzed. Informational assumptions of the model are critically evaluated. It is shown that the assumption that agents cannot observe the state variables of the economy is incompatible with the rational expectations hypothesis.

In Section 5.4.2, an extension of the model formulated in Section 5.1 that allows for differences in supply parameters is considered. It is demonstrated that the parameters of the rational expectations equilibrium forecast functions depend, in addition to the moments of random variables in the model, on all of the supply parameters in the economy. It is argued that from an "empirical" point of view the assumption of rational expectations is not plausible in this model. Furthermore, the imposition of this assumption in the model would undermine the fundamental notion that decentralized markets economize on information required by agents in making their economic decisions. Finally, it is argued that it is precisely this notion of decentralization that Lucas used in the defense of the assumptions in his models.

Section 5.5 contains some discussion of the applicability of rational expectations models to the evaluation of effects of macroeconomic policy and to the modeling of a decentralized market economy.

5.1. A representative model

The purpose of this section is to set up a representative model of the class of models originally formulated by Lucas (1973). The model allows an analysis of the rational expectations equilibrium and learning problems in a variety of models used in the literature (e.g., Lucas, 1973; Barro, 1976; Sargent, 1979, p. 379).

Suppliers of a single good are assumed to be located in a large number of physically separated competitive markets, indexed by $z = 1, \ldots, N$. Demand is distributed unevenly across markets. Hence, prices of the one good vary across markets.

The quantity supplied in market z, $y_t^s(z)$, is assumed to be governed by

$$y_t^s(z) = \alpha[P_t(z) - F_z P_t] + u_t^s + \epsilon_t^s(z) \tag{1}$$

where α is a supply parameter; $P_t(z)$ is the market clearing price in z at t; P_t is the general price level defined as an average (across markets) of $P_t(z)$; $F_z P_t$ is an average of forecasts of P_t in z; u_t^s is an aggregate supply shock, $u_t^s \sim N(0, \sigma_{u_s}^2)$; $\epsilon_t^s(z)$ is a relative, market-specific supply shock, $\epsilon_t^s(z) \sim N(0, \sigma_{\epsilon_s}^2)$.[2,3,4]

$F_z P_t$ will be called an *average forecast function in z,* and a realization of $F_z P_t$ will be called an *average opinion in z.*[5] I also define an *economy-wide average opinion* by

$$FP_t = \frac{1}{N} \sum_{z=1}^{N} F_z P_t \tag{2}$$

The quantity demanded in market z, $y_t^d(z)$, is assumed to be governed by

$$y_t^d(z) = \beta [M_t - P_t(z)] + u_t^d + \epsilon_t^d(z) \tag{3}$$

where β is a demand parameter; M_t is the money supply at t; u_t^d is an aggregate demand shock, $u_t^d \sim N(0, \sigma_{u_d}^2)$; $\epsilon_t^d(z)$ is a relative, market-specific demand shock, $\epsilon_t^d(z) \sim N(0, \sigma_{\epsilon_d}^2)$.

We define $y_t(z)$ to be an equilibrium level of output in market z at t and y_t to be an economy-wide average of $y_t(z)$. We also denote the information set available to agents in z at t by $I_t(z)$ and assume that $I_t(z) = \{P_t(z), P_{t-1}(z), \ldots, M_{t-1}, M_{t-2}, \ldots, P_{t-1}, P_{t-2}, \ldots, y_{t-1}, y_{t-2}, \ldots\}$. As is well known, the lack of information on contemporaneous M_t and P_t plays a crucial role in this model.

[2] All random variables in this model are uncorrelated serially and with each other.

[3] All variables in this chapter are expressed in logarithms.

[4] In the rational expectations literature, $F_z P_t$ has been defined as $E[P_t \mid I_t(z)]$, where $I_t(z)$ denotes an information set available in z at t. This formulation of the supply function in (1) has been justified in the literature by an appeal to Lucas and Rapping's model (1969) of labor supply and Friedman's postulate (1968) of informational differences between workers and employers. Bull and Frydman (1983) argued that those two justifications are incompatible. They suggested that the model cannot be interpreted as a general equilibrium model of the multicommodity world. They also demonstrated that, under the assumption of rational expectations, the parameter α depends on the variance of aggregate demand. The standard analysis of the model (e.g., Lucas, 1973) implicitly presumes that α is a function of only the parameters of preference and production functions.

[5] The assumption that market z is competitive implies that there are many suppliers in market z. Thus, α is an average (across individual agents) in z of supply parameters, and $F_z P_t$ is an average (across individual agents) of forecasts of P_t. The form of the function $F_z P_t$ will be discussed in more detail in Section 5.2 of this chapter.

Finally, the money supply process is assumed to be governed by

$$M_t = \mu + x_t \qquad (4)$$

where μ is a constant; $x_t \sim N(0, \sigma_x^2)$.[6]

5.1.1. The rational expectations equilibrium price function

From (4) and the market clearing condition $y_t(z) = y_t^s(z) = y_t^d(z)$ we obtain the following expression for the market clearing price:

$$P_t(z) = \frac{1}{\alpha + \beta} \left[\beta\mu + \alpha F_z P_t + \beta x_t + u_t + \epsilon_t(z) \right] \qquad (5)$$

where $u_t = u_t^d - u_t^s$, $u_t \sim N(0, \sigma_u^2)$, $\sigma_u^2 = \sigma_{u_s}^2 + \sigma_{u_d}^2$; $\epsilon_t(z) = \epsilon_t^d(z) - \epsilon_t^s(z)$, $\epsilon_t(z) \sim N(0, \sigma_\epsilon^2)$, $\sigma_\epsilon^2 = \sigma_{\epsilon_s}^2 + \sigma_{\epsilon_d}^2$.

We also have

$$P_t = \frac{1}{\alpha + \beta} \left[\beta\mu + \alpha F P_t + \beta x_t + u_t \right] \qquad (6)$$

Expressions (5) and (6) imply that

$$P_t(z) = P_t + \frac{\alpha}{\alpha + \beta} \left[F_z P_t - F P_t \right] + \frac{1}{\alpha + \beta} \epsilon_t(z) \qquad (7)$$

Lucas (1973) assumed that individual agents know the relevant parameters of the model. In the present context, this entails knowledge of α, β, μ, σ_x^2, σ_u^2, and σ_ϵ^2. Even with this assumption, expression (7) implies that the individual forecast function in z cannot be well specified without additional assumptions on the forecast functions used by agents in other markets (as summarized in $F P_t$). Following Lucas, we assume that $F_z P_t = E[P_t \mid I_t(z)]$ for all $z = 1, \ldots, N$.[7] This assumption directly leads to the following definition:

Definition of the rational expectations equilibrium price functions: The (rational expectations) equilibrium price functions $P_t^*(z)$ and P_t^* are the price functions such that if $F_z P_t^* = E[P_t^* \mid P_t^*(z)]$ for all z,[8] then

---

[6] The assumption in (4) simplifies an analysis in this chapter. The usual assumption in this class of models is that the money supply process follows a random walk.

[7] Lucas (1973) defined $P_t(z) = P_t + z$, where z is the relative demand shock. Note that this formulation is not simply a consequence of uneven distribution of demands. It also requires that $F_z P_t = E[P_t \mid I_t(z)]$ for all z, which is an equilibrium condition.

[8] It is clear that in this model only $P_t^*(z)$ is relevant for forecasting P_t^* on the basis of $I_t(z)$.

$$P_t^*(z) = \frac{1}{\alpha + \beta} \{\beta\mu + \alpha E[P_t^* \mid P_t^*(z)] + \beta x_t + u_t + \epsilon_t(z)\} \qquad (8)$$

and

$$P_t^* = \frac{1}{N} \sum_{z=1}^{N} P_t^*(z) \qquad (9)$$

for all realizations of x_t, u_t, and $\epsilon_t(z)$ (except on a set of probability zero).

We use the method of undetermined coefficients to obtain expressions for $P_t^*(z)$ and P_t^*. Thus, assume that

$$E[P_t^* \mid P_t^*(z)] = \beta_0^* + \beta_1^* P_t^*(z) \qquad (10)$$

Using (10) in (8) yields

$$P_t^*(z) = \frac{1}{\beta + \alpha(1 - \beta_1^*)} [\alpha\beta_0^* + \beta\mu + \beta x_t + u_t + \epsilon_t(z)] \qquad (11)$$

Averaging $P_t^*(z)$ across markets gives

$$P_t^* = \frac{1}{\beta + \alpha(1 - \beta_1^*)} [\alpha\beta_0^* + \beta\mu + \beta x_t + u_t] \qquad (12)$$

Taking the conditional expectation of P_t^* on $P_t^*(z)$ and using (10) and (11) results in the system of two equations for β_0^* and β_1^*. The solutions are given by

$$\beta_0^* = \mu(1 - \theta) \qquad (13)$$

$$\beta_1^* = \theta \qquad (14)$$

where

$$\theta = \frac{\beta^2 \sigma_x^2 + \sigma_u^2}{\beta^2 \sigma_x^2 + \sigma_u^2 + \sigma_\epsilon^2} \qquad (15)$$

Expressions (10)–(14) imply the following expressions for the rational expectations equilibrium price functions:

$$P_t^*(z) = \mu + \frac{1}{\beta + \alpha(1 - \theta)} [\beta x_t + u_t + \epsilon_t(z)] \qquad (16)$$

and

$$P_t^* = \mu + \frac{1}{\beta + \alpha(1 - \theta)} [\beta x_t + u_t] \qquad (17)$$

5.2.   An analysis of the possibility of learning

The fundamental assumption in the rational expectations literature is that individual agents know the relevant parameters of the rational expectations equilibrium forecast function. We note that in the model set up in Section 5.1, all of the markets are in the rational expectations equilibrium in every period if and only if individual agents are using the forecast functions in (10). Thus, the assumption that individual agents know β_0^* and β_1^* can be justified if it can be shown that agents can learn those parameters on the basis of the information available to them when the markets are not in the rational expectations equilibrium. In this section we shall examine the possibility of modeling such learning processes.

I assume that although individual agents do not already know the relevant parameters, they know that the behavior of prices and quantities is governed by the functional relationships given in (1), (3), (5), and (6). Individual agents are also assumed to know that the random variables M_t, u_t^s, u_t^d, $\epsilon_t^s(z)$, and $\epsilon_t^d(z)$ have properties specified in Section 5.1. These relationships will be called *the structure of the model*. Because individual agents do not know the relevant parameters, they cannot form the equilibrium forecast functions in (10). In such a situation, an average opinion function in (2) can be written as

$$F_z P_t = W_t^{(z)} \delta_{t-1}^{(z)} \tag{18}$$

where $\delta_{t-1}^{(z)}$ is a vector of parameters; $W_t^{(z)}$ is a vector of variables used in market z in forming a forecast of P_t.[9]

Because the forecasts of P_t in z are formed on the basis of information available in z, the vector $W_t^{(z)} \subseteq I_t(z)$.[10] Also, the coefficients $\delta_t^{(z)}$ will, in general, be based on information in $I_{t-1}(z)$ and updated every time period.

Muth (1961) postulated that "expectations since they are informed predictions of future events, are essentially the same as the predictions of relevant economic theory." In the present discussion we can analogously consider the possibility of "rational learning," that is, learning on the basis of the correct specification of the structure of the model.[11]

---

[9] See Section 5.2.2 for an example of such an average opinion function.

[10] The formulation in (18) also allows for a "constant" term in $F_z P_t$. This term represents any additional information not in $I_t(z)$ considered relevant by agents in z in forecasting P_t. Examples of such extraneous information include "rumors," government announcements of policy changes, and so forth.

[11] Obviously, if a model formulated in Section 5.1 is not the "relevant economic model," the price functions in (16) and (17) are not the "objective" price functions, and learning in that model becomes irrelevant. See Chapter 1 in this book for a discussion of this point.

5.2.1. An analysis of the possibility of learning on the basis of the correct specification of the model

I can immediately present the following proposition:

Proposition 1
Individual agents in market z can form consistent estimators of β_0^* and β_1^* on the basis of the correct specification of the structure of the model if and only if every agent has information on either an average forecast function in z and an economy-wide average opinion or an average opinion in z and an economy-wide average forecast function in every time period.[12]

Proof
See the Appendix.[13]

In the model formulated in Section 5.1, the markets were assumed to be physically isolated. This assumption played an essential role in a justification of the crucial feature of the model, that is, the "confusion" between absolute and relative price movements. Furthermore, individual agents in every market z do not have information on an economy-wide average opinion.[14] We conclude that individual agents cannot form consistent estimators of the parameters β_0^* and β_1^* of the rational expectations equilibrium forecast function on the basis of the correct specification of the model and information in $I_t(z)$.

We can use Proposition 1 to specify information required for learning on the basis of the correct specifications in a variety of models used in the literature. Although the model formulated by Barro (1976) contains more elaborate supply and demand functions and the forecasts of next period's price level rather than contemporaneous price level, Proposition 1 can easily be seen to be directly applicable to the Barro model. Sargent (1979, p. 379) specified the supply function with market-specific supply shocks. His model can be obtained by setting $u_t^s \equiv 0$ in (1). The following corollary is pertinent to Sargent's model.

[12] Individual agents are said to have information on an average forecast function if they know the values of the coefficients and variables in this function.

[13] If $F_z P_t$ does not depend on $P_t(z)$, the proof is identical with the proof of Proposition 2 in Frydman (1982a). Simultaneity of $P_t(z)$ and P_t necessitates a stronger assumption in this chapter that an average forecast function rather than an average opinion be known. Also, if other variables in $I_t(z)$ are included in $F_z P_t$, the proof follows with minor modifications.

[14] From an "empirical" point of view, information on realizations of FP_t is not available in any of the presently existing market economies.

Corollary 1.1

Let $u_t^s \equiv 0$. Then individual agents in z can form consistent estimators of β_0^* and β_1^* on the basis of the correct specification of the structure of the model if and only if every agent has information on an average forecast function in z in every time period.

Proof
See the Appendix.

The original model formulated by Lucas (1973) does not contain supply shocks in the supply function, but it contains a lagged output variable. Consequently, the rational expectations solution for P_t [Lucas, 1973, equation (12)] contains the parameter λ of the lagged output variable. It is easily seen that Corollary 1.1 is also applicable to Lucas's model.

The crucial notion that underlies models proposed by Lucas is that "the situation as perceived by individual suppliers will be quite different from the aggregate situation as seen by an outside observer" (Lucas, 1973, p. 133). The observation that there is a difference between the situation of individual suppliers and aggregate market outcomes also underlies the analysis in this chapter.[15] In fact, it is precisely this point that leads to serious problems in the modeling of learning. Furthermore, as King (1981) has noted, "one plausible rationalization [of Lucas's model] is that aggregate information is not acquired as a consequence of individual exchange." Clearly, information on the average forecast function is not acquired during trading in the decentralized, competitive markets. The argument in the proof of Proposition 1 also implies that information on the average forecast function in z cannot be inferred from observations of market prices, $P_t(z)$. Therefore, Proposition 1 and Corollary 1.1 imply that individual agents cannot learn the relevant parameters on the basis of the correctly specified structure of the model.

An important implication of Proposition 1 is that individual agents cannot use regression techniques to form standard "optimal" forecasts.[16] This result is presented without proof in the following corollary.

[15] I would like to emphasize, however, that I do not presume that an "outside observer" is able to analyze and predict completely the market behavior of *individual agents*. For further remarks, see Section 5.5. An example of a rigorous analysis of the model incorporating this point has been presented by Frydman (1982*a*).

[16] This class of forecast functions has been widely used as "optimal" forecasts in the literature (e.g., Sargent, 1979, Chapter X). In this chapter we shall not attempt to critically evaluate this notion of "optimality." The term "optimal" forecast will be used in the sense of the minimum mean square error forecast.

Corollary 1.2
Suppose that individual agents in z do not have information on $F_z P_t$ and FP_t. Then they cannot consistently estimate all of the parameters of $E[P_t \mid P_t(z)]$.

The minimum mean square error forecasting criterion has been used in the rational expectations literature to formalize the notion that individual agents "optimally" utilize information available to them. This optimality criterion plays a crucial role in the definition of the rational expectations equilibrium. Corollary 1.2 implies that when individual agents do not already know the relevant parameters, they cannot use regression techniques to form the minimum mean square error forecasts. We shall next consider a class of "nonoptimal" forecasting procedures.

5.2.2. Forecasting on the basis of misspecified models and the fundamental indeterminacy of the average opinion functions

Because agents in the model have to form forecasts of P_t to make their output decisions, they will forecast according to some forecasting rule. These rules are not based on any well-defined and generally accepted optimality criteria. Thus, an "outside observer" and other agents cannot, in general, ascertain the structure of the average opinion function. This conclusion provides additional support for the validity of the results obtained in the previous section. We recall that inability to learn and forecast optimally was shown to be a consequence of the fact that individual agents in decentralized competitive markets cannot ascertain the structure of the average opinion function on the basis of information available to them.

We shall now consider the problem of indeterminacy of the average opinion functions using an example of a large class of "nonoptimal" forecast functions.

Least-squares forecasting and the indeterminacy of the average opinion functions: Consider the following individual forecast function in market z at t:

$$F_z P_t = \tilde{\delta}_{0t-1}^{(z)} + \tilde{\delta}_{1t-1}^{(z)} P_t(z) = W_t^{(z)} \tilde{\delta}_{t-1}^{(z)} \tag{19}$$

where $\tilde{\delta}_{t-1}^{(z)}$ is computed using the standard least-squares formula:

$$\tilde{\delta}_{t-1}^{(z)} = (W_{(t-1)}^{(z)\prime} W_{(t-1)}^{(z)})^{-1} W_{(t-1)}^{(z)\prime} P_{(t-1)} \tag{20}$$

where

$$W_{(t-1)}^{(z)} = \begin{bmatrix} 1 & P_0(z) \\ \vdots & \\ 1 & P_{t-1}(z) \end{bmatrix} \quad \text{and} \quad P_{(t-1)} = \begin{bmatrix} P_0 \\ \\ P_{t-1} \end{bmatrix}$$

If the forecast functions in all markets are assumed to be given by (19), then an economy-wide average forecast function is given by

$$FP_t = \frac{1}{N} \sum_{z=1}^{N} F_z P_t \tag{21}$$

In this model, every agent is assumed to be acting individually. This raises the question whether or not the additional assumption that an economy-wide average forecast function is given by (21) would not lead an individual agent to adopt a different forecast function than the one in (19). The least-squares updating formula (Friedman, 1979, p. 35) implies that

$$FP_t = FP_{t-1} + \gamma'_{1t} + \gamma'_{2t} P_{t-1} \tag{22}$$

where

$$\gamma'_{1t} = \frac{1}{N} \sum_{z=1}^{N} [(W_t^{(z)} - W_{t-1}^{(z)}) \delta_{t-1}^{(z)} - W_t^{(z)} \gamma_{t-1}^{(z)} F_z P_{t-1}]$$

$$\gamma_{t-1}^{(z)} = \frac{(W_{(t-2)}^{(z)\prime} W_{(t-2)}^{(z)})^{-1} W_{t-1}^{(z)\prime}}{1 + W_{t-1}^{(z)} (W_{(t-2)}^{(z)\prime} W_{(t-2)}^{(z)})^{-1} W_{t-1}^{(z)\prime}}$$

and

$$\gamma'_{2t} = \frac{1}{N} \sum_{z=1}^{N} W_t^{(z)} \gamma_{t-1}^{(z)}$$

Expression (22) shows that FP_t is a linear function of FP_{t-1} and P_{t-1}.[17] Although individual agents in z do not observe realizations of FP_{t-1}, observations on P_{t-1} provide information on FP_{t-1}. Rearranging an expression for P_{t-1} [see (6)] and replacing FP_{t-1} in (22) yields

$$FP_t = \gamma''_{1t} + \gamma''_{2t} P_{t-1} - \frac{\beta}{\alpha} x_{t-1} - \frac{1}{\alpha} u_{t-1} \tag{23}$$

where $\gamma''_{1t} = \gamma'_{1t} - (\beta/\alpha)\mu$; $\gamma''_{2t} = \gamma'_{2t} + (\alpha+\beta)/\alpha$. Plugging (23) into (6) yields

$$P_t = \gamma_{1t} + \gamma_{2t} P_{t-1} + \eta_t \tag{24}$$

where

$$\gamma_{1t} = \frac{\alpha}{\alpha+\beta} \gamma''_{1t}; \quad \gamma_{2t} = \frac{\alpha}{\alpha+\beta} \gamma''_{2t}; \quad \eta_t = \frac{1}{\alpha+\beta} [\beta(x_t - x_{t-1}) + (u_t - u_{t-1})]$$

[17] The analysis here is confined to linear functions, because the definition of rational expectations equilibrium also presupposes linearity.

First we note that the parameters of $E[P_t \mid P_t(z)]$, which agents are trying to estimate by (19), are unknown functions of time. Moreover, an "estimator" $\tilde{\delta}_{t-1}^{(z)}$ in (19) is biased, and the extent of the bias cannot be ascertained by any agent. It is also clear that forecasts formed according to (19) cannot be justified by an appeal to any generally acceptable individual optimality criterion. The only justification for the use of (19) appears to be that every agent infers from the knowledge of the structure of the model [see (5) and (6)] that $P_t(z)$ is correlated with P_t, and therefore it uses $P_t(z)$ to gain some information on P_t. Expression (24) shows that if every agent uses the forecast function in (19), P_t is correlated not only with $P_t(z)$ but also with P_{t-1}. Because the correlation between P_t and $P_t(z)$ justified the use of $P_t(z)$ in forecasting P_t, the very same argument requires that under the assumption that the average forecast functions are given by (19) and (20), P_{t-1} should also be used in forecasting P_t. Thus, individual agents in market z would be led to the following average forecast function:

$$F_z P_t = \hat{\delta}_{0t-1}^{(z)} + \hat{\delta}_{1t-1}^{(z)} P_t(z) + \hat{\delta}_{2t-1}^{(z)} P_{t-1} \tag{25}$$

where $\hat{\delta}_{t-1}^{(z)} = (\hat{\delta}_{0t-1}^{(z)}, \hat{\delta}_{1t-1}^{(z)}, \hat{\delta}_{2t-1}^{(z)})$ is defined analogously to (20). Furthermore, it can easily be seen from the definition of γ_{1t}' in (22) that if every agent used the forecast function in (25), P_t would linearly depend not only on $P_t(z)$ and P_{t-1} but also on P_{t-2}. Continuing the same line of reasoning, P_t would in general be a linear function of all of the past prices. Because there is no general procedure for choosing an "optimal" number of variables in a "regression," the particular subsets of $\{P_{t-1}, P_{t-2}, \ldots\}$ used by individual agents cannot be determined in the model. This conclusion implies that the structure of the average forecast function is indeterminate in the model.[18]

The convergence of the coefficients $\tilde{\delta}_{t-1}^{(z)}$ seems difficult to analyze analytically, because their behavior is governed by a system of highly nonlinear stochastic difference equations. Moreover, from the point of view of plausibility of the assumption that markets are in the rational expectations equilibrium in every period and the consequent usefulness of the model to analyze effects of changes in policy regimes, the question of the number of time periods required for convergence is critical.[19,20]

[18] Also note that in the case of least-squares forecasting, an average forecast function is given by a highly nonstationary autoregressive process. This suggests that the assumption made by Townsend (1981 and Chapter 9) that the average forecast function is given by a stationary moving average process might be difficult to justify.

[19] Lucas (1975) emphasized that this class of models is "motivated entirely by practical considerations" (p. 180). See Section 5.5 for further discussion of this point.

[20] An example of a computer simulation of the model suggests that if one arbi-

Furthermore, even if for a particular *necessarily arbitrary* choice of forecast functions, $\tilde{\delta}_{t-1}^{(z)}$ could be shown to converge to β_0^* and β_1^*, this convergence result could not substantiate the claim that convergence to the rational expectations equilibrium is, in general, likely to take place. Such a claim would not be valid because the least-squares procedures in this model are not based on any optimality criterion and the structure of the average forecast functions (i.e., the variables used in forecasting) is indeterminate.[21]

An analysis of this section implies that the behavior of prices and outputs crucially depends on the forecasting rule used by agents. This implication of the analysis is briefly discussed in the next section.

5.2.3. *Forecasting on the basis of misspecified models and the autoregressive behavior of aggregate output and price levels*

The rational expectations price P_t^* and a corresponding output y_t^* are uncorrelated over time. The autoregressive behavior of output and prices has been justified in the rational expectations literature by an appeal to the serial correlation of the exogenous shocks, the costs of adjustment in capital formation (Sargent, 1979, p. 330), and the existence of staggered wage contracts (Taylor, 1980).[22]

An analysis of least-squares forecasting [see (24) and (25)] suggests

trarily restricts the class of forecast functions to (19), the behavior of $\tilde{\delta}_{t-1}^{(z)}$ indicates "some tendency" toward convergence. However, $\tilde{\delta}_{t-1}^{(z)}$ *did not* converge in 5,000 periods.

[21] The question of convergence to the rational expectations equilibrium for a restricted class of forecast functions of the form in (19) in a simple model of the asset market has recently been analyzed by Bray (1982). She made a number of restrictive assumptions in her model. In particular, she assumed that the rate of return of an asset is distributed as an i.i.d. random variable and that the agents already hold rational expectations on the mean of the rate of return and asset prices. With these assumptions, she proved that convergence would take place if a specific condition on the parameters of the model is satisfied. She also suggested that if this condition is not satisfied, the parameters of the least-squares forecast function appear to diverge. See also Bray and Kreps (1981) for further analysis.

It should be noted that in the model of this chapter, P_t is nonstationary and endogenously determined.

[22] Sargent (1979, p. 377) and Barro (1977) criticized the contract explanation of persistence in output for "attributing suboptimal decision rules to agents." I shall argue in the next section that "optimal" decisions attributed to agents in the rational expectations literature cannot be made by agents in decentralized markets. This argument casts doubt on the validity of Barro's and Sargent's criticisms of long-term contracts as necessarily "suboptimal."

that if individual agents do not already know the parameters of the model, autoregressive behavior of aggregate output and price level may simply be a consequence of an attempt by agents to learn and forecast on the basis of misspecified models. Clearly, if $FP_t = \gamma_{1t} + \gamma_{2t} P_{t-1} + \gamma_{3t} P_{t-2} + \cdots$, then the resulting observed series of P_t and y_t will be autoregressive. This is true even though in this model exogenous variables are not serially correlated and there are no wage contracts and lags in capital formation. This conclusion obtained in the case of least-squares forecasting seems generally valid, because the only way for agents to learn about their environment is to use the history of the variables they can observe.[23]

5.3. Optimality of individual behavior and the rational expectations hypothesis

Muth (1961) formulated the "rational expectations" hypothesis by postulating "that expectations of firms (or, more generally, the subjective probability distribution of outcomes) tend to be distributed, for the same information set, about the prediction of the theory (or the objective probability distribution of outcomes)." He did not link this hypothesis with the basic economic assumption that individual agents behave optimally. In fact, Muth explicitly warned against "confusing this purely descriptive hypothesis with a pronouncement as to what firms ought to do" (Muth, 1961, p. 316). Lucas (1972, 1973, 1975) provided the link between individual optimal behavior and the rational expectations hypothesis by postulating a specific expectational mechanism used by individual agents. He supposed that individual agents form their rational expectations equilibrium forecasts by minimizing the expected value of the square of the forecast error conditional on information available to them. In order to give this assumption "an operational meaning," Lucas restricted the analysis of his models "to the situation in which the relevant distributions have settled down to stationary values and can thus be 'known' by traders" (Lucas, 1975, p. 1121). The major problem with this justification of the rational expectations hypothesis is that "the relevant distributions" can be at their "stationary values" if and only if every

[23] Note that the autoregressive behavior of aggregate output and price level implied by least-squares forecasting is not claimed here to correspond to the "observed" autoregressive behavior. Taylor (1980) carefully studied this problem in the model with contract behavior. Taylor's analysis appears to be an exception in the rational expectations literature. An analysis of the question whether or not particular forecast functions lead to the "observed" autoregressive behavior of aggregate output and price level is outside the scope of this chapter.

agent already "knows" the parameters of these stationary distributions. Stated differently, the markets are in the rational expectations equilibrium if and only if every agent forms its expectations according to its rational expectations equilibrium forecast function. Thus, the assumption that relevant distributions have settled down to stationary values cannot be used to give "operational meaning" to the assumption that agents "know" the parameters of those distributions.[24]

A potential avenue to escape this dilemma is to suppose that agents act "as if" they form rational expectations equilibrium forecasts. It has been suggested in the literature that the assumption of rational expectations is simply an extension of "the maximizing assumption to the use of information" (Kantor, 1979, p. 1429).[25] Futia elaborated on this point, arguing that "the assumption implicit in the rational expectations hypothesis that economic agents are very competent statisticians is *no different in kind* from the assumption that they are very competent mathematical programmers – something implicit in a literal interpretation of utility and profit maximizing hypothesis" (Futia, 1981, p. 27, emphasis added). In order to compare the utility maximization hypothesis with the rational expectations hypothesis, one has to adopt a criterion for evaluating economic assumptions. In his analysis of market processes, Hayek (1948b, p. 46) suggested such a criterion. He argued that an assumption is "justified" if it can "be regarded as likely to be true; and it must be possible, at least in principle, to demonstrate that it is true in particular cases." Adopting Hayek's criterion, it is obvious that individual agents can, in principle, maximize utility, because maximization of utility involves strictly individual decisions. In contrast, the formation of equilibrium forecasts requires knowledge of the parameters of the equilibrium distribution. As we demonstrated in the previous section, the assumption that agents know those parameters cannot "be regarded as likely to be true" in the context of decentralized competitive markets. Thus, the assumption that agents act as if they form rational expectations equilibrium forecasts is fundamentally "different in kind" from the assumption of utility maximization.

Let us further emphasize that we assumed in Section 5.2 that individuals are "very competent statisticians" and that they know a great deal about their environment. Recall that individual agents are assumed

---

[24] For an example of this problem, see an analysis of the Lucas business cycle model in Section 5.4 of this chapter.

[25] Note that Lucas (1975, p. 1121) was aware of the fact that there is a difference between optimality "in the conventional sense, given objectives and expectations" and in the sense "that available information is optimally utilized in forming expectations."

to know the structure of the model and the nonlinear estimation procedures, and to be able to deduce the consequences of least-squares forecasting. Even under these assumptions, as shown in Section 5.2, agents cannot forecast optimally and learn θ. Furthermore, we showed that the assumption that individual agents use $E[P_t^* \mid P_t^*(z)]$ to generate their predictions is not implied by the assumption that individual agents process information available to them in an "optimal way."[26] [See Lucas (1975, p. 213) for this interpretation.) We conclude that the specification of the individual forecast function as $E[P_t^* \mid P_t^*(z)]$ appears to be simply an ad hoc specification of individual forecasting behavior. Moreover, this specification cannot be regarded as likely to characterize forecasting behavior of agents in decentralized competitive markets. Further support for this conclusion is provided in the next section, where the information requirements of the rational expectations equilibrium are analyzed in Lucas's model (1975) of the business cycle and in an extension of the model formulated in Section 5.1.

5.4.   Decentralization and informational requirements of the rational expectations equilibrium

The distinction between information available to individual agents and information on the aggregate state of an economy is one of the fundamental characteristics of the decentralized market economies. Lucas formalized this distinction by assuming that "information is imperfect, not only in the sense that the future is unknown, but also in the sense that no agent is perfectly informed as to the current state of the economy" (Lucas, 1975, p. 1113). As we showed in Section 5.2, the difficulties of learning the relevant parameters of the rational expectations equilibrium forecast functions are precisely due to the decentralized nature of market economies. Thus, the assumption that markets are in the rational expec-

---

[26] Let me add that the idea of "processing" of information by agents has been formalized in a puzzling way in the rational expectations literature. The term "running a regression" has been loosely used as an "operational" procedure by means of which individual agents can obtain rational forecasts (e.g., Barro, 1976, p. 9; Lucas, 1975, p. 1126; Sargent, 1979, Chapter X). Of course, because all of these authors assume that individual agents know the "true" values of the parameters of the relevant conditional expectations, no regressions have to be "run" (as these authors are aware). Moreover, if the agents do not know these parameters, regression techniques do not yield unbiased and consistent estimators of the parameters of the minimum mean square error forecast function (see Corollary 1.2).

tations equilibrium in every period seems incompatible with the "fact" that information differs across agents in decentralized markets. An equilibrium model of the business cycle represents another example of this problem.

5.4.1. The rational expectations hypothesis and an equilibrium model of the business cycle

Lucas (1975) developed an equilibrium model of the business cycle "in which unsystematic monetary shocks and an accelerator effect interact to generate serially correlated 'cyclical' movements in real output." Agents in the model are assumed to be randomly distributed over a large number of markets indexed by z. In every period they produce output and accumulate money and capital.[27] Capital accumulated in a given market stays there when agents move to other markets. The behavior of agents is assumed to be governed by demand functions for money and capital. The money supply is assumed to follow a random walk. The deviations of the money stock and capital stock in market z from economy-wide averages of money stock and capital stock, respectively, are assumed to be equal to normally distributed random variables. The specifications of the asset demand functions and the money supply process imply the following solutions for the equilibrium "set of functions which specify prices and asset movements given the current state" of the economy (Lucas, 1975, p. 1123-4). These functions are given by

$$k_{t+1}(z) = \Pi_{10} + \Pi_{11}\hat{k}_t + \Pi_{12}\hat{m}_t + \Pi_{13}[k_t + u_t(z)]$$
$$+ \Pi_{14}[m_t + x_t + \theta_t(z)] \tag{26}$$

and

$$p_t(z) = \Pi_{20} + \Pi_{21}\hat{k}_t + \Pi_{22}\hat{m}_t + \Pi_{23}[k_t + u_t(z)]$$
$$+ \Pi_{14}[m_t + x_t + \theta_t(z)] \tag{27}$$

where $k_t(z)$ is the money stock in z; k_t is an economy-wide average of $k_t(z)$; $u_t(z) = k_t - k_t(z)$, $u_t(z) \sim N(0, \sigma_u^2)$; m_t is the money supply; $x_t \sim N(\mu, \sigma^2)$; $m_t(z)$ is the money stock in market z; $\theta_t(z) = m_{t+1} - m_{t+1}(z)$, $\theta_t(z) = \rho\theta_{t-1}(z) + \epsilon_t(z)$, $\epsilon_t(z) \sim N(0, \sigma_\epsilon^2)$, in addition, $\sigma_{u\theta} \neq 0$; $\hat{k}_t$ and $\hat{m}_t$ are economy-wide averages of forecasts of k_t and m_t.

The crucial informational assumptions of the model are the following:

[27] The reader is referred to Lucas's article (1975) for a complete statement of the model. We focus here only on the essential elements required for a discussion in this section.

(A1)   "The behavior of each trader is rational both in the conventional sense of optimal, given objectives and expectations, and in the Muthian sense [Muth (1961)] that available information is used optimally."

In an attempt to give *"operational meaning"* to (A1), Lucas restricted the analysis "to the situation in which the relevant distributions have settled down to the stationary values and can thus be 'known' by traders" (Lucas, 1975, p. 1121, emphasis added).

(A2)   Agents can observe realizations of $p_t(z)$.

(A3)   Agents cannot observe realizations of m_t, k_t, $m_t(z)$, and $k_t(z)$.

(A4)   "Each agent summarizes the price history $(p_{t-1}, p_{t-2}, \ldots)$ observed by him in a pair $(\hat{k}_t, \hat{m}_t)$, his unbiased estimate of the current values of the aggregate state variables, (k_t, m_t) .... Prior to trading each period, these estimates are 'pooled' by traders by simple averaging, so that a single pair $(\hat{k}_t, \hat{m}_t)$ of numbers describes the perceptions of *all* agents" (Lucas, 1975, p. 1123).

Assumptions (A3) and (A4) require additional comments. The assumption that agents cannot observe the aggregate money stock has been criticized in the literature, because the money supply data are easily available. Lucas's response (1977) was explicitly based on the observation that in a decentralized economy aggregate statistics are of "no importance" to individual traders, because they "will process [only] those prices of most importance to [their] decision problems" (Lucas, 1977, p. 21). He also appealed to decentralization of the economy when he suggested that "the monetary 'state' of the economy" should be described "as being determined by some *unobservable* monetary aggregate, loosely related to observed aggregates over short periods but closely related secularly" (Lucas, 1977, p. 24).

Assumption (A4) is mentioned by Lucas only in passing. First, we note that agents can form unbiased estimates of k_t and m_t only if (A1) holds. Second, this assumption cannot be justified "empirically," because institutions for "pooling" of such information do not exist. Finally, if, as suggested by Lucas, agents in the decentralized economy do not pay attention to information on aggregate variables, it is difficult to understand why at the same time they would try to form estimates of those variables.

Assumptions (A1)–(A4) play a crucial role in Lucas's derivation of the "dynamics of the cycle." This "dynamics" is based on updating by agents of their estimates of k_t and m_t in (26) and (27). The updated forecasts, obtained by the signal extraction procedure, are based on observations of local prices $p_t(z)$ and knowledge of $\hat{m}_t$ and $\hat{k}_t$ and the moments of the distributions of the relevant random variables.

We now show that the assumption that agents "know" the moments of the relevant distributions cannot be reconciled with the assumption that agents cannot observe m_t, k_t, $m_t(z)$, and $k_t(z)$. First, following Lucas, suppose that "the relevant distributions have settled down to the stationary values." Assumption (A1) entails knowledge of the following covariance matrix (Lucas, 1975, p. 1123):

$$\Sigma = \begin{bmatrix} \sigma_k^2 & \sigma_{km} & 0 & 0 & 0 \\ \sigma_{km} & \sigma_m^2 & 0 & 0 & 0 \\ 0 & 0 & \sigma^2 & 0 & 0 \\ 0 & 0 & 0 & \sigma_\theta^2 & \sigma_{u\theta} \\ 0 & 0 & 0 & \sigma_{u\theta} & \sigma_u^2 \end{bmatrix} \tag{28}$$

It is obvious that if agents cannot observe m_t, k_t, $\theta_t(z)$, and $u_t(z)$ they cannot directly estimate the covariances in Σ. In addition, equilibrium relationships in (26) and (27) would not allow the inference of those parameters in the absence of observations of $k_t(z)$, $m_t(z)$, k_t, and m_t. *Note that this conclusion is valid even if all of the markets are assumed to be somehow in the rational expectations equilibrium for an infinite number of periods.* Thus, in contrast to the situation analyzed in Section 5.2, agents cannot estimate the relevant parameters even on the basis of equilibrium observations. We conclude that assumptions (A1) and (A3) cannot be reconciled in this model. Furthermore, if the agents cannot "know" the relevant parameters, the markets will not be in the rational expectations equilibrium in every period.

We have already noted that Lucas justified assumption (A3) by an appeal to the fact that the economy is decentralized. An analysis of learning in Section 5.2 also rested on the decentralization of markets. Therefore, the assumption that agents form rational expectations appears to conflict with the fact that the economy is decentralized. This conclusion is further elucidated in the next section, where we consider an extension of the model formulated in Section 5.1.

5.4.2. *The rational expectations hypothesis in a representative model with differences in supply parameters*

The rational expectations literature has emphasized one important characteristic of the decentralized market economies, namely the distinction between "local" and "aggregate" information. Another important feature of decentralized markets is that behavior of agents is characterized by different demand and supply parameters. This feature has been entirely neglected in the rational expectations literature. For example, in a model (representative of this literature) formulated in Section 5.1, demand and supply parameters were assumed to be the same in all markets. In this section we analyze an extension of the model formulated in Section 5.1 that allows for differences in supply parameters.[28]

Suppose that the quantity supplied in market z is governed by

$$y_t^s(z) = \alpha_z[P_t(z) - F_z P_t] + u_t^s + \epsilon_t^s(z) \tag{29}$$

where α_z is the supply parameter in market z and α_z is not necessarily equal to $\alpha_{z'}$ for $z \neq z'$; all other symbols are defined in Section 5.1.[29]

We shall now compute the coefficients of the rational expectations equilibrium forecast functions in the model composed of (29), (3), and (4). Assume that the individual equilibrium forecast function in market z is given by

$$F_z P_t = E[P_t^* \mid P_t^*(z)] = \beta_{0z}^* + \beta_{1z}^* P_t(z) \tag{30}$$

Equating $y_t^s(z)$ in (29) with $y_t^d(z)$ in (3) and using (4) and (30) yields

$$P_t^*(z) = \delta_{0z}^* + \frac{1}{\delta_{1z}^*}[\beta\mu + \beta x_t + u_t + \epsilon_t(z)] \tag{31}$$

where $\delta_{1z}^* = \beta + \alpha_z(1 - \beta_{1z}^*)$ and $\delta_{0z}^* = \alpha_z \beta_{0z}^*/\delta_{1z}^*$. Averaging $P_t^*(z)$ across markets gives

$$P_t^* = \delta_0^* + \delta_1^*[\beta\mu + \beta x_t + u_t] \tag{32}$$

where $\delta_0^* = (1/N) \sum_{z=1}^{N} \delta_{0z}^*$ and $\delta_1^* = (1/N) \sum_{z=1}^{N} 1/\delta_{1z}^*$. Taking the conditional expectation of P_t^* on $P_t^*(z)$ for every z results in the system of $2N$ equations for β_{0z}^* and β_{1z}^*, $z = 1, \ldots, N$. These equations are given by

$$\beta_{1z}^* = \theta[\beta + \alpha_z(1 - \beta_{1z}^*)] \frac{1}{N} \sum_{k=1}^{N} \frac{1}{\beta + \alpha_k(1 - \beta_{1k}^*)} \tag{33}$$

$$\beta_{0z}^* = \frac{1}{N} \sum_{k=1}^{N} \frac{\beta\mu(1-\theta) + \alpha_k \beta_{0k}^* - \alpha_z \beta_{0z}^* \theta}{\beta + \alpha_k(1 - \beta_{1k}^*)} \tag{34}$$

where $\theta = (\beta^2 \sigma_x^2 + \sigma_u^2)/(\beta^2 \sigma_x^2 + \sigma_u^2 + \sigma_\epsilon^2)$, $z = 1, \ldots, N$.

By inspection it can be shown that the following expression for β_{0z}^* satisfies (34):

$$\beta_{0z}^* = \mu(1 - \beta_{1z}^*) \tag{35}$$

Thus, the system (33)–(34) is recursive. If equations (33) have a unique solution, this solution can be written as[30]

---

[28] An analysis is identical if differences in demand parameters are introduced in addition to differences in supply parameters.

[29] The model could be further complicated by introducing technical change, which would make α_z a function of time. An analysis of this section also applies to such cases at each point in time.

[30] If the unique solutions do not exist, the argument in this section will be even

$$\beta^*_{1z} = f_z(\alpha_1, \ldots, \alpha_N, \theta, \mu, \beta) \quad (z=1,\ldots,N) \tag{36}$$

In order to illustrate these solutions, consider a specific example when $\alpha_1 = \cdots = \alpha_{N/2} = \alpha_z$ and $\alpha_{(N/2)+1} = \cdots = \alpha_N = \alpha_k$. In this case, explicit solutions for β^*_{1z} and β^*_{1k} can be obtained. They are given by

$$\beta^*_{1z} = \theta \frac{2\beta + \alpha_z + \alpha_k}{2\beta + \alpha_k(2-\theta) + \theta\alpha_z}$$

$$\beta^*_{1k} = \theta \frac{2\beta + \alpha_z + \alpha_k}{2\beta + \alpha_z(2-\theta) + \theta\alpha_k} \tag{37}$$

We conclude that agents in market z can use the rational expectations equilibrium forecast function in (30) if and only if they know, in addition to β, μ, and θ, the values of the supply parameters in *all* other markets. Furthermore, the assumption that agents form rational expectations has no "operational meaning" in this model because agents in the decentralized economy simply do not have information on behavioral parameters of other agents. Finally, the imposition of the assumption of rational expectations in this model would undermine the fundamental notion that decentralized markets economize on information required by agents in making their economic decisions. We recall (see Section 5.4.1) that it is precisely this notion that Lucas used in the defense of the assumptions in his models.

5.5.   Concluding remarks

The analysis in this chapter has a number of implications for modeling a decentralized market economy and an assessment of the analysis of macroeconomic policies derived in the rational expectations literature. Each of these large issues requires separate treatment. My remarks here will necessarily have to be brief.

5.5.1.   *The rational expectations hypothesis and the evaluation of effects of macroeconomic policy*

Lucas (1975, p. 1114)

motivated...the attempt to discover [the rational expectations] equilibrium account of the business cycle...*entirely by practical considerations.* The problem of quantitatively assessing hypothetical countercyclical policies (say, a monetary growth rule or a fiscal stabilizer) involves imagining how agents will behave in a situation which has never been observed. To do this successfully, one must have

stronger, because in such a situation agents in market z would have to know which solutions were chosen by agents in other markets.

some understanding of the way agents' decisions have been made in the past and some method of determining how these decisions would be altered by a hypothetical change in policy. Insofar as our descriptions of past behavior rely on arbitrary mechanical rules of thumb, illusions, and unspecified institutional barriers, this task will be made difficult, or impossible [emphasis added].

The analysis in this chapter suggests that the rational expectations hypothesis does not, in general, characterize expectations formation of agents in decentralized markets. Therefore, rational expectations models do not seem to provide an "understanding of the way agents' decisions have been made in the past" and how they are likely to react to policy changes. It seems clear that agents react to policy changes and, thus, that the task of assessing the results of policy is difficult. This task, however, cannot be accomplished by models attributing to agents decisions that they cannot, *even hypothetically or in principle,* carry out.

5.5.2. *Modeling of individual behavior in decentralized markets*

The conclusion that the rational expectations hypothesis appears to be incompatible with the fundamental characteristics of the decentralized market economy suggests that the question of modeling individual forecasts has not been satisfactorily solved by the REH.

In searching for the alternative approaches, we might, perhaps, recall that Hayek (1948a) presented an argument that *precise* modeling of individual expectations and acquisition of knowledge by *individual agents* is impossible.[31,32] This impossibility played a crucial role in Hayek's analysis of superiority of decentralized market economies over centrally planned economies. It would be unfortunate if one of the leading approaches to the study of decentralized market economies were subject conceptually to the same criticism as leveled by Hayek against the proponents of socialist planning. These issues are, however, outside the bounds of this chapter.

Appendix

Proof of Proposition 1

Sufficiency
Suppose that individual agents know the functions $F_z P_l$ ($l = t, t-1, \ldots$) and the realizations of FP_l ($l = t-1, t-2, \ldots$). An analogous proof can be

[31] For important arguments on this point, see Hayek (1978a,b), Keynes (1936, p. 162), and Knight (1921). Also see Chapter 1 of this book.

[32] An attempt to provide a formulation of forecasting behavior that does not presume the possibility of precise modeling of individual expectations is presented in a specific model by Frydman (1982b).

carried out for the case when agents know functions FP_l ($l = t-1, t-2, \ldots$) and realizations of $F_z P_l$ ($l = t, t-1, \ldots$).

For convenience, we rewrite the expressions for β_0^* and β_1^*:

$$\beta_0^* = \mu(1-\theta) \tag{A1}$$

and

$$\beta_1^* = \theta \tag{A2}$$

where

$$\theta = \frac{\beta^2 \sigma_x^2 + \sigma_u^2}{\beta^2 \sigma_x^2 + \sigma_u^2 + \sigma_\epsilon^2} = \frac{\theta_1}{\theta_2} \tag{A3}$$

We first consider consistent estimation of α, β, and μ. Because individual agents know that $P_t(z)$ is correlated with P_t, we suppose that the average forecast function in z is given by

$$F_z P_t = \delta_{0t-1}^{(z)} + \delta_{1t-1}^{(z)} P_t(z) \tag{A4}$$

Substituting (A4) into (5) and solving for $P_t(z)$ yields

$$P_t(z) = \frac{\beta\mu + \alpha\delta_{0t-1}^{(z)}}{\beta + \alpha(1 - \delta_{1t-1}^{(z)})} + \eta_t \tag{A5}$$

where $\eta_t = (1/[\beta + \alpha(1 - \delta_{1t-1}^{(z)})])\{[\beta x_t + u_t + \epsilon_t(z)]$. Note that $E[\eta_t \mid \delta_t^{(z)}] = 0$. Because individual agents are assumed to know $\delta_t^{(z)}$ in every time period, they can consistently estimate α and β on the basis of (A5) using the generalized nonlinear least-squares procedure (Malinvaud, 1970). Note that μ and σ_x^2 can also be consistently estimated from the past money supply data. Thus, denote consistent estimators of α, β, and μ by $\hat{\alpha}$, $\hat{\beta}$, and $\hat{\mu}$. Then $\theta_2 = \beta^2 \sigma_x^2 + \sigma_u^2 + \sigma_\epsilon^2$ can be consistently estimated by

$$\hat{\theta}_2 = \frac{1}{t} \sum_{l=1}^{t} [P_l(z)(\hat{\beta} + \hat{\alpha}) - \hat{\beta}\hat{\mu} - \hat{\alpha} F_z P_l]^2 \tag{A6}$$

Finally, because individual agents are assumed to know FP_l, $\theta_1 = \beta^2 \sigma_x^2 + \sigma_u^2$ can be consistently estimated by

$$\hat{\theta}_1 = \frac{1}{t-1} \sum_{l=1}^{t-1} [P_l(\hat{\beta} + \hat{\alpha}) - \hat{\beta}\hat{\mu} - \hat{\alpha} FP_l]^2 \tag{A7}$$

and a consistent estimator of θ is given by

$$\hat{\theta} = \frac{\hat{\theta}_1}{\hat{\theta}_2} \tag{A8}$$

Necessity
Suppose that individual agents know the coefficients and variables used in $F_z P_l$ ($l = t, t-1, \ldots$). Then, by the procedure detailed in the sufficiency

proof, α, β, μ, and $\beta^2\sigma_x^2 + \sigma_u^2 + \sigma_\epsilon^2$ can be consistently estimated on the basis of (5). Also, σ_x^2 can be consistently estimated on the basis of the past money supply data. To prove the necessity, suppose that individual agents do not know the values of FP_l $(l = t-1, t-2, \ldots)$. Then they cannot distinguish the influence of FP_l and $\beta x_l + u_l$ on P_l [in (6)] for $l = t-1, t-2, \ldots$. Thus, σ_u^2 cannot be consistently estimated on the basis of the correct specification in (6). By an identical argument, σ_u^2 cannot be consistently estimated on the basis of economy-wide average output equations or separate aggregate demand and supply equations. [For an example of an aggregate demand equation, see (A9).] Therefore, if individual agents do not know an economy-wide average opinion, they cannot form a consistent estimator of θ on the basis of the correct specification of the model and information available to them.   Q.E.D.

Proof of Corollary 1.1

Necessity
The necessity follows directly from the necessity part of Proposition 1.

Sufficiency
Suppose that individual agents know the functions $F_z P_l$ $(l = t, t-1, \ldots)$. Then, from the sufficiency proof of Proposition 1, they can consistently estimate α, β, μ, and $\theta_2' = \beta^2\sigma_x^2 + \sigma_{u_d}^2 + \sigma_\epsilon^2$. Averaging across markets of market demand functions in (3), we obtain

$$y_t = \beta(\mu - P_t) + \beta x_t + u_t^d \tag{A9}$$

From (A9), consistent estimators of $\theta_1' = \beta^2\sigma_x^2 + \sigma_{u_d}^2$ and $\theta = \theta_1'/\theta_2'$ can be obtained. They are given by

$$\hat{\theta}_1' = \frac{1}{t-1} \sum_{l=1}^{t-1} [y_l - \hat{\beta}(\hat{\mu} - P_l)]^2 \tag{A10}$$

and

$$\hat{\theta} = \frac{\hat{\theta}_1'}{\hat{\theta}_2'}   \text{Q.E.D.} \tag{A11}$$

References

Barro, Robert J. (1976). "Rational Expectations and the Role of Monetary Policy." *Journal of Monetary Economics,* 2:1–32.

(1977). "Long-Term Contracting, Sticky Prices, and Monetary Policy." *Journal of Monetary Economics,* 3:305–16.

Bray, Margaret (1982). "Learning, Estimation and Stability of Rational Expectations." *Journal of Economic Theory,* 26:318–39.

Bray, Margaret, and David M. Kreps (1981). "Rational Learning and Rational Expectations." Research paper No. 616, Graduate School of Business, Stanford University.

Bull, Clive, and Roman Frydman (1983). "The Derivation and Interpretation of the Lucas Supply Function." *Journal of Money, Credit and Banking,* February, pp. 82-95.

Friedman, Benjamin J. (1979). "Optimal Expectations and the Extreme Information Assumptions of 'Rational Expectations' Macromodels." *Journal of Monetary Economics,* 5:23-42.

Friedman, Milton (1968). "The Role of Monetary Policy." *American Economic Review,* 58:1-17.

Frydman, Roman (1982*a*). "Towards an Understanding of Market Processes: Individual Expectations, Learning and Convergence to Rational Expectations Equilibrium." *American Economic Review,* 72:652-68.

(1982*b*). "Subjective Forecasts and Output-Inflation Relationship." Unpublished mimeograph, Department of Economics, New York University.

Futia, Carl A. (1981). "Information and the Trade Cycle." Bell Laboratories discussion paper 182.

Hayek, Friedrich A. (1948*a*). *Individualism and Economic Order.* University of Chicago Press.

(1948*b*). "Economics and Knowledge." In *Individualism and Economic Order,* edited by F. A. Hayek, pp. 33-56. University of Chicago Press.

(1948*c*). "The Use of Knowledge in Society." In: *Individualism and Economic Order,* edited by F. A. Hayek, pp. 77-91. University of Chicago Press.

(1948*d*). "The Meaning of Competition." In: *Individualism and Economic Order,* edited by F. A. Hayek, pp. 92-106. University of Chicago Press.

(1978*a*). "The Pretence of Knowledge." In: *New Studies in Philosophy, Politics, Economics and History of Ideas,* F. A. Hayek, pp. 23-34. University of Chicago Press.

(1978*b*). "Competition as a Discovery Procedure." In: *New Studies in Philosophy, Politics, Economics and History of Ideas,* F. A. Hayak, pp. 179-90. University of Chicago Press.

Kantor, Brian (1979). "Rational Expectations and Economic Thought." *Journal of Economic Literature,* December, pp. 1422-41.

Keynes, John M. (1936). *The General Theory of Employment, Interest and Money.* New York: Harcourt Brace & World.

King, Robert G. (1981). "Monetary Information and Monetary Neutrality." *Journal of Monetary Economics,* 7:195-206.

Knight, Frank H. (1921). *Risk, Uncertainty and Profit.* No. 16 in series of reprints of scarce tracts in economics, London School of Economics.

Lucas, Robert E., Jr. (1972). "Expectations and Neutrality of Money." *Journal of Economic Theory,* 4:103-24; reprinted in R. E. Lucas, Jr. (1981). *Studies in Business-Cycle Theory.* Cambridge, Mass.: M.I.T. Press.

(1973). "Some International Evidence on Output-Inflation Tradeoffs." *American Economic Review,* 63:326-34; reprinted in R. E. Lucas, Jr. (1981). *Studies in Business-Cycle Theory.* Cambridge, Mass.: M.I.T. Press.

(1975). "An Equilibrium Model of the Business Cycle." *Journal of Political Economy,* 83:1113-44; reprinted in R. E. Lucas, Jr. (1981). *Studies in Business-Cycle Theory.* Cambridge, Mass.: M.I.T. Press.

(1977). "Understanding Business Cycles." In: *Stabilization of Domestic and International Economy, Vol. 5,* Carnegie-Rochester Series on Public Policy, edited by K. Brunner and A. H. Meltzer, pp. 7-29. Amsterdam: North Holland; reprinted in R. E. Lucas, Jr. (1981). *Studies in Business-Cycle Theory.* Cambridge, Mass.: M.I.T. Press.

Lucas, Robert E., Jr., and Leonard A. Rapping (1969). "Real Wages, Employment and Inflation." *Journal of Political Economy,* 77:721–54; reprinted in R. E. Lucas, Jr. (1981). *Studies in Business-Cycle Theory.* Cambridge, Mass.: M.I.T. Press.

Malinvaud, Edmond (1970). "The Consistency of Nonlinear Regressions." *Annals of Mathematical Statistics,* 41:956–69.

Muth, John F. (1961). "Rational Expectations and the Theory of Price Movements." *Econometrica,* 29:315–35.

Phelps, Edmund S. (1970). "The New Microeconomics in Employment and Inflation Theory." In: *Microeconomic Foundations of Employment and Inflation Theory,* E. S. Phelps et al., pp. 1–23. New York: Norton.

Phelps, Edmund S., et al. (1970). *Microeconomic Foundations of Employment and Inflation Theory.* New York: Norton.

Sargent, Thomas J. (1979). *Macroeconomic Theory.* New York: Academic Press.

Taylor, John B. (1980). "Aggregate Dynamics and Staggered Contrasts." *Journal of Political Economy,* 88:1–23.

Townsend, Robert M. (1978). "Market Anticipations, Rational Expectations and Bayesian Analysis." *International Economic Review,* 19:481–94.

(1981). "Forecasting the Forecasts of Others: Formulation and Analysis of Equilibrium Time Series Models" (to be published in *Journal of Political Economy,* 83).

CHAPTER 6

Convergence to rational expectations equilibrium

MARGARET BRAY

The use of the rational expectations hypotheses is now so standard in both the microeconomic and the macroeconomic literature that authors no longer feel the need to justify and explain the hypothesis. Nevertheless, this chapter discusses the arguments for using the rational expectations hypothesis in the light of recent work by myself and others on the question of how agents learn to form rational expectations (Bray and Kreps, 1981; Bray, 1982). See also Blume, Bray, and Easley (1982) for a survey of the literature on the subject.

Sargent and Wallace (1976) provide a variety of reasons for using the rational expectations hypothesis. They argue that it provides identifying restrictions for econometric work and a partial explanation for the finding that macroeconometric models fail tests for structural stability. Most fundamentally, they write that the rational expectations hypothesis "accords with the economist's usual practice of assuming that people behave in their own best interests." This could mean that people act in their own best interests given their perception of the nature of the world; indeed, this is the nature of the Bayesian theory of decision making under uncertainty that underlies so many economic models. However, something more is entailed in the rational expectations hypothesis. Lucas (1976) writes:

Unfortunately, the general hypothesis that economic agents are Bayesian decision makers has, in many applications, little empirical content: without some way of inferring what an agent's subjective view of the future is, this hypothesis is of no help in understanding his behavior. Even psychotic behavior can be (and today, is) understood as "rational", given a sufficiently abnormal view of relevant probabilities. To practice economics, we need *some* way (short of psychoanalysis, one hopes) of understanding *which* decision problem agents are solving.

John Muth (1961) proposed to resolve this problem by identifying agents' subjective probabilities with observed frequencies of the events to be forecast, or with "true" probabilities, calling the assumed coincidence of subjective and "true" probabilities *rational expectations*. Evidently, this hypothesis will not be of value in understanding psychotic behavior. Neither will it be applicable in situations in which one cannot guess which, if any, observable frequencies are relevant: situations which Knight called "uncertainty". It will *most* likely be

123

useful in situations in which the probabilities of interest concern a fairly well defined recurrent event, situations of "risk" in Knight's terminology. In situations of risk, the hypothesis of rational behavior on the part of agents will have usable content, so that behavior may be explainable in terms of economic theory. In such situations, expectations are rational in Muth's sense. In cases of uncertainty, economic reasoning will be of no value.

I have quoted Lucas at length because he makes the essential point that if the rational expectations hypothesis is taken to mean that subjective beliefs correspond to objective probabilities, it lacks content unless the stochastic process generating outcomes and expectations is in some rather general sense stationary. In a completely nonstationary world, it is impossible to identify probabilities with observed frequencies.

By observing the history of a stationary world, people can eventually learn the objective probability distributions by using Bayesian or classical statistical techniques. This suggests that although people may not initially hold rational expectations, they must eventually come arbitrarily close to doing so. This intuition based on textbook theorems on the asymptotic properties of estimators is somewhat misleading. As Lucas points out so forcefully in his critique of econometric policy evaluation (1976), the reduced form of an econometric model is not stationary if people change the way in which they form expectations. Lucas considers changes in expectations induced by changes in policy. However, the process of learning also changes the way people form expectations, introducing a nonstationarity into the situation.

Consider, for example, the following somewhat simplified version of the aggregate macroeconomic model of Sargent and Wallace (1975).

Aggregate supply

$$y_t = a_1 + a_2(p_t - {}_t p_{t-1}^*) + u_{1t} \quad (a_i > 0, \ i = 1, 2) \tag{1}$$

Aggregate demand

$$y_t = b_1 + b_2[r_t - ({}_{t+1}p_{t-1}^* - {}_t p_{t-1}^*)] + u_{2t} \quad (b_1 > 0, \ b_2 < 0) \tag{2}$$

Portfolio balance

$$m_t = p_t + c_1 y_t + c_2 r_t + u_{3t} \quad (c_1 > 0, \ c_2 < 0) \tag{3}$$

Here y_t, p_t, and m_t are the natural logarithms of output, the price level, and the money supply, and r_t is the nominal rate of interest (not its logarithm). The variable ${}_{t+i}p_{t-j}^*$ is the expectation of the log of the price level at $t+i$, the expectation being held at $t-j$. Sargent and Wallace assume that the noise variables u_{1t}, u_{2t}, and u_{3t} are serially uncorrelated. I shall make the somewhat stronger assumption that they form a stationary sequence of independent zero mean random variables with finite variance.

Solving for p_t,

$$p_t = J_0(_t p_{t-1}^*) + J_1(_{t+1} p_{t-1}^*) + J_2 m_t + J_3 + e_t \tag{4}$$

where

$$J_0 = D[b_2 + a_2(1 + b_2 c_1 c_2^{-1})] \tag{5}$$

$$J_1 = -Db_2 \tag{6}$$

$$J_2 = Db_2 c_2^{-1} \tag{7}$$

$$J_3 = D[b_1 - a_1(1 + b_2 c_1 c_2^{-1})] \tag{8}$$

$$e_t = D[-u_{1t}(1 + b_2 c_1 c_2^{-1}) + u_{2t} - b_2 c_2^{-1} u_{3t}] \tag{9}$$

and

$$D = [b_2 c_2^{-1} + a_2(1 + b_2 c_1 c_2^{-1})]^{-1}$$

If the authorities follow the optimal policy under rational expectations recommended by Sargent and Wallace, holding the money supply constant so that $m_t = m$ for all t, in the rational expectations equilibrium

$$p_t = \frac{J_2 m + J_3}{1 - J_0 - J_1} + \frac{e_t}{1 - J_0 - J_1} \tag{10}$$

and

$$_t p_{t-1}^* = _{t+1} p_{t-1}^* = \frac{J_2 m + J_3}{1 - J_0 - J_1} \equiv p^* \tag{11}$$

The deviation of the logarithm of the price level from its mean is a sequence of independent identically distributed random variables $\{e_t/(1 - J_0 - J_1)\}$.

An outside observer of the rational expectations equilibrium could estimate the mean log price level and form an unbiased predictor of the logarithm of future price levels as $(1/t) \sum_{i=1}^t p_i$. However, the inference problem for people in the model is not so simple. If they do not form rational expectations, the price level is not the same as it would be in the rational expectations equilibrium. If they change their expectations as they learn, the price level is no longer stationary. The maintained hypothesis, that the economy is in a rational expectations equilibrium, under which $(1/t) \sum_1^t p_i$ is an unbiased predictor of the logarithm of the price level, does not hold if people use $(1/t) \sum_1^t p_i$ rather than the rational expectation p^* as a predictor. If people do not initially know that p^* is the rational expectation, how can they ever learn to expect that log price level when the logarithms of the prices that they do observe do not have p^* as their mean?

It can in fact be shown that if

$$_tp^*_{t-1} = {}_{t+1}p^*_{t-1} = \frac{1}{t-1} \sum_1^{t-1} p_i \tag{12}$$

expectations become rational in the limit in the sense that both $_tp^*_{t-1}$ and $_{t+1}p^*_{t-1}$ tend to their rational expectations value.

This result is implied by the following theorem, which is proved in the Appendix to this chapter.

Theorem

If a stochastic process can be written as

$$p_t = Ap^e_{t-1} + b + u_t$$

where $p^e_{t-1} = [1/(t-1)] \sum_{i=1}^{t-1} p_i$, A is a deterministic matrix, b is a deterministic column vector, $\{u_t\}$ is a sequence of independent zero mean random column vectors satisfying $Eu'_t u_t < \sigma^2 < \infty$ for some σ^2 and all t, and $I - \frac{1}{2}(A + A')$ is positive definite, then p^e_t converges to $(I - A)^{-1}b$ almost surely.

Note that if $p^e_t = (I - A)^{-1}b$, expectations are rational. In the case where A is a scalar, as in the Sargent-Wallace example, the convergence condition is $A < 1$, which, referring to equations (4) and (12), is in fact $J_0 + J_1 < 1$. It is easy to verify that the sign conditions imposed by Sargent and Wallace imply that the convergence condition is satisfied.

The result is perhaps surprising as the estimation technique is based on a misspecification of the situation, although the estimation technique is not completely ad hoc in the sense that it is based on a correct specification of the rational expectations equilibrium. People using this technique are in fact following Sargent's recommendation (1981) of estimating a model as if it were in its rational expectations equilibrium, and they are fortunate in knowing the correct specification of the rational expectations equilibrium.

This convergence result is similar in spirit to that of Bray (1982), which deals with a simple asset market model in which a group of traders try to estimate the price–return relationship using a naive econometric technique, ordinary least squares. In this case, also, the estimation technique could appropriately be used by an outside observer using data generated by repeated realizations of the rational expectations equilibrium, but, as used by traders in the model, it is based on a misspecification of the situation. There is also a stability condition (Bray, 1982) that essentially requires that the traders who are learning do not form too large a proportion of the market.

These results can be interpreted as support for the use of the rational expectations hypothesis, because they suggest that, despite the complications introduced by the feedback from expectations to outcomes under learning, people may learn to form rational expectations using relatively simple and standard statistical techniques. But two examples do not constitute a theory. The stability condition in the Sargent-Wallace example is always satisfied, given the economically plausible sign restrictions, but in other examples instability may be a real possibility. Blanchard (1976) and Blume and Easley (1982) provide examples in which learning methods based on misspecified models do not yield rational expectations even in the limit, and this I think is not surprising.

An alternative approach to the issue is to assume that people estimate models based not on the correct specification of the rational expectations equilibrium but on the correct specification of the situation in which they are learning. This is a very complicated inference problem. Sargent (1981) discusses whether or not econometricians should, as a practical matter, try to take learning into account in estimating models. He argues that there is in general no closed-form prediction formula describing how people should optimally form expectations when they are ignorant about certain parameters, and he continues:

The fact that there is no closed-form prediction formula for sufficiently general cases implies that it is impossible to derive closed-form versions of decision rules (and hence equilibria). As we shall see, for the kind of empirical work we are advocating, it is important to have a closed form for the mapping from the parameters of the objective functions and the dynamic constraints to the decision rule. From this viewpoint, the suggestion that one ought to build a learning mechanism into rational expectations models is not useful in suggesting practical econometric alternatives to the procedures recommended here.

Sargent goes on to argue that neglect of learning does not matter enormously, as Bayesian learning ultimately leads people to form rational expectations, and so the econometric estimates produced by ignoring learning are consistent. This line of argument may be comforting to the econometrician faced with the impossible practical problem of specifying a model that incorporates learning, but it leaves the theorist supporting a hypothesis that maintains that people act as if they have solved an inference problem that is too complicated for econometricians, working in full knowledge of the structure of the model, to write down a closed-form solution.

The problem is in fact more complicated than Sargent suggests. From the point of view of people in the model, the correct specification is not given exogenously; it depends on how they and other people are learning, on their specification of likelihood functions, their priors, their priors about each other's priors, and so on ad infinitum. The correct Bayesian learning process is an equilibrium, in fact a rational expectations equilibrium, in which people are subjectively uncertain not only about the variables that are usually treated as stochastic in rational expectations models but also about the parameters of the model. The equilibrium is less informationally demanding than the conventional rational expectations equilibrium in the sense that people are not assumed to know the numerical values of parameters. However, it demands that people have a quite fantastic degree of understanding about the structure of their world.

Equilibrium may not be unique, in which case, even given complete information about parameters, people would not know which equilibrium they were in, and indeed would not be in a rational expectations equilibrium at all unless they all happened to believe that they were in the same equilibrium.

There may also be problems with the existence of an equilibrium with learning; no general existence theorems have been proved. However, granted existence and uniqueness, there are results on the convergence of equilibria with learning to standard rational expectations equilibria. Friedman (1979) and Taylor (1975) consider models in which people's expectations do not affect the variables they form expectations about. In these cases, learning does not introduce any nonstationarity into the relationships that people are estimating, and convergence to rational expectations equilibrium follows from standard results on the asymptotic properties of estimators.

Townsend (1978) analyzes an example in which people incorporate the effects of their own and each other's learning into their learning process, and he also demonstrates convergence to rational expectations equilibrium. Bray and Kreps (1981) argue that in general the martingale convergence theorem implies that Bayesian posteriors must converge and that, given further assumptions (in particular, continuity), this convergence generates rational expectations in the limit.

The theory of the stability of rational expectations equilibrium is in a somewhat unsatisfactory state. It is eminently plausible that people will not persist indefinitely in using a *stationary* forecasting rule that generates nonrational expectations that are systematically confounded by events; rational expectation seems to be the only type of expectations formation in a long-run stationary equilibrium that is compatible with the general assumption of optimizing behavior. However, this assertion does not rule out the possibility that people try to learn and understand what is going on, and continually change the way in which they form expectations, never reaching a stationary equilibrium. Making the assumption that agents follow a correct Bayesian learning process does generate convergence to a stationary rational expectations equilibrium, but, in my opinion, applying this assumption to the very complicated situations that can be generated even by rather simple models with learning is pushing the general presumption of optimizing behavior to the point where it loses many of its attractions. In some cases, irrational learning based on standard statistical techniques has been shown to generate rational expectations in the limit, but in other cases irrational learning does not generate rational expectations, and at present we lack any general theory about what distinguishes these cases.

Appendix

This appendix contains the proof of the following result.

Theorem
If

$$p_t = A p^e_{t-1} + b + u_t \tag{A1}$$

where

$$p^e_{t-1} = \frac{1}{t-1} \sum_{i=1}^{t-1} p_i \tag{A2}$$

and A is a deterministic matrix, b is a deterministic vector, $\{u_t\}$ is a sequence of independent random vectors satisfying $E u'_t u_t < \sigma^2 < \infty$ for some σ^2 and all t, and $I - \frac{1}{2}(A + A')$ is positive definite, then p^e_{t-1} converges to $(I-A)^{-1} b$ almost surely.

Proof
It is convenient to work in terms of a variable x_t defined by

$$x_t = p^e_t - (I-A)^{-1} b = \frac{1}{t} \sum_1^t p_i - (I-A)^{-1} \tag{A3}$$

The theorem is proved by showing that x_t tends to the zero vector almost surely.
Equations (A1) and (A2) imply that

$$x_{T+1} = \left(I - \frac{1}{T+1} B\right) x_T + \frac{1}{T+1} u_{T+1} \tag{A4}$$

where

$$B = I - A$$

so by the assumption of the theorem, $\frac{1}{2}(B + B')$ is positive definite.
Equation (A4) implies that for any integers $t > T > 0$,

$$x_t = \prod_{i=T+1}^{t} \left(I - \frac{1}{i}B\right)x_T + z_{Tt} \tag{A5}$$

where

$$z_{Tt} = \sum_{i=T+1}^{t-1} \prod_{j=i+1}^{t} \left(I - \frac{1}{j}B\right)\frac{1}{i}u_i + \frac{1}{t}u_t \tag{A6}$$

The theorem follows from two lemmas:

Lemma 1

$$\lim_{t \to \infty} \left\| \prod_{i=T+1}^{t} \left(I - \frac{1}{i}B\right) \right\| = 0 \tag{A7}$$

Lemma 2
Given any ϵ and $\delta > 0$, if T is sufficiently large,

$$P\left(|z_{Tt}| < \frac{\epsilon}{2} \quad \text{for all} \quad t > T\right) \geqslant 1 - \delta \tag{A8}$$

Now equation (A5) implies that

$$|x_t| < \left\| \prod_{i=T+1}^{t} \left(I - \frac{1}{i}B\right) \right\| |x_T| + |z_{Tt}| \tag{A9}$$

It also implies that for each T, x_T has finite variance; so Chebyschev's inequality implies that there is a number L such that

$$P(|x_T| < L) \geqslant 1 - \delta$$

and so for sufficiently large t, using Lemma 1,

$$P\left[\left\| \prod_{i=1+T}^{t} \left(1 - \frac{1}{i}B\right) \right\| |x_T| < \frac{\epsilon}{2} \right] \geqslant 1 - \delta \tag{A10}$$

Equations (A8), (A9), and (A10) taken together imply that x_t tends to zero almost surely, as required.

Proof of Lemma 1
By definition,

$$\left\| I - \frac{1}{i}B \right\| = \max_x \left(\frac{x'\left(I - \frac{1}{i}B\right)'\left(I - \frac{1}{i}B\right)x}{x'x} \right)^{1/2}$$

$$= \left(1 - \frac{2}{i}\frac{x'(B'+B)x}{2x'x} + \frac{1}{i^2}\frac{x'B'Bx}{x'x}\right)^{1/2} \tag{A11}$$

By assumption, $\frac{1}{2}(B'+B)$ is positive definite; so there is a positive scalar α [the minimal eigenvalue of $\frac{1}{2}(B'+B)$] such that for all nonzero x,

$$\frac{\frac{1}{2}x'(B'+B)x}{x'x} \geqslant \alpha > 0 \tag{A12}$$

Also, if $\|B\| = \beta$

$$\frac{x'B'Bx}{x'x} \leqslant \beta^2 \tag{A13}$$

Thus, from (A11)–(A13),

$$\left\|I - \frac{1}{i}B\right\| \leqslant \left(1 - \frac{2\alpha}{i} + \frac{\beta^2}{i^2}\right)^{1/2} \tag{A14}$$

and so

$$\log\left(\left\|\prod_{T+1}^{t}\left(I - \frac{1}{i}B\right)\right\|\right) \leqslant \log \prod_{T+1}^{t}\left\|I - \frac{1}{i}B\right\|$$

$$\leqslant \sum_{T+1}^{t} \log\left(1 - \frac{2\alpha}{i} + \frac{\beta^2}{i^2}\right)^{1/2}$$

$$\leqslant -\alpha \sum_{T+1}^{t} \frac{1}{i} + \frac{\beta^2}{2} \sum_{T+1}^{t} \frac{1}{i^2}$$

Thus, as α is strictly positive and $\sum_{T+1}^{t} 1/i$ tends to infinity while $\sum_{T+1}^{t} 1/i^2$ tends to a finite limit as t tends to infinity, the last term tends to $-\infty$, which establishes the lemma.

Proof of Lemma 2
Let

$$\left.\begin{array}{l} w_{TT} = 0 \\[2mm] w_{Tt} = z_{Tt} - \displaystyle\sum_{i=T+1}^{t} \frac{1}{i} u_i \end{array}\right\} \tag{A15}$$

Equations (A6) and (A15) imply that

$$w_{Tt} = \left(I - \frac{1}{t}B\right)w_{Tt-1} - \frac{1}{t}B\sum_{T+1}^{t-1} \frac{u_i}{i}$$

Thus, using the triangle inequality and equation (A14) and recalling that $\|B\| = \beta$,

$$|w_{Tt}| < \left(1 - \frac{2\alpha}{t} + \frac{\beta^2}{t^2}\right)^{1/2}|w_{Tt-1}| + \frac{1}{t}\beta\left|\sum_{T+1}^{t-1} \frac{u_i}{i}\right| \tag{A16}$$

Using (A16), and noting that $|w_{TT}| = 0$, a simple induction argument establishes that there is a number η such that if for all $t > T$,

$$\left| \sum_{T+1}^{t} \frac{u_i}{i} \right| < \eta < \frac{\epsilon}{4}$$

then $|w_{Tt}| < \epsilon/4$, and so, from (A15), $|z_{Tt}| < \epsilon/2$ for all $t > T$.

Now, using Kolmogorov's inequality (which can be applied because the u_i's are by assumption independent) and recalling that by assumption $Eu_i'u_i \leqslant \sigma^2$,

$$P\left(\left| \sum_{T+1}^{t} \frac{u_i}{i} \right| < \eta \quad \text{for all} \quad t > T \right) \geqslant 1 - \frac{1}{\eta^2} \sum_{T+1}^{\infty} \frac{Eu_i'u_i}{i^2}$$

$$> 1 - \frac{\sigma^2}{\eta^2} \sum_{T+1}^{\infty} \frac{1}{i^2} > 1 - \delta$$

if T is sufficiently large, which is the desired result.

References

Blanchard, O.(1976). "The Non-transition to Rational Expectations." Unpublished manuscript, Department of Economics, Massachusetts Institute of Technology.

Blume, L. E., M. M. Bray, and D. Easley (1982). "Introduction to the Stability of Rational Expectation Equilibrium." *Journal of Economic Theory,* 26:313-17.

Blume, L. E., and D. Easley (1982). "Learning to be Rational." *Journal of Economic Theory,* 26:340-51.

Bray, M. M. (1982). "Learning, Estimation and the Stability of Rational Expectations." *Journal of Economic Theory,* 26:318-39.

Bray, M. M., and D. M. Kreps (1981). "Rational Learning and Rational Expectations." Research paper No. 616, Graduate School of Business, Stanford University.

Chung, K. L. (1974). *A Course in Probability Theory,* 2nd ed. New York: Academic Press.

Friedman, B. M. (1979). "Optimal Expectations and the Extreme Informational Assumptions of Rational Expectations Macromodels." *Journal of Monetary Economics,* 5:23-42.

Lucas, R. E. (1976). "Econometric Policy Evaluation: A Critique." In: *The Phillips Curve and Labor Markets,* edited by K. Brunner and A. M. Meltzer, pp. 19-46.

(1977). "Understanding Business Cycles." In: *Stabilization of the Domestic and International Economy,* edited by K. Brunner and A. M. Meltzer, pp. 7-29. Amsterdam: North Holland.

Sargent, T. W. (1981). "Interpreting Economic Time Series." *Journal of Political Economy,* 89:213-48.

Sargent, T. W., and N. Wallace (1975). "Rational Expectations, the Optimal Monetary Instrument, and the Optimal Money Supply Rule." *Journal of Political Economy,* 83:241-54.

(1976). "Rational Expectations and the Theory of Economic Policy." *Journal of Monetary Economics,* 2:169-83.

Taylor, J. B. (1975). "Monetary Policy during a Transition to Rational Expectation." *Journal of Political Economy,* 83:1009-21.

Townsend, R. M. (1978). "Market Anticipations, Rational Expectations, and Bayesian Analysis." *International Economic Review,* 19:481-94.

Comment

ROY RADNER

I

In the recent work on rational expectations equilibrium in economic systems, two somewhat different phenomena are usually combined: (1) In an economic system that extends over several time periods, the behavior of agents at any one date will depend on their expectations of endogenous (as well as exogenous) random variables at future dates; in equilibrium, the stochastic process of the endogenous random variables should be such as to be consistent with those expectations. (2) If different agents have different information about the random variables in the system, some agents may be able to use their own information about endogenous random variables to infer something about the information held by other agents; in equilibrium, these inferences should be consistent with the joint distribution of the endogenous random variables and all of the agents' information.[1]

If only the first phenomenon is present, I shall say that we are dealing with a case of *homogeneous information*; otherwise, I shall speak of *heterogeneous information*. In both cases, the behavior of an agent depends on his own "model" of the joint distribution of information and endogenous random variables; in a *rational expectations equilibrium* (REE) these models are correct. This naturally leads to the question: If the system is not in equilibrium, are there "reasonable" processes of adjustment (sometimes called "learning") on the part of the agents such that the system does converge to an REE? For the case of homogeneous information, Margaret Bray's chapter provides a simple example for which the answer to this question is yes.

In this discussion I shall try to place Bray's result in a slightly broader context, and I shall do this partly in a formal way. In the process, I shall state her result more or less precisely, but I shall also focus on three points: (1) the importance of the distinction between homogeneous and heterogeneous information in models of rational expectations equilibrium, (2) problems of existence and uniqueness, and (3) desirable properties of boundedly rational forecast functions.

The views expressed here are those of the author and do not necessarily reflect the views of Bell Laboratories or the Bell System.

[1] For a fuller account of these concepts, see Radner (1982).

II

Consider an economic system with an exogenous stationary time series, (e_t), and an endogenous time series, (p_t). Let

H_{it} be the information history available to agent i at date t

F_{it} be agent i's forecast of p_t, based on $H_{i,t-1}$

F_t be a weighted average of the agents' forecasts, F_{it}

Assume that, given the history of endogenous variables through date $(t-1)$ and the history of the exogenous variables through date t, the endogenous variable p_t is determined by the following equation:

$$p_t = h + kF_t + e_t \qquad \qquad \text{(D1)}$$

where h and k are given parameters of the system. Equation (D1) will typically correspond to the "reduced form" of some set of simultaneous equations. We shall say here that the system is in a rational expectations equilibrium if

$$F_{it} = E(p_t \mid H_{i,t-1}) \quad \text{for all } i \text{ and } t \qquad \qquad \text{(D2)}$$

(The present model is special in that the reduced form is linear, and the REE condition involves only the conditional expectations of p_t, not its entire conditional distributions.)

The special case of homogeneous information will be defined by supposing that, at each date, all agents have the same information:

$$H_{it} = H_t \quad \text{for all } i$$

It follows in this case that their forecasts at each date will also be the same, provided they all have the same model of the economic system, so that

$$F_{it} = F_t \quad \text{for all } i$$

In Bray's example, the exogenous random variables (e_t) are independent and identically distributed; we may without loss of generality take them to have mean zero. If we confine our attention to REEs in which the process of endogenous random variables (p_t) is stationary, then it follows that, for an REE,

$$p_t = p^* + e_t \quad \text{where } p^* = \frac{h}{1-k} \qquad \qquad \text{(D3)}$$

(provided k is different from 1).

What about learning? Bray explores the hypothesis that each agent uses the "reasonable" forecast function

$$F_t = \frac{p_1 + \cdots + p_{t-1}}{t-1} = \bar{p}_{t-1} \tag{D4}$$

In other words, each agent forecasts the next price to be the arithmetic mean of the previous prices. In this case the reduced form (D1) is

$$p_t = h + k\bar{p}_{t-1} + e_t \tag{D5}$$

Bray shows that, in this case, if k is less than 1, then the forecasts $\bar{p}_t$ converge to p^* almost surely. Note that in REE, the conditional expectation of p_t given H_{t-1} is exactly p^*, so that in Bray's example, *the economic system converges to an REE if the agents follow Bray's learning rule.*

III

In the analysis of REE models, the case of heterogeneous information seems to be essentially different from the case of homogeneous information. Not only is the analysis more difficult, but there seem to be more obstacles in the way of existence, uniqueness, and stability. In other words, the introduction of heterogeneity of information may profoundly affect the behavior of the system, if, as is assumed in the REE paradigm, the agents attempt to learn from prices about other agents' information.

In microeconomic models of the two-period general equilibrium sort, with heterogeneous information, the question of existence has now been thoroughly explored by Beth Allen, James Jordan, and others; see Jordan and Radner (1982) for an overview. This work shows that although the existence of REE cannot be guaranteed, even under "classical" hypotheses, existence is "generic"[2] except in the case in which the dimension of the price space is equal to the dimension of the space of all of the agents' information. On the other hand, this work also shows that the original definition of REE that many of us have been using is defective in that it admits REEs that could not be implemented by any reasonable market mechanism. (This point was first emphasized by Avram Beja.) I have no space here to describe the attempts to repair this defect, but in any case I doubt that the last word has been said on the subject.

The general infinite horizon case presents even more serious difficulties with respect to existence. (Note that Bray's example has an infinite horizon.) Once we depart from the assumption of independence of the

---

[2] Roughly speaking, a property of an economic system is "generic" if it holds when the parameters of the system are in general position.

exogenous disturbances (e_t) – although maintaining the assumption of stationarity – the work of Carl Futia shows that we can quickly get into trouble with nonuniqueness or even nonexistence of REE. Furthermore, the nonexistence of REE can occur on "large" sets in the parameter space of the model. The possibility that exogenous disturbances in the economy are higher-order autoregressive processes cannot be ruled out as absurd a priori, although it is usually ruled out in theoretical models. Hence, the conditions for the existence of REE may have economic as well as mathematical interest.

IV

Given the state of affairs in the theory of existence and uniqueness of REE, it is no wonder that we know so little about adjustment and learning. In the linear example described in Section II, with homogeneous information and independent and identically distributed (i.i.d.) exogenous variables, it would seem to me that Bray's theorem could be generalized to a multivariate model. From a technical point of view, the problem is one of solving linear stochastic difference equations with exogenous, but time-varying, coefficients. On the other hand, in the heterogeneous information case, even in one dimension, with i.i.d. exogenous variables, the analysis is apparently much more difficult. Bray has a positive convergence result for a linear example along these lines (Bray, 1982). The technical problem is again one of solving linear stochastic difference equations, but in this case with *endogenous* coefficients, and the generalization to multivariate systems seems at this point difficult, if not altogether problematical.

V

In her chapter, Bray has discussed the difficulties inherent in attempts to construct a theory of *rational* learning out of REE, and her positive result demonstrates the convergence of the system to an REE when the agents use a particular "boundedly rational" forecast function. Even Herbert Simon has not yet provided us with a precise description of bounded rationality, and I shall not try to do so here. However, there is one aspect of the Bray forecast function that worries me. I suppose that most of us would regard the underlying structure and randomness of the economy as only *approximately stationary,* at best. Therefore, a boundedly rational learning procedure should be able to adapt reasonably well to slow changes in the underlying structure. Because the Bray forecast function gives equal weight to all past periods, it might not perform as well under a slowly varying structure as would, say, some kind of "adaptive" formula that gave declining weights to observations in the more distant past. With such forecast functions, however, it seems unlikely that the economy would converge to an REE in a *strictly stationary* environment. It would be interesting to explore this apparent conflict in a precise model, and the one in Bray's chapter seems well suited to such an exploration.

VI

As a concluding thought, I shall quote Margaret Bray's own comment that "two examples do not constitute a theory." We pride ourselves on having a decentralized economy, and even so-called centralized economies are informationally decentralized to an important degree. Decentralization means heterogeneous information, and given the pervasiveness and importance of heterogeneous information in our economy, the theory of REE will have to come to grips with this phenomenon if it is to be an important part of economic analysis. But perhaps this is expecting too much. A simple linear model with homogeneous information – as in Bray's chapter – may still do good service as a parable of a situation in which most of the agents in a particular market observe a few important "public" time series and are content to use their observations to forecast the future without making serious efforts to infer other agents' information from that public information. Within that narrower domain, the "example" analyzed in this chapter by Bray promises to lead to significant generalizations.

References

Allen, Beth (1982). "Strict Rational Expectations Equilibria with Diffuseness." *Journal of Economic Theory,* 27:20–46.

Beja, Avram (1976). "The Limited Information Efficiency of Market Processes." Working paper No. 43, Research Program in Finance, University of California, Berkeley (unpublished).

Futia, Carl (1981). "Rational Expectations in Stationary Linear Models." *Econometrica,* 49:171–92.

Jordan, James S., and R. Radner (1982). "Rational Expectations in Microeconomic Models: An Overview." *Journal of Economic Theory,* 26:201–23.

Radner, R. (1982). "Equilibrium under Uncertainty." In: *Handbook of Mathematical Economics, Vol. II,* Chapter 20, edited by K. J. Arrow and M. D. Intriligator, pp. 923–1006. Amsterdam: North Holland.

CHAPTER 7

A distinction between the unconditional expectational equilibrium and the rational expectations equilibrium

ROMAN FRYDMAN

A number of investigators have recently argued that learning and convergence to rational expectations equilibrium are problematic.[1] These results suggest that despite the great popularity of minimum mean square error forecasts and the associated notion of the rational expectations equilibrium, the problems of modeling expectations and a definition of an appropriate notion of equilibrium in stochastic models are still important areas of investigation.

Typical linear stochastic macroeconomic or market models contain expectational variables, *forecasts,* which are *the averages of individual expectations.* This formulation suggests a possibility of defining a notion of stochastic equilibrium in terms of the behavior of averages of forecasts.

In this chapter we shall define a simple notion of "aggregate" equilibrium. It is called the *unconditional expectational equilibrium,* and it is defined by the requirement that in the context of a specific model, forecasts of the endogenous variable be equal to the expected value of the probability distribution of this variable.

It should be emphasized that the unconditional expectational equilibrium concept pertains to the behavior of *averages* of individual expectations. Therefore, there is no presumption that it is based on the optimality of individual behavior.

The unconditional expectational equilibrium coincides with the rational expectations equilibrium in models containing exogenous variables that are independently and identically distributed (i.i.d.). However, it is clear that in more general models these two definitions of equilibria lead

I would like to thank Clive Bull and Edmund Phelps for helpful comments and discussions. I am indebted to Roy Radner for pointing out an error in the previous version of a proof of the proposition. I retain responsibility for remaining errors and any opinions expressed in this chapter.

[1] For example, see Cyert and DeGroot (1974), Blume and Easley (1982), Bray (1982), Frydman (1982), and other chapters in this book.

to different stochastic processes characterizing the behavior of endogenous variables. The difficulties of convergence to rational expectations equilibrium raise the question of convergence to unconditional expectational equilibrium.

In Chapter 6 of this book, Bray demonstrates in a version of the Sargent and Wallace (1975) model that a simple forecast rule leads to convergence to the rational expectations equilibrium. The forecast rule is that agents forecast future price levels using the average of past prices. Because in Bray's model the only exogenous variable is a constant, the rational expectations equilibrium coincides in her model with the unconditional expectational equilibrium. However, because the agents use only the means of past values of endogenous variables, one would not expect that Bray's result would hold in a more general class of models.

Here we shall set up a model with non-i.i.d. exogenous variables and demonstrate that, under certain conditions, the forecast rule proposed by Bray leads to convergence to the unconditional expectational equilibrium, but not to the rational expectations equilibrium.[2] Next, we shall briefly discuss some implications of a distinction between the unconditional expectational equilibrium and the rational expectations equilibrium. We suggest that the unconditional expectational equilibrium provides an interpretation of an alternative hypothesis in the standard test of rational expectations. We also point out an implication of a distinction between the two notions of equilibrium for an analysis of the effectiveness of monetary policy based on a feedback rule.

7.1.   A model and equilibria

Consider the following semireduced form of a simultaneous equations model containing expectational variables:[3]

$$y_t = (Fy_t)B + x_t\Gamma + u_t \ (t=1,\ldots,T) \tag{1}$$

where y_t is a vector of m endogenous variables at time t; Fy_t is a vector of forecasts of y_t formed at $t-1$; x_t is a vector of G exogenous variables; u_t is a vector of m disturbance terms, B and Γ are $(m \times m)$ and $(G \times m)$ matrices, respectively, of coefficients.

Assume that (i)

---

[2] It is clear that in models with non-i.i.d. exogenous variables, a forecast rule more general than Bray's should be used in an analysis of convergence to the rational expectations equilibrium. However, the literature does not contain any results on convergence to the rational expectations equilibrium when the rational forecast function contains more than one parameter. See footnote 23 in Chapter 1 for further discussion of this point.

[3] See Wallis (1980) for a discussion of this formulation.

$$E(u_t)=0, \quad \text{Cov}(u_t)=\Sigma \quad (t=1,\ldots,T)$$

$$E(u_t u_t')=0 \quad (t\neq t')$$

(ii) x_t is generated by the following vector ARMA process:

$$x_t=\Phi(L)x_t+\Theta(L)\epsilon_t+\epsilon_t \tag{2}$$

where ϵ_t is a white-noise process independent of u_t, and $\Phi(L)$ and $\Theta(L)$ are polynomials in the lag operator L of degree p and q, respectively, namely,

$$\Phi(L)=-\Phi_1 L-\cdots-\Phi_p L^p \quad \Theta(L)=\Theta_1 L+\cdots+\Theta_q L^q \tag{3}$$

We now turn to a discussion of equilibria in this model.

7.1.1. Definition of the rational expectations equilibrium

The functions $y_t(x_t,u_t)$ are called the rational expectations equilibrium functions, y_t^*, if

$$Fy_t^*=E[y_t^*\mid\Omega_{t-1}] \tag{4}$$

and

$$y_t^*=E[y_t^*\mid\Omega_{t-1}]B+x_t\Gamma+u_t \tag{5}$$

for all realizations of u_t and x_t (except on a set with probability zero). $\Omega_{t-1}=(x_{t-1},x_{t-2},\ldots,\epsilon_{t-1},\epsilon_{t-1},\ldots)$ denotes the information set available at time $t-1$.

In the model (1)–(3), the solution for y_t^* can be written as

$$y_t^*=x_t\Gamma(I-B)^{-1}+u_t-\epsilon_t\Gamma(I-B)^{-1}B \tag{6}$$

Next we define the concept of the unconditional expectational equilibrium.

7.1.2. Definition of the unconditional expectational equilibrium

The functions $y_t(x_t,u_t)$ are called the unconditional expectational equilibrium functions, $\bar{y}_t$, if

$$F\bar{y}_t=E(\bar{y}_t) \tag{7}$$

and

$$\bar{y}_t=E(\bar{y}_t)B+x_t\Gamma+u_t \tag{8}$$

for all realizations of x_t and u_t (except on a set with probability zero).

Note that in the unconditional expectational equilibrium, agents forecast future values of y_t on the basis of the expected values of those variables. In contrast, the rational forecasts defined in (4) and (5) are expectations of future values of endogenous variables conditional on the information available to agents. An empirical implication of this distinction between the two equilibrium concepts is discussed in Section 7.4.

In the model (1)–(3), a solution for $\bar{y}_t$ can be written as

$$\bar{y}_t = E(x)\Gamma(I-B)^{-1}B + x_t\Gamma + u_t \tag{9}$$

Comparing (6) and (9), we conclude that $y_t^* = \bar{y}_t$ if and only if the only exogenous variables in the model are i.i.d.

7.2.   Convergence to the unconditional expectational equilibrium

Consider the following forecast rule for Fy_t:

$$Fy_t = \frac{1}{t}\sum_{i=0}^{t-1} y_i \tag{10}$$

We can now present the proposition.

Proposition
Let Fy_t be given by (10). If eigenvalues $\lambda_1, \ldots, \lambda_m$ of B are such that $|\lambda_i| < 1$ for all i, then Fy_t converges almost surely to $E(\bar{y}_t) = E(x)\Gamma(I-B)^{-1}$.

Proof
See the Appendix.

7.3.   The unconditional expectational equilibrium and the short-run effectiveness of monetary policy based on the feedback rule

We noted earlier that in the unconditional expectational equilibrium, forecasts are based on the unconditional (rather than conditional) expectations of endogenous variables. It can easily be shown that under the assumption of the unconditional expectational equilibrium the parameters of the monetary policy feedback rule will influence the time path of aggregate output. In order to illustrate this point, consider the following simple macroeconomic model:

$$q_t = \alpha(p_t - Fp_t) + u_t \tag{11}$$

$$q_t + p_t = m_t + v_t \tag{12}$$

where q_t is the log of aggregate output; p_t is the log of the price level; m_t

is the log of the money supply; v_t is a velocity shock, $E(v_t) = 0$, $\text{Var}(v_t) = \sigma_v^2$; u_t is a supply shock, $E(u_t) = 0$, $\text{Var}(u_t) = \sigma_u^2$, $E[u_t v_t] = 0$; Fp_t is the forecast of p_t formed at time $t-1$.

As is well known, the model in (11) and (12) implies the ineffectiveness of monetary policy (based on the feedback rule) under rational expectations. In such a case, the expression for q_t is given by

$$q_t = \frac{1}{1+\alpha} u_t + \frac{\alpha}{1+\alpha} v_t \tag{13}$$

Under the assumption of the unconditional expectational equilibrium,

$$Fp_t = E(p_t) \tag{14}$$

Using (11) and (12), we get

$$Fp_t = E(m_t) \tag{15}$$

Finally, using (15) in (11) and (12) yields

$$q_t = \frac{\alpha}{1+\alpha} [m_t - E(m_t)] + \frac{1}{1+\alpha} u_t + \frac{\alpha}{1+\alpha} v_t \tag{16}$$

If the money supply is given by the feedback rule, say $m_t = \Omega_{t-1} \Phi$, where Φ is a vector of parameters, it is clear from (16) that parameters in Φ influence the behavior of output.

7.4. An empirical implication of a distinction between the unconditional expectational equilibrium and the rational expectations equilibrium

The ARMA representation for x_t in (2) and the assumption of rational expectations imply a set of restrictions given in (6) on the variance-covariance structure of the process generating endogenous variables of the model.[4] This set of restrictions constitutes the null hypothesis in the standard test of rational expectations. The unrestricted representations of y_t constitute a class of alternative hypotheses. We observe from (9) that the ARMA representation for x_t and the assumption of the unconditional expectational equilibrium imply an unrestricted variance-covariance representation for y_t. Therefore, the assumption of the unconditional expectational equilibrium is consistent with the class of alternative hypotheses in the standard test of the rational expectations hypothesis.

---

[4] See Wallis (1980) for a detailed analysis.

Appendix

In the proof of the proposition, we shall need the following lemma:

Lemma
Let B be a square matrix. There exist matrices A and Q such that

$$B = QAQ^{-1}$$

where

$$A = \begin{bmatrix} \lambda_1 & a_{12} & \cdots & a_{1m} \\ & \ddots & \ddots & \\ & & & \lambda_m \end{bmatrix}$$

$\sum_{i \neq j = 1}^{m} |a_{ij}| \leqslant \epsilon$, where ϵ is any preassigned constant; $\lambda_1, \ldots, \lambda_m$ are eigenvalues of B.

Proof
See Bellman (1960, p. 205).

Proof of the proposition
Define

$$w_t = y_t - E(x)\Gamma(I - B)^{-1} \tag{A1}$$

From (1) we get

$$\bar{w}_t = \frac{1}{t} \sum_{i=0}^{t-1} \bar{w}_i B + \frac{1}{t} \sum_{i=1}^{t} [x_i - E(x)]\Gamma + \frac{1}{t} \sum_{i=1}^{t} u_i \tag{A2}$$

where $\bar{w}_{t-1} = (1/t) \sum_{i=0}^{t-1} w_i$.

   (i) Show that $\bar{w}_t$ is bounded almost surely (a.s.) for all t. Using the lemma, we obtain

$$z_t = \frac{1}{t} \sum_{i=0}^{t-1} z_i A + \frac{1}{t} \sum_{i=1}^{t} v_t \tag{A3}$$

where

$$z_t = \bar{w}_t Q \tag{A4}$$

and

$$v_t = [x_t - E(x)]\Gamma Q + u_t Q \tag{A5}$$

Consider the first component of z_t, $z_t^{(1)}$. From the structure of A in the lemma, and denoting by $v_t^{(1)}$ the first component of v_t, we obtain

$$z_t^{(1)} = \frac{1}{t} \sum_{i=0}^{t-1} z_i^{(1)} \lambda_1 + \frac{1}{t} \sum_{i=1}^{t} v_i^{(1)} \tag{A6}$$

Next we define

$$z_t^{(1)'} = z_t^{(1)} - \frac{1}{t} \sum_{i=1}^{t} \frac{v_i^{(1)}}{1-\lambda_1} \tag{A7}$$

Plugging (A7) into (A6) results in the following expression for $z_t^{(1)'}$:

$$z_t^{(1)'} = \frac{1}{t} \sum_{i=0}^{t-1} z_i^{(1)'} \lambda_1 \tag{A8}$$

Expression (A8) implies the following inequality:

$$|z_t^{(1)'}| \leqslant \left(\frac{t+\lambda_1}{t+1} \right)^t |z_1^{(1)'}| \tag{A9}$$

(A9) and $|\lambda_1| < 1$ implies that $z_t^{(1)'}$ is bounded a.s.

In order to demonstrate a.s. boundedness of $z_t^{(1)}$, we note that x_t is a strictly stationary process and $E|v_1^{(1)}| < \infty$. Therefore, from the Birkhoff-Khinchine law of large numbers for stationary processes (Gikhman and Skorokhod, 1969, p. 129), we conclude that

$$\frac{1}{t} \sum_{i=1}^{t} [x_i - E(x)] \Gamma Q_{\cdot 1} \to 0 \text{ a.s.} \tag{A10}$$

From the law of large numbers for independently distributed random variables,

$$\frac{1}{t} \sum u_i Q_{\cdot 1} \to 0 \text{ a.s.} \tag{A11}$$

Thus, from (A5), (A7), (A10), (A11), and a.s. boundedness of $z_t^{(1)'}$, we conclude that $z_t^{(1)}$ is bounded a.s.

A similar argument can be used to demonstrate that all other components of z_t are bounded a.s.

Finally, we conclude from (A4) that $\bar{w}_t$ is bounded a.s.

(ii) show that $\bar{w}_t$ converges a.s. Transformation of (A2) yields

$$\bar{w}_{t+1} - \bar{w}_t = \frac{B-1}{t+1} \bar{w}_t + \frac{1}{t+1} \eta_t \tag{A12}$$

where

$$\eta_t = [x_t - E(x)] \Gamma + u_t \tag{A13}$$

Because $\bar{w}_t$ and η_t are bounded a.s., (A13) implies that $\bar{w}_t$ converges a.s., say to $\bar{w}$.

(iii) Show that $\bar{w} = 0$. Expression (A2), the Birkhoff-Khinchine law of large numbers, and the standard law of large numbers imply that

$$\bar{w} = \bar{w}B \tag{A14}$$

Because $I - B$ is nonsingular, (A14) implies that $\bar{w} = 0$. Thus,

$$Fy_t = \frac{1}{t} \sum_{i=0}^{t-1} y_i \to E(x)\Gamma(I - B)^{-1} \quad \text{a.s.} \quad \text{Q.E.D.}$$

References

Bellman, R. (1960). *Introduction to Matrix Analysis*. New York: McGraw-Hill.

Blume, L. E., and D. Easley (1982). "Learning to Be Rational." *Journal of Economic Theory,* 26:340-51.

Bray, M. (1982). "Learning, Estimation and the Stability of Rational Expectations." *Journal of Economic Theory,* 26:318-39.

Cyert, R. M., and M. H. DeGroot (1974). "Rational Expectations and Bayesian Analysis." *Journal of Political Economy,* 82:521-36.

Frydman, R. (1982). "Towards an Understanding of Market Processes: Individual Expectations, Learning and Convergence to the Rational Expectations Equilibrium." *American Economic Review,* 72:652-68.

Gikhman, I. I., and A. V. Skorokhod (1969). *Introduction to the Theory of Random Processes*. Philadelphia: Saunders.

Sargent, T. J., and N. Wallace (1975). "'Rational Expectations,' the Optimal Memory Instrument, and the Optimal Money Supply Rule." *Journal of Political Economy,* 83:241-54.

Wallis, K. F. (1980). "Econometric Implications of the Rational Expectations Hypothesis." *Econometrica,* 48:49-74.

CHAPTER 8

On mistaken beliefs and resultant equilibria

ALAN KIRMAN

Recently, with the growing interest in the notion of rational expectations and with the emphasis on the influence of expectations on inflation, the literature on these subjects has raised, not always explicitly, a fundamental problem for economic theory. This question may be phrased as follows. If agents in an economic model start out with personal, possibly mistaken, beliefs and then learn, to what extent will their learning lead them to a knowledge of the true situation, and will they be led to an equilibrium corresponding to a situation in which they have complete information? This question is not as trivial as it might appear precisely because of the nature of economic situations. Agents learn by observing and modifying their behavior in consequence, but in most economic situations what they observe is conditioned by their own behavior. This feedback and its consequences were explicitly discussed in a recent study by Bray (1981). In that study, despite mistaken beliefs, the agents are led to a rational expectations equilibrium, that is, one in which their subjective beliefs coincide with the objective situation. However, at each point in time before reaching the equilibrium there is a discrepancy between the two. In other cases it is easy to see that the feedback mechanism may prevent convergence occurring at all. Another alternative, one that is the main subject of this chapter, is that the model may be led to an outcome that is unrelated to any "real" equilibrium. Thus, instead of learning progressively about the "true" situation, the beliefs of the agents may drive the model to some other outcome. In particular, given the agents' *beliefs,* this outcome may be completely rational, in the sense that what they observe confirms their beliefs. Thus, in a certain sense, rather than the agents learning about the model, the model learns from the agents, and the outcome is conditioned by their view of the world, mistaken or otherwise. Thus, we have a situation corresponding to the idea of "self-

I wish to thank for their help and suggestions Françoise Fogelman, David Hendry, Claude Oddou, Martine Quinzii, Alfredo Pastor, and the participants in the University of Essex seminar. This research was financed by a contract with the Commisariat Génèral du Plan, Paris.

fulfilling expectations" even though individuals are misinformed. It may well be argued that because agents are frequently less than perfectly informed, such situations may be commonplace.

To see how such situations can arise in economic models, we must look at the way in which imperfect information is incorporated in those models and the impact of learning in such situations.

Because there is no place for such a notion in the standard general equilibrium model, the usual approach is to introduce uncertainty into the model, in particular by introducing a stochastic element in the determination of the outcome. Better information then consists of being able to narrow down the possible outcome to some subset of possibilities. Thus, if an agent knows the probability distribution over all outcomes, he will be able with good information to restrict his attention to the probability of the outcomes in some subset, that is, to condition the probabilities on that set. Suppose that the individual does not know the "true" probability distribution, will he be led, for example, by learning, to know it? There are, of course, well-known cases in which a Bayesian approach would lead one to a true knowledge of the situation. However, even in the simple case where there is a "true" stochastic process and an individual tries to learn about it, it is not at all clear that he will, in general, be led to the truth. Rothschild (1973) gave an example in which although, in the long run, an individual will be led to the true distribution, he may, for perfectly rational reasons, stop learning and be left acting with a false impression of his environment.

In this sort of model there is a "true" process, and agents try to learn about it. The problem reduces to one in statistics. We can start with any of three cases, and the problem would seem to fall into a well-defined part of the statistical literature. The first case is one where individuals know the true model, and the only uncertainty for them is that engendered by the underlying stochastic process. The second is a situation in which the individuals know the nature of the process but do not know the parameters and, over time, try to learn about the values of those parameters. The third case is one in which the individuals do not know, a priori, even the true nature of the model facing them and start out with a misspecified model. In this case the natural question is, Will observation over time lead them to reject the specification that they originally chose?

It is this third case that interests us here. Before going any further, the very definition of equilibrium is put in question. If, without uncertainty (e.g., in a model of imperfect competition) individuals misspecify the model with which they are faced and then act accordingly, then what constitutes an equilibrium? It is clear that a situation in which each individual, given the model he has in mind, maximizes and in which no individual has an incentive to move constitutes an equilibrium. If the beliefs of the individuals are sufficiently far from reality, such an equilibrium is likely to be very different from an equilibrium of the true model.

Now, if we allow agents to modify their behavior in function of what they observe, we are faced with the questions posed earlier. Will this lead the model to converge to some solution, will it be related to an equilibrium of the true model, or will the model fluctuate, and will the agents be led to reject the models that they have postulated?

The idea that an equilibrium can, or indeed should, be defined in terms of the subjective views of the agents, as opposed to the objective reality, is, of course, not new. In a study by Negishi (1961), agents maximize with respect to models that do not, in general, correspond, except at one point, with the reality. If they were to be aware of the reality, they would wish to change their behavior. The literature on conjectural demand by Clower, Hahn, and others has, again, at its heart, such a situation. In these models, however, a static equilibrium is described, and there is no modification of behavior in the light of experience. What is said is that if agents were in this position, they would have no incentive to move.

This approach has been taken further, and a number of studies have examined models in which agents learn from observations about misspecified models. Among these, the studies of Cyert and DeGroot (1971, 1973, 1974) and of Arrow and Green (1973) are of particular interest. In the various models discussed, there may be no convergence at all, convergence to an equilibrium that is unrelated to the "true" equilibrium, or, in special cases, convergence to the true equilibrium itself.

Now, as we have observed, there is a strong interrelation in the economic models between the observer and the observed, and it is this that contributes to the difficulty these agents will have in rejecting their "perceived" but wrong models.

The fundamental problem is this: The agents have in mind a certain model; they modify this model in the light of what they observe. But, in general, what they observe is the consequence of their own and the other observers' behavior. If their own behavior is continuous with respect to what they observe and they believe that the underlying process is continuous, then, in general, it will not be possible for them to reject their models, and moreover they may well converge to a situation in which they believe themselves to be optimizing, that is, to an equilibrium that is rational in the sense described earlier.

In the rational expectations literature the equilibrium is one in which what people believe is coherent with what they observe, but the question is still largely open as to how one might arrive at such a situation. In the study by Bray (1981), agents proceed by a learning process and arrive at a rational expectations equilibrium. At each point in their learning process the agents may have a mistaken model, but they nevertheless arrive at a "true" equilibrium. The only problem here is that to prove this convergence Bray allows the agents to have, for the estimation procedure, information about the true underlying process. It may well be that if their knowledge were wholly subjective, the process would still converge to the true equilibrium, but this is not proved. Similar results were obtained by Lewis (1981), who also raised the sort of question we pose here.

In another framework, Azariadis and Guesnerie (1981) showed in a simple overlapping generations model that there exist equilibria in which agents may have wrong and conflicting models (sunspots and moonspots) and yet in which these models are confirmed by observations.

In an earlier study (Kirman, 1975) it was shown that in a simple duopoly model, misspecification would lead to outcomes unrelated to "true" equilibria but dependent on initial conditions. The general case had to be treated by numerical means. A number of studies by Gates and associates (1977, 1978, 1981) have shown, in a general version of this model, convergence in special cases. Furthermore, they characterize the limits of the convergence and define an extended notion of solution that incorporates, as well as the classic solutions, all the limit points of their process.

What may happen in the models described is closely related to an important problem in the statistical literature, which is the extent to which an individual may be led to reject a misspecified model as he accumulates observations. With the increased interest in the way in which economic agents learn about their environment, such questions as we have suggested assume more importance. In the rest of this chapter we shall discuss a problem that has arisen in economic theory in the area of monopolistic competition and shall show that a simple learning process does not lead the agents in the model to rectify their misspecification and that the model may well be led, despite attempts to learn by the agents, to solutions that satisfy the agents but have nothing to do with the equilibria of the correctly specified model. Furthermore, we shall show that there is a large class of possible equilibria. It is well established that in order for agents who have specified a particular model to establish predictive failure, some perturbation in the underlying data-generating process is necessary. Now, in our simple example the data are generated by the agents themselves. Now, provided that there is no perturbation (i.e., change in the behavior of one of the agents), no other agent will be led to modify what he is doing. Hence, the agents are trapped in a situation that might be thought of as a misinformed equilibrium in which no agent has any reason to change his behavior. The point is not to show that persistent misspecification will lead to perverse situations (this is almost self-evident) but rather that such misspecification may, by rigorous criteria, be perfectly justified.

In the last part of this chapter we shall indicate that this result depends neither on the simplicities of the model nor on the naivety of the learning process.

The model that we have chosen arises naturally from a discussion in a recent study, where Roberts and Sonnenschein (1977) showed up a fundamental weakness in the traditional theory of monopolistic competition. They pointed out that proofs of the existence of general equilibrium in models that incorporate imperfectly competitive firms use, in an essential way, the continuity of the reaction function of such firms. This continuity is (in the existing literature) either assumed more or less directly or derived from assumptions, as in Negishi (1961), about the demand conditions that are not derived from the basic data of the model. In Negishi's model, firms perceive inverse demand functions that are linear, and even though it may not be the case that their demand is, in fact, linear, nevertheless at equilibrium there exist linear demand functions for each firm such that the quantity they produce is optimal, and hence none of them have any incentive to move. In other words, each firm perceives a linear demand function and produces accordingly, and the "true" model generates data that confirm the perception. If the firms were aware of the true model, they might well have an incentive to modify their behavior, but given what they believe to be the demand facing them, their behavior is optimal.

The problem raised by Roberts and Sonnenschein is that, were all the relevant data known to the two firms in a simple duopoly model, even with the most standard assumptions on technology and preferences, the reaction curves of the firms would no longer be continuous, and hence equilibrium need not exist. Thus, once one removes the sort of misapprehension assumed in Negishi's model, there may well be no equilibrium.

Roberts and Sonnenschein suggested several answers to this dilemma: first, to find restrictions that make firms' reaction functions continuous, or rather make the reaction curves convex-valued, although such conditions are likely to be extremely restrictive; second, to continue to assume directly convex-valuedness and to admit that cases where this does not hold are out of reach, or, third, and most important from our point of view, to drop the assumption of full information about demand conditions. In particular, one might start with the assumption that firms have "perceived demand curves" that might, for example, be linear. Now, as Roberts and Sonnenschein observed: "Of course, these perceived curves are completely ad hoc, although one might attempt to construct a theory to explain them. Within such a theory, however, one would presumably want to allow for learning leading to the perceived curves more and more closely approximating the true relationships. In this case, one is confronted again with the original problem of nonexistence.''

The purpose of this part of this chapter is to show that even in the most simplified model, misspecification of functions will not necessarily be corrected as learning takes place. Worse, a perfectly reasonable learning process may lead to a result that bears no relation to any standard non-cooperative or cooperative equilibrium. Thus, the participants, in our case the noncompetitive firms, will get apparently better and better approximations of demand curves that are not in fact the "true" ones and will finish in a situation from which they believe it would not be profitable to move.

In particular, we shall show that in a simple price-setting duopoly model, any of a whole class of pairs of prices can result as the limit of a simple econometric learning process. In other words, if we choose any limit prices from this class, we can find initial prices from which the learning process will lead us to those chosen.

The model developed here is basically that studied by Kirman (1975), in the same spirit as those of Arrow and Green (1973), and which has recently been studied by Gates and associates (1977, 1978, 1981).

8.1.   The model

We consider a symmetric duopoly in which the demand functions for firms 1 and 2 are given by the "true model"[1]:

$$d_1[p_1(t), p_2(t)] = \alpha - \beta p_1(t) + \gamma p_2(t) \tag{1}$$

$$d_2[p_1(t), p_2(t)] = \alpha - \beta p_2(t) + \gamma p_1(t) \tag{2}$$

We also assume, in the tradition of Cournot, that production is costless, and hence the goal for each of the two firms if they knew the true model would be to maximize revenue given the price of the opponent.

Now suppose that the two firms, through ignorance or inertia, are unaware that their demand depends on each other's actions. In a duopoly situation, such an assumption is difficult to accept, but it is more plausible in a several firm situation in which each firm feels unable to take explicit account of the behavior of all the opponents and hence focuses on the "own-price" demand curve and adds a random term to take

---

[1] The motivation for introducing a time subscript will become evident later in the chapter.

account of the, to him, unpredictable behavior of the other firms. It changes nothing in our results to consider an n-firm model, as do Gates and associates (1977, 1978), and the notion that some firms should in such a situation omit the prices of some of their rivals is perfectly plausible.[2]

Thus, in our case, the two firms will have the following "perceived model":

$$d_1[p_1(t)] = a_1 - b_1 p_1(t) + \epsilon_1(t) \tag{3}$$

$$d_2[p_2(t)] = a_2 - b_2 p_2(t) + \epsilon_2(t) \tag{4}$$

where the firms assume, in the best economic tradition, that the error terms are normally distributed with mean zero; that is,

$$\epsilon_i(t) \sim N(0, \sigma_i^2)$$

The problem now is, if the firms have no information about their respective parameters a_i and b_i, how should or would they set about trying to establish their true values? Kirman (1975) showed that if both firms knew, or rather believed with certainty, that $b_i = \beta$, then a reasonable Bayesian learning process would lead them, despite their misspecification of the model, to the Cournot equilibrium of the "true" game.

More interesting is the case in which the firms have no information about the values of the parameters and try to learn from experience about them. How will the model then evolve? At each period, given the quantities observed at each price, the firms will make their estimates of the two parameters of their perceived demand curves, and we shall call these estimates $\hat{a}_i(t)$ and $\hat{b}_i(t)$. If we assume that each firm simply wishes to maximize expected profit in the next period, then, given the assumption that $E[\epsilon_i(t)] = 0$, the optimal price is clearly given by

$$p_i(t) = \frac{\hat{a}_i(t)}{2\hat{b}_i(t)} \tag{5}$$

So, at each period, given its estimates, each firm will charge a price, and the demand realized as a result of these prices will, of course, be given by the true model specified by equations (1) and (2). This new observation of a price–quantity pair will lead to a revision of the estimates of the parameters and, in turn, to new prices and so forth.

As mentioned, it was shown by Kirman (1975) that a reasonable learning process would make the sequence of prices converge to

---

[2] Later in the chapter we suggest adding an error term to the two equations. This makes the result here more cumbersome but more plausible. The reader who does not like the behavior of the residuals in what directly follows may have to bear this in mind.

$$p_1^* = p_2^* = \frac{\alpha}{2\beta - \gamma}$$

the Cournot solution, provided that $\hat{b}_i(t) = \beta$ for all t.

A sensible learning process for the case where there is ignorance of both the parameters would be for each firm to try to fit the observed data by means of least squares. Faced with the model they believe they observe, this behavior on the part of firms can be justified from a Bayesian point of view; see, for example, Zellner (1971). A consideration of general forms of updating and learning that include this type of process can be found in Aoki (1976). The model we consider is a special case of that developed by Gates, Rickard, and Wilson (1977),[3] in which they allow for n firms and variable weights for preceding observations. As we shall see, they were obliged to confine their attention to particular cases to obtain analytic results.

In our particular model, we can specify the ordinary least square estimates for a_i and b_i as follows:

$$\hat{b}_i(t) = - \frac{\sum_{k=1}^{t-1} [d_i(k) - \bar{d}_i(t)][p_i(k) - \bar{p}_i(t)]}{\sum_{k=1}^{t-1} [p_i(k) - \bar{p}_i(t)]^2} \tag{6}$$

and

$$\hat{a}_i(t) = \bar{d}_i(t) + \hat{b}_i(t)\bar{p}_i(t) \quad (i = 1, 2) \tag{7}$$

where

$$\bar{d}_i(t) = \frac{\sum_{k=1}^{t-1} d_i(k)}{t-1} \quad \text{and} \quad \bar{p}_i(t) = \frac{\sum_{k=1}^{t-1} p_i(k)}{t-1}$$

It may add something to the intuitive interpretation of the estimates to observe that (6) can be rewritten for firm 1, for example, as

$$\hat{b}_1(t) = \beta - \gamma \frac{\sum_{k=1}^{t-1} [p_1(k) - \bar{p}_1(t)][p_2(k) - \bar{p}_2(t)]}{\sum_{k=1}^{t-1} [p_1(k) - \bar{p}_1(t)]^2} \tag{8}$$

and symmetrically for firm 2.

The significance of this expression is that it makes it quite clear precisely where the "misbehavior" in the system comes from. The second term in (8) is nothing other than the covariance of the prices or the bias due to the omission of a variable and, as a result, is familiar to econometricians. It is precisely the fact that the prices are indeed closely related that generates problems in the evolution of the system.

That the whole system is recurrent is evident, because at each period each firm sets

---

[3] Referred to for convenience as G.R.W.

$$p_i(t) = \frac{\hat{a}_i(t)}{2\hat{b}_i(t)} \tag{9}$$

Hence, from the equation for the true demand (1), we have for firm 1, for example,

$$p_1(t) = \frac{\begin{aligned}&[\alpha + \gamma \bar{p}_2(t)] \sum_{k=1}^{t-1} [p_1(k) - \bar{p}_1(t)]^2 \\ &\quad - \gamma \bar{p}_1(t) \sum_{k=1}^{t-1} [p_1(k) - \bar{p}_1(t)][p_2(k) - \bar{p}_2(t)]\end{aligned}}{\begin{aligned}&2\beta \sum_{k=1}^{t-1} [p_1(k) - \bar{p}_1(t)]^2 \\ &\quad - \gamma \sum_{k=1}^{t-1} [p_1(k) - \bar{p}_1(t)][p_2(k) - \bar{p}_2(t)]\end{aligned}}$$

and symmetrically for firm 2.[4]

This recurrence relation is a special case of that given by G.R.W. (1977). It is apparent that even in this form it is not a trivial matter to establish convergence or to establish the nature of the set of limit points of such a process.

By simulation, it becomes clear that the process does indeed converge given an arbitrary set of starting conditions; that is, $p_1(1)$, $p_1(2)$, $p_2(1)$, and $p_2(2)$; see Kirman (1975) and G.R.W. (1977). However, the problem of establishing convergence analytically remains unresolved.

Evidently, there are special cases that can be disposed of quickly. For example, consider the special case where

$$p_1(1) = p_2(1) \quad \text{and} \quad p_1(2) = p_2(2)$$

In this case, examination of the recurrence relation shows that the process converges to limit prices

$$p_1^* = p_2^* = \frac{\alpha}{2(\beta - \gamma)} \tag{10}$$

that is, to the solution where the two firms collude and act as a joint monopoly. Thus, behaving the same at the outset, even unwittingly, will lead to maximization of joint profit from the third period on.

Note that in this case the final outcome is not dependent on the particular prices chosen, merely on the fact that the prices chosen by the two firms are the same initially. In general, it is not true that limit prices are independent of initial prices. Simulation shows clearly that although there is convergence, in general the limit is determined by the initial conditions. This is true even when one varies the weights attached to various observations or shortens the "memory" of the firms; this is discussed in detail by G.R.W. (1977).

---

[4] Thus, the underlying data-generating process is a nonlinear dynamic model. The evolution of the estimators and in consequence the prices can also be seen by considering updating formulas.

What analytic results do we then have on the general behavior of the process? Apart from the special case of identical starting points for the two firms, we have as a trivial consequence the results mentioned earlier (Kirman, 1975), Proposition 1.

Proposition 1

If $\hat{b}_1(3) = \hat{b}_2(3) = \beta$, then $\lim_{t \to \infty} p_1(t) = \lim_{t \to \infty} p_2(t) = \alpha/(2\beta - \gamma)$ (i.e., the Cournot solution).

Furthermore, we know Proposition 2.

Proposition 2

From G.R.W. (1977, 1978), if the econometric estimates $\hat{a}_i(\tau)$ and $\hat{b}_i(\tau)$ are obtained from observation 1 and observation t only, then the processes $p_1(t)$ and $p_2(t)$ converge for a set of initial prices of nonzero measure.

This result is obtained by applying G.R.W.'s (1977) Theorem 3 to our special model; a proof of this theorem is to be found in G.R.W. (1978). The obvious criticism of this result is that the retention of the first observation is clearly unrealistic, and it is evident that in such a case the limit demand curve must depend on initial conditions, because the estimated demand curve pivots about the initial point and must inevitably pass through that point. Thus, although the fact such a process converges is interesting, and perhaps rather remarkable, the fact that the limit will depend on the initial conditions is all too clear.

We can add to these results by showing that, whereas the learning process may indeed be very stable in the sense that it converges, the outcome of the process is indeterminate. Thus, the learning process does not lead to knowledge of the "true model" as one might have hoped. We note first that associated with any pair of positive prices p_1^* and p_2^* are estimates of a_1, b_1, a_2, and b_2, that is, perceived demand curves that will sustain p_1^* and p_2^* as an equilibrium.

Proposition 3

For any positive p_1^* and p_2^* there exist numbers a_1^*, b_1^*, a_2^*, and b_2^* such that if for some $\bar{t}$

$$\hat{a}_1(\bar{t}) = a_1^*, \quad \hat{b}_1(\bar{t}) = b_1^*, \quad \hat{a}_2(\bar{t}) = a_2^*$$

and

$$\hat{b}_2(\bar{t}) = b_2^*$$

then

$$p_1(t) = p_1^* \quad \text{and} \quad p_2(t) = p_2^* \quad \text{for all} \quad t > \bar{t}$$

Proof
Let

$$b_1^* = -\beta + \frac{\alpha + \gamma p_2^*}{p_1^*}$$

$$b_2^* = -\beta + \frac{\alpha + \gamma p_1^*}{p_2^*}$$

and

$$a_1^* = 2(\alpha - \beta p_1^* + \gamma p_2^*)$$

$$a_2^* = 2(\alpha - \beta p_2^* + \gamma p_1^*)$$

It is clear then that

$$p_1^* = \frac{a_1^*}{2b_1^*} \quad \text{and} \quad p_2^* = \frac{a_2^*}{2b_2^*}$$

and that if

$$\hat{a}_1(\bar{t}) = a_1^*, \quad \hat{a}_2(\bar{t}) = a_2^*, \quad \hat{b}_1(\bar{t}) = b_1^*, \quad \hat{b}_2(\bar{t}) = b_2^*$$

then

$$\hat{a}_1(\bar{t}+1) = a_1^*, \quad \hat{a}_2(\bar{t}+1) = a_2^*, \quad \hat{b}_1(\bar{t}+1) = b_1^*, \quad \text{and} \quad \hat{b}_2(\bar{t}+1) = b_2$$

and similarly for all $t \geqslant \bar{t}$.

Having established that any pair of prices can be sustained as an equilibrium, we shall now show that there is a significant set of prices such that any pair of prices in this set is a limit point for our particular econometric learning process. In other words, given p_1^* and p_2^* in this set, we can find initial prices such that starting from these prices the process will lead us to p_1^* and p_2^*. We note first that for our learning process to start, there must be at least two initial observations; in fact, of course, the number of initial observations is arbitrary, and we shall need three for our purpose. Our proof is based on showing that immediately after the initial observations the process has reached its limit point and remains there, in our case, from the fourth period onward. Such a proof is not possible if we allow only two initial observations. This does not rule out the possibility that there may well be initial pairs of prices for each firm from which the process could start and eventually converge to the limit prices in question, but it would not do so at the third step.

In fact, our result is stronger than this, because the region of final prices is the same for any evolution of the process that terminates after a finite number of steps. It should be possible therefore to use a limiting argument to show that, in fact, all terminating prices lie in this region.

Our result may be interpreted as follows. Associated with any pair of prices p_1^* and p_2^* is a pair of demand curves as given in Proposition 3, defined by the parameters a_1^*, b_1^*, a_2^*, and b_2^*. If the slopes b_1^* and b_2^* of the two firms' demand curves do not differ "too much" from the true slope β, then there will be initial prices from which the firms will be led to p_1^* and p_1^* as an equilibrium. The greater the interdependence of the two firms, as represented by γ, the larger the mistake permissible in the estimate b_1^*. For example, if $\gamma=0$, then no mistake is permissible, and the only limit prices possible are those for which $b_1^*=b_2^*=\beta$.

Proposition 4

For any p_1^* and p_2^*, let a_1^*, a_2^*, b_1^*, b_2^* be as defined in Proposition 3. If for any given p_1^* and p_2^* the following condition holds

$$\gamma^2 \geqslant (\beta-b_1^*)(\beta-b_2^*)>0$$

then there exist vectors of initial prices

$$p_1=[p_1(1),p_1(2),p_1(3)]$$

and

$$p_2=[p_2(1),p_2(2),p_2(3)]$$

such that

$$\hat{a}_1(4)=a_1^*, \quad \hat{b}_1(4)=b_1^*$$
$$\hat{a}_2(4)=a_2^*, \quad \hat{b}_2(4)=b_2^*$$

and hence

$$p_1(4)=p_1^* \quad \text{and} \quad p_2(4)=p_2^*$$

Thus,

$$p_1(t)=p_1^* \quad \text{and} \quad p_2(t)=p_2^* \quad \text{for all } t \geqslant 4$$

Proof

Given p_1^* and p_2^*, we must find vectors p_1 and $p_2 \in R^3$ such that the following hold:[5]

$$\hat{a}_1(4)=a_1^*, \quad \hat{b}_1(4)=b_1^*$$
$$\hat{a}_2(4)=a_2^*, \quad \hat{b}_2(4)=b_2^* \tag{11}$$

Now, we know from (7) that

[5] $\hat{a}_i(t)$ and $\hat{b}_i(t)$ are as defined in equations (6) and (7).

$$\hat{a}_1(4) = \bar{d}_1 + \hat{b}_1(4)\bar{p}_1 \quad \text{and} \quad \hat{a}_2(4) = \bar{d}_2 + \hat{b}_2(4)\bar{p}_2 \tag{12}$$

where

$$\bar{d}_1 = \frac{\sum_{t=1}^{3} d_1[p_1(t), p_2(t)]}{3}$$

$$\bar{p}_1 = \frac{\sum_{t=1}^{3} p_1(t)}{3}$$

and similarly for $\bar{d}_2$ and $\bar{p}_2$. Substituting from (11) and (12) and using the definitions of a_1^*, a_2^*, b_1^*, and b_2^* gives us

$$\bar{p}_1 = p_1^* \quad \text{and} \quad \bar{p}_2 = p_2^* \tag{13}$$

Hence, we require two vectors p_1 and p_2 with means p_1^* and p_2^*, respectively. Now define

$$X = (p_1 - p_1^*)$$

where $(p_1 - p_1^*)$ is the vector $[p_1(1) - p_1^*, \; p_1(2) - p_1^*, \; p_1(3) - p_1^*]$. Similarly, define

$$Y = (p_2 - p_2^*)$$

Now, given that, we must have

$$\hat{b}_1(4) = b_1^* \quad \text{and} \quad \hat{b}_2(4) = b_2^*$$

then, from (8), we have

$$b_1^* = \beta - \gamma \frac{X \cdot Y}{\|X\|^2}$$

and

$$b_2^* = \beta - \gamma \frac{X \cdot Y}{\|Y\|^2}$$

that is,

$$(\beta - b_1^*)\|X\|^2 = (\beta - b_2^*)\|Y\|^2 = \gamma X \cdot Y$$

Thus, the vectors X and Y must satisfy

$$\|X\|^2 = \frac{\beta - b_2^*}{\beta - b_1^*} \|Y\|^2 = \frac{\gamma}{\beta - b_1^*} X \cdot Y$$

and for this to have a solution, we have the condition

$$(\beta - b_1^*)(\beta - b_2^*) > 0 \tag{14}$$

If we define

$$Z = \sqrt{\frac{\beta - b_2^*}{\beta - b_1^*}}\, Y$$

$$\epsilon = \frac{\beta - b_1^*}{|\beta - b_1^*|}$$

and

$$\delta = \frac{\epsilon \gamma}{\sqrt{(\beta - b_1^*)(\beta - b_2^*)}}$$

then we need vectors X and Z satisfying the system

$$\bar{X} = 0, \quad \bar{Z} = 0$$

and   (15)

$$\|X\|^2 = \|Z\|^2 = \delta X \cdot Z$$

and for this system to have a nontrivial solution, we have the condition

$$\delta \geqslant 1$$

that is,

$$\gamma^2 \geqslant (\beta - b_1^*)(\beta - b_2^*) \tag{16}$$

hence, from (14) and (16), the theorem follows.

The reader may check that no nontrivial vector of initial conditions in R^2 can be found, but that expanding the number of initial conditions beyond 3 to any finite number does not weaken the condition of the theorem.

The shaded areas in Figures 8.1 and 8.2 represent attainable limit prices for different values of the parameters α, β, and γ. The Cournot solution is a reference point and is given by

$$p_1^* = p_2^* = \frac{\alpha}{2\beta - \gamma}$$

In Figure 8.1 we have the normal "stable" situation, with $\beta > \gamma$, whereas in Figure 8.2 we have $2\beta < \gamma$. It is of some interest to note that the situation in Figure 8.2, which is normally regarded as highly unstable, because both firms have an interest in pushing up prices, does, within the context of our model, have a wide range of limit prices.

The theorem shows that there is a significant set of possible limit prices and hence that the process may well converge to a solution that is no way a solution of the true system. Two questions remain open. If we specify starting conditions and then let the process evolve, can we obtain price

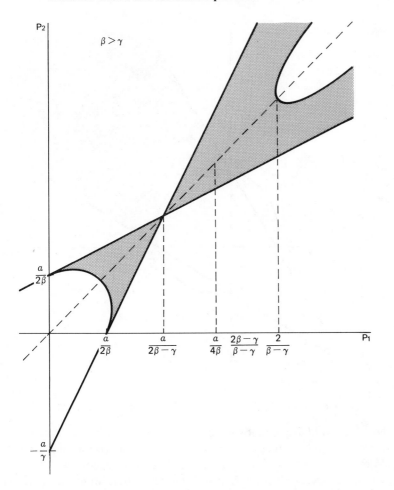

Figure 8.1. Attainable limit prices for different values of α, β, and γ.

pairs outside the shaded area? The foregoing remarks suggest that the answer to this is no.

Second, does the process necessarily converge from any arbitrary initial conditions? Even in this simple example this problem seems to be complicated to solve.

8.2.   More general frameworks[6]

The interest of the example in the previous section turns on how dependent the results are on the particular behavior of the individuals in the

[6] I am grateful to Mr. Lai Tung, who did the computational work for this section.

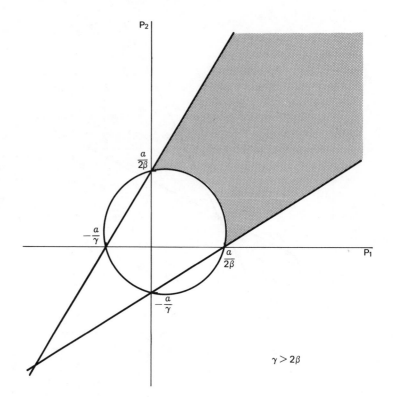

Figure 8.2. Attainable limit prices for different values of α, β, and γ.

model. One could argue that such or simpler behavior is widely assumed in the theoretical literature and that to assume a more technical approach would be to attribute an unrealistically high level of sophistication to the firms in the model. Indeed, in Negishi's model (1961), for example, firms must have fixed and unchangeable ideas about the "wrong" demand curves.

Nevertheless, the basic argument of this chapter would be undermined if it could be shown that by the adoption of standard techniques the firms would be led to discover the error of their ways and to modify their models accordingly. Three questions can be asked. First, are there statistical tests that would lead to rejection of the hypotheses that are made by the firms in formulating their models? Second, are there statistical results that would indicate the nature of the misspecification if the answer to the first question is in the affirmative? Third, are there standard procedures that, even if the second question cannot strictly be answered by yes, would lead an econometrician to find the "true" model?

Before looking at the answers to these questions, let us look at what it is that intuitively leads one to realize that "something is wrong." What happens is that as the prices converge, the residuals become smaller in absolute size. It is this striking feature that would lead the observant firm to reflect on the problem. Now, whereas the absolute values of the residuals diminish, standard tests of serial correlation will not necessarily lead to rejection of the hypothesis that the error terms are serially independent. This, of course, depends on the relative speed at which the errors and the difference between them go to zero. Furthermore, the convergence is not monotonic. However, any sensible test would lead one to reject the hypothesis that σ^2, the variance of the error terms, is constant over time.

Having observed this fact, is there any formal result that would lead the firms to the appropriate specification? The answer seems to be no, unless the error terms in the *true model* are generated by a nonstationary process.[7]

Yet, faced with such a situation, the firms would presumably try some procedure to eliminate the contradiction. We tried first the obvious solution.

8.2.1. *Modified approach: generalized least squares with $\sigma_t^2 = \sigma^2/t$*

Observing the structure of the error terms, the firms might simply suppose that the process generating them has a variance that diminishes over time. To see the consequences of this, we simulated the model assuming that the error terms in the observed models were independently distributed, but with variance $\sigma_t^2 = \sigma^2/t$. The results would not lead one to reject this hypothesis, and even though using generalized least squares in this way with a diagonal variance–covariance matrix implies simply giving greater weight to later observations, convergence was always to prices different from the standard solutions of the true model. Thus, the retention of early observations does not seem to account for the determination of the limit prices.

8.2.2. *Modified approach: addition of lagged demand*

An alternative approach that has been suggested for the firms is to estimate a model

$$a_i + b_i p_i(t) + c_i d_i(t-1) + \epsilon_t$$

This would insert a variable that it is thought would act as a close proxy

[7] For a discussion of this sort of problem, see Hendry (1979).

for the omitted price term. Simulation of this model led again to convergence to limit prices dependent on the initial conditions and, with generalized least squares, no obviously curious behavior of the residuals. Thus, firms would not be led to doubt the veracity of their model.

8.2.3. *Modified approach: addition of an error term to the true model*

As suggested earlier, we might suppose that there is in fact an error term in the true model. That is, the model for firm 1, for example, would be

$$d_1(t) = \alpha - \beta p_1(t) + \gamma p_2(t) + \mu_t \quad \text{where} \quad \mu \sim N(0, \sigma^2)$$

In this case, simulation shows that even the most suspicious firm will have its fears allayed, because as prices converge rapidly, all that is left in the residuals is the true random variable. Thus, nothing would make the firms realize that they had misspecified their model. Once again, the limit points of this process depended on initial conditions, contradicting the argument that the problem in the early model was that late in the process one observed only a very small region of the price–demand space.

All this suggests that an increase in the sophistication of the methods employed by the firms would not lead to a result different from that in the first part of the chapter and, second, that a small increase in the realism of the true model would remove the feature that would lead the firms to question their own models.

There are a number of questions that merit further investigation. Suppose, for example, that some firms start with very general models and include many other prices as their explanatory variables. If some of their competitors follow a static strategy, this generality will not help, because they could be led to reject, as insignificant, prices that do, in reality, enter into the real model. Thus, a model in which some firms try to adapt their models and others do not would be of interest.

Another project worth undertaking would be to consider a model in which one firm or several firms are perfectly informed either about the nature of the true model or about the behavior of their competitors, or both, and then to investigate the consequences of such firms' adopting optimal strategies.

One further rather simple point has to be made. In fact, a firm can never include the current price of its competitors in its model. It must use last period's price. A natural question is whether the use of lagged prices of other firms in an *n*-firm model would lead to convergence even with complete information.

8.2.4. An alternative approach: long-term profit maximization

A different problem is posed by the assumption that firms maximize short-term profits. If the firms were to maximize profits in the long run, they would be prepared to gain information in the short run at the expense of a loss in short-term profits.

The analysis of the appropriate behavior in this sort of situation is very complicated and leads one to have to find new estimates of the parameters of the model. Such behavior is usually ruled out directly as being too complicated (e.g., Rothschild, 1973), but nevertheless it would be of interest to know if the conclusions of this chapter would be modified by analyzing such a case. This will be the subject of a future study.

8.3. Conclusion

What is clear from this analysis of an admittedly simplistic model is that a reasonable learning process will not necessarily overcome the problem of misspecification. Furthermore, improving the learning process or complicating the model to make the firm's behavior more plausible does not change the results. Thus, Roberts and Sonnenschein's (1977) suggestion that firms will come to learn the "true" model facing them even from a misspecified start has to be accepted with reservations. This is comforting from one point of view, because even in cases where equilibrium in the Cournot sense does not exist, such an oligopoly model may converge to a situation with which all the participants are satisfied, in the sense that none of them feels any incentive to move. On the other hand, and more disquieting, is the observation that in the model in this chapter, for example, a whole class of outcomes may be a final "equilibrium," and which of these is actually observed is determined by the arbitrary initial conditions. Thus, stability is paid for in terms of indeterminateness. There would seem to be no reason why such conclusions should not be applicable to economic models in general. If this is true, then we should perhaps be more concerned about the characterization of possible equilibria than about the existence or stability of equilibria in the more restricted traditional sense.

References

Aoki, M. (1976). *Optimal Control and System Theory in Dynamic Economic Analysis.* New York: American Elsevier.
Arrow, K., and J. Green (1973). "Notes on Expectations Equilibria in Bayesian Settings."

Working paper 33, Institute for Mathematical Studies in the Social Sciences, Stanford University.

Azariadis, C., and R. Guesnerie (1981). "The Persistence of Self-fulfilling Theories." Discussion paper, C.E.P.R.E.M.A.P., Paris.

Bray, M. (1981). "Learning, Estimation, and the Stability of Rational Expectations." Discussion paper, Faculty of Economics and Politics, University of Cambridge.

Cyert, R. M., and M. H. DeGroot (1971). "Interfirm Learning and the Kinked Demand Curve." *Journal of Economic Theory*, 3:272–87.

(1973). "An Analysis of Cooperation and Learning in a Duopoly Context." *American Economic Review*, 63:26–37.

(1974). "Rational Expectations and Bayesian Analysis." *Journal of Political Economy*, 82:521–36.

Gates, D. J., J. A. Rickard, and D. J. Wilson (1977). "A Convergent Adjustment Process for Firms in Competition." *Econometrica*, 45:1349–64.

(1978). "Convergence of a Market Related Game Strategy." *Journal of Mathematical Economics*, 5:97–110.

Gates, D. J., and M. Westcott (1981). "Extended Optima and Equilibria for Continuous Games. I: General Results. II: A Class of Economic Models. III: Comparison with Bargaining Experiments." *Journal of the Australian Mathematical Society, Series B*, 23:187–209.

Hendry, D. F. (1979). "The Behaviour of Inconsistent Instrumental Variables – Estimators in Dynamic Systems with Autocorrelated Errors." *Journal of Econometrics*, 9:295–314.

Kirman, A. P. (1975). "Learning by Firms about Demand Conditions." In: *Adaptive Economic Models*, edited by R. H. Day and T. Groves, pp. 137–56. New York: Academic Press.

Lewis, G. (1981). "The Phillips Curve and Bayesian Learning." *Journal of Economic Theory*, 24:240–64.

Negishi, T. (1961). "Monopolistic Competition and General Equilibrium." *Review of Economic Studies*, 28:196–201.

Roberts, J. and H. Sonnenschein (1977). "On the Foundations of the Theory of Monopolistic Competition." *Econometrica*, 45:101–14.

Rothschild, M. (1973). "Models of Market Organization with Imperfect Information: A Survey." *Journal of Political Economy*, 81:1283–308.

Zellner, A. (1971). *An Introduction to Bayesian Inference in Econometrics*. New York: Wiley.

Comment

JERRY GREEN

The chapter by Kirman offers us some interesting results in the theory of learning by agents whose view of their economic environment is through their own misspecified models. It is built around an example, a simple duopoly model with linear demand curves dependent on the two prices charged, but with potentially different coefficients. In this specification, each of the competitors does not recognize the dependence of his demand on the other duopolist's price. Because this price is varying as the learning process proceeds, and is an unobservable variable, the model is underidentified.

The chapter considers various mechanical rules for repeated estimation of the parameters in the perceived models and various testing procedures for evaluating the maintained hypotheses of these models. These rules have been shown to lead to convergence of beliefs. However, the limiting prices are not optimal, were the true model and its parameters common knowledge. In this respect, the chapter is a generalization of the results of Arrow and Green (1973) and the study by Gates, Rickard, and Wilson (1977). Kirman's chapter confirms our intuition that the limit points of these learning procedures are not independent of the initial beliefs.

I think the chapter is valuable in that it demonstrates the robustness of these learning models to some further tests for consistency that the competitors might apply based on their own data. For example, it allows for a time-varying variance term in the perceived specification.

Yet the chapter fails to be convincing in its insistence on myopic optimization of the profit criterion with respect to the price chosen at every stage of the learning process. Consider the following strategy for estimating the price coefficient in the perceived model. At the first stage, charge an outrageously high price. Then revert to myopic optimization. The initial observation generated is very informative about the price parameter. Will the information so gathered be worth the cost? What will its feedback effects be on the information gathered by the other competitor? Clearly, at a zero discount rate, it is worth gathering information in this way. Because the hypothesis that the linear specification of demand is maintained, a finite loss in profit at the initial date is offset by the superior information that is obtained and can be reused into the indefinite future. (Of course, defining an optimal learning rule of this form might be a formidable task.)

But at positive discount rates this result is in doubt. It involves trading a finite loss in profit as the first step against a finite (discounted) gain in the future. Moreover, it is not even clear that there is *any* positive departure from myopic optimization that is beneficial to the duopolists. Small departures involve second-order small losses in profit at the initial date, but also generate only second-order small benefits in terms of increases in the precision of estimation of parameters.[1]

---

[1] Roy Radner pointed this out in conference, and I am grateful to him for clarifying this point. It is also of interest to consider the comparison between this type of learning strategy and the two-armed bandit problem studied by Rothschild (1971): "A Two-Armed Bandit Theory of Market Pricing." Working paper No. 10, Mathematical Social Science Ford Workshop, University of California, Berkeley.

Therefore, it seems to me that the principal question left open in the wake of Kirman's chapter is whether active nonmyopic learning rules exist that can actually be beneficial to the participants when the model set forth is given a genuine dynamic optimization structure. If so, one must view the results of this chapter with some caution, as the misspecification becomes more likely to be discovered.

CHAPTER 9

Equilibrium theory with learning and disparate expectations: some issues and methods

ROBERT M. TOWNSEND

9.1. Introduction

Motivated by certain stylized facts or observations, and perhaps by a desire to develop models that offer a reliable guide for policy, economists have developed equilibrium models that are more and more sophisticated in their treatment of time and imperfect information. The profession has witnessed a movement from static models to dynamic models with perfect foresight and, more recently, with the advances of Muth (1961), Lucas and Prescott (1971), and Lucas (1972, 1975), among others, to dynamic models with uncertainty and rational expectations.[1] Muth's work (1961) was motivated by two major conclusions from studies of expectations data: "1. Averages of expectations in an industry are more accurate than naive models and as accurate as elaborate equation systems, although there are considerable cross-sectional differences of opinion. 2. Reported expectations generally underestimate the extent of changes that actually take place." Muth goes on to invoke his rational expectations hypothesis, "that the expectations of firms (or, more generally, the subjective probability distribution of outcomes) tend to be distributed, for the same information set, about the prediction of the theory (or the 'objective' probability distributions of outcomes)" and to establish that both the periodic movement of time series displayed in so-called corn–hog cycles and the second preceding observation can be explained

Helpful comments from Lars Peter Hansen, Thomas J. Sargent, John Taylor, Roswell G. Townsend, and the participants of the conference in New York and a seminar at the University of Pennsylvania, and support from the National Science Foundation and the Alfred P. Sloan Foundation, are all gratefully acknowledged. The author assumes full responsibility for any errors, as well as for the views expressed here.

[1] Needless to say, this chapter does not attempt to trace the development of the rational expectations equilibrium notion or to tie together the microeconomic and macroeconomic literatures.

with that hypothesis. Similarly, Lucas and Prescott's work (1971) was motivated by econometric considerations, a desire to develop a guide as to how variables measuring anticipated future demand should be placed in industry investment rules; in making forecasting considerations explicit, they invoked the more general rational expectations hypothesis that the entire subjective and objective probability distributions be equal. Finally, Lucas's work (1972, 1975) on business cycles was motivated by the desire to explain certain key cross-correlation and serial-correlation properties of prices, unemployment, and output and to develop models with implications about the way in which reduced-form equations might change with changes in the systematic component of stabilization policy. Thus, Lucas developed formal equilibrium analysis consistent with rational but disparate expectations across decision makers.

Despite these advances, there remains some concern with the use of the rational expectations hypothesis. It is perhaps unwise to attempt to speak for others, but this concern itself may be motivated by economic observations. Rational expectations, it is thought, require essentially uniform beliefs at some level and imply more stationarity or stability of time series than is consistent with even casual observations. Put rather crudely, decision makers do not agree about things that keep moving around. Indeed, it is easy to read Keynes (1936) on the role of expectations in stock markets and Pigou (1929) on the role of expectations in industrial fluctuations and sustain the view that equilibrium analysis is inappropriate. It was Keynes's view that with the opening of stock exchanges, investors shift from a concern with long-term determinants of profitability or yield to a concern with short-term movements in the market prices themselves. Thus, conventional valuation will be "established as the outcome of the mass psychology of a large number of ignorant individuals which is liable to change violently as the result of a sudden fluctuation in opinion due to factors which do not really make much difference to prospective yield." In this environment, Keynes believed that even expert professionals "possessing judgment and knowledge beyond that of the average private investor" would be forced to concern themselves with average opinion. Similarly, Pigou (1929) argued that the key feature of cycles is that decision makers are unaware of what others are doing and are thus bound to make mistakes, that is, to make forecast errors; of course, this is also a key idea in Lucas (1975). Further, Pigou argued that these errors can be mutually generated, that is, with errors of optimism generated by errors of pessimism, and so on.

The research program of which this chapter is a part continues in the tradition of enriching equilibrium theory, extending it to the point that it might begin to address some of the observations that Keynes and Pigou had in mind. Thus, it follows Muth, Lucas, and Prescott, among others, adopting a strategy described by Hayek (1939), offering precise equilibrium constructs to explain relatively complicated dynamic phenomena. Of course, the equilibrium constructs of this chapter should not be taken as literal descriptions of the way the world works; as in Muth, it is not asserted here that the system of equations resembles the scratchwork of entrepreneurs in any way. Moreover, one can argue, as did Muth (1961), that rationality of expectations is a logical (albeit somewhat extreme) specification to examine, an assumption that can be modified: "Systematic biases, incomplete or incorrect information, poor memory, etc. can be examined with analytical methods based on rationality."

For this research program to be successful, equilibrium models with learning and with disparate but rational expectations must be tractable. Unfortunately, such models are not currently regarded as tractable by many in the economics profession, perhaps for a variety of reasons. First, models with learning are frequently used to address the question whether or not there will be convergence to rational expectations equilibria. Indeed, Muth (1961) and Lucas and Prescott (1971) suggested that rational expectations should be regarded as the natural outcome of some unspecified process of learning and adapting on the part of decision makers. But attempts to model that process have produced mixed conclusions; see Arrow and Green (1973), Cyert and DeGroot (1974), Townsend (1978), DeCanio (1979), Bray and Kreps (1981), Blume and Easley (1982), Bray (1982), and Frydman (1982). In general, convergence to (strong-form) rational expectations seems problematical, and there remain many open questions concerning how best to model learning processes and to pose stability questions. Second, equilibrium models with rational but disparate expectations often seem to require that decision makers not only forecast underlying economic state variables but also forecast the forecasts of others. This can be viewed as quite demanding. [See also B. Friedman (1979).] Third, economy-wide average forecasts can become an object of speculation in these models, and this in turn can lead to an infinite regress problem in which decision makers forecast the forecasts of forecasts of others, and so on. Finally, and related, Lucas (1975), Chari (1979), and Futia (1981) have indicated analytical difficulties in solving for closed-form solutions in models in which decision makers forecast from *endogenous* time series, encountering the infinite regress problem, nonlinear equations, or an infinite number of state variables.[2]

Thus, on the one hand, there is the hope that one might explain the

[2] This reference is somewhat misleading, because in one way or another these authors *do* solve their respective problems. The solution procedures offered here are not unrelated.

movement of economic time series in equilibrium models with learning and with disparate but rational expectations; on the other hand, there is the view that such models are difficult to solve. This chapter takes a step toward resolving this dilemma by devoting much of its attention to the formulation-analysis issue. That is, the basic intent of the research of which this chapter is a part is to find constructs and techniques that will prove useful in a variety of economic models. In this regard, these efforts have been somewhat successful; it is argued here that the class of linear dynamic models with learning and with disparate but rational expectations is indeed tractable under a wide variety of information speci-fications. Moreover, these models do deliver qualitatively interesting time series, as hoped. In particular, even in a simple setting, they deliver waves of optimism and pessimism and cyclical fluctuations in output.

This chapter proceeds by fixing a simple, partial equilibrium, industry model that might be suggested by a reading of Muth (1961), a basic struc-ture with shocks to demand that are the sum of a (relatively) permanent component and a transitory component. There follows an investigation of what problems arise and what formulation-solution techniques are needed as the information structure is varied in the simple model. With arbitrary prior beliefs on the initial demand shock, there *is* an infinite regress problem in forecasts. But that problem has a natural solution, at least in principle, in an infinite-dimensional space (see Section 9.3). Moreover, statistical decision theory frequently can be used to pin down the source of prior beliefs, and in that way one can return to finite-dimensional state space methods, such as the Kalman filtering algorithm – Bayes's rule for linear dynamic systems (see Sections 9.4, 9.5, and 9.6). In particular, recursive structures with informed and uninformed traders are tractable. And even when simple Kalman filtering is inapplicable, the infinite regress problem can be solved by a nonlinear technique in a finite-dimensional space, the space of undetermined coefficients for moving average representations of economy-wide average forecasts (see Section 9.7).

In all these information specifications, decision makers take as given linear laws of motion of state variables, such as shocks and forecasts, that they do and/or do not see, and more often than not these laws have time-invariant coefficients. That is, as in Muth's early formulation (1961), state variables take on period-by-period realizations as if gen-erated from well-defined stationary stochastic processes. These "self-fulfilling" stochastic processes are the analogues of the "self-fulfilling" price distributions in relatively static rational expectations models. It should be noted also that to the extent that the state variables are unob-served, the information specifications here contain unobserved components or latent variables. Such latent variable constructs have become increasingly useful to economists studying social phenomena; see, for example, Friedman (1957) and Muth (1960) on permanent income, Crawford (1976) and Jovanovic (1978) on labor turnover and job match, and Kydland and Prescott (1981) and Meltzer (1981) on fluctuations. For a more comprehensive discussion of the relationship between economic models with uncertainty and statistical decision theory see Prescott and Townsend (1980).

Finally, it may be emphasized again that in this chapter the interest in equilibrium models with learning and with disparate but rational expectations is motivated by the search for abstractions with testable implications, that is, abstractions capable of explaining the movement of economic time series. On this account, dynamic linear equilibrium models show some promise, and on this account (but certainly not others) the issue of whether or not there is convergence to strong-form rational expectations outcomes loses some of its interest (see Section 9.5). In particular, there can be convergence in such models to a steady state suitable for econometric purposes – the variance–covariance matrices of beliefs settle down, so that coefficients in the laws of motion are time-invariant. But in such a steady state, means of beliefs are subject to economic and measurement error shocks and thus move around in an interesting way, a movement that is not predicted in strong-form rational expectations equilibrium (of the same model). In fact, as noted earlier, such shocks can induce oscillations and the waves of optimism and pessimism that Pigou (1929) had in mind. More generally, the research program of which this chapter is a part builds on the contributions of Hansen and Sargent (1980a, 1980b, 1981) and Sargent (1978, 1981a) on the formulation and estimation of dynamic linear rational expectations models, incorporating learning and information discrepancies across decision makers. Of course, all this work is designed to circumvent Lucas's critique (1976) of conventional econometric policy evaluation.

9.2. The basic model

Following Muth (1961), a linear partial equilibrium framework is adopted. Each of a set of firms maximizes expected profit, a function that is quadratic in output. This produced commodity is sold in a competitive market with stochastic demand. Production decisions must be made prior to the realization of the demand. Subsequent to the realization of demand, the market clearing price is the one that would be determined by a Walrasian auctioneer. There are no contingent commodity markets. Under these assumptions, the production decision of each firm is a linear function of the expected price. In terms of generality, neither the linearity nor the partial equilibrium approach nor the exogenous restriction on markets nor the risk neutrality is satisfactory.

It is assumed that there are many firms, so that each regards his own contribution to market output and his influence on market beliefs as negligible. Formally, this is accomplished by supposing that the set of firms I is the unit interval. That is, firm i has label $i \in [0, 1]$. Let q_{it} denote the output of firm i at time t. Let P_t denote the market price of the commodity output at time t. Output q_{it} must be chosen prior to the realization of P_t. Prior to its realization, suppose each firm i believes that P_t is a real-valued random variable with mean $E_{it}(P_t)$. Each firm acts to maximize $E_{it}(P_t)q_{it} - (1/2a)(q_{it})^2$, where $a > 0$, with respect to q_{it}. This yields the linear decision rule $q_{it} = aE_{it}(P_t)$. Also, let $Q_{it} = \int q_{it} \, di$ denote aggregate or average output at time t, where it is supposed, both here and later, that such Lebesgue integration is well defined.

In conjunction with market clearing (i.e., supply equals demand), price P_t is determined by the linear demand schedule $P_t = \theta_t + \epsilon_t - bQ_t$, where $b > 0$. Here $\{\epsilon_t\}$ is a sequence of independent and identically distributed random variables, completely transitory shocks, each of which is normally distributed with mean zero and variance σ_ϵ^2. Parameter θ_t, the relatively permanent shock, follows the first-order Markov process $\theta_{t+1} = \rho\theta_t + v_{t+1}$, where $|\rho| < 1$ and $\{v_t\}$ is a sequence of independent and identically distributed random variables, each with mean zero and variance σ_v^2, independent of the $\{\epsilon_t\}$. Finally, it should be noted that the basic model and all of its information variants that follow have steady states of zero. Thus, variables should be interpreted as deviations from means both here and later.

9.3.   Arbitrary prior beliefs and the infinite regress problem in expectations: a solution[3]

Now suppose that at the end of each period t, firms see P_t but do not see (directly) aggregate output Q_t. Suppose also that both the relatively permanent and transitory components of demand, θ_t and ϵ_t, are unobserved. Then, in choosing output $q_{i,t+1}$ at the beginning of period $t+1$, firm i will attempt to forecast P_{t+1}, which, under market clear-

---

[3] This section builds on the work of Townsend (1978), where the solution procedure was first described. However, the discussion here is marked by a strikingly simpler and more conventional definition of equilibrium – one that removes strategic considerations among decision makers (as described later). With this definition, it is easier to describe the solution algorithm, one that handles the added generality here of a Markov process on θ_t.

ing, is a linear combination of the forecast of θ_{t+1} and Q_{t+1}, namely, $E_{i,t+1}(P_{t+1}) = E_{i,t+1}(\theta_{t+1}) - bE_{i,t+1}(Q_{t+1})$. But how does the firm forecast Q_{t+1}? Taking account of the symmetry of the situation, we might suppose that each firm recognizes that all the other firms are attempting to solve a similar forecasting problem. Hence, if firm i's output decision $q_{i,t+1}$ depends at least on $E_{i,t+1}(\theta_{t+1})$, aggregate output Q_{t+1} must depend at least on market anticipations of θ_{t+1}, namely, $\int E_{j,t+1}(\theta_{t+1}) \, dj$. So firm i will attempt to forecast this market anticipation, $E_{i,t+1} \int E_{j,t+1}(\theta_{t+1}) \, dj$. But again, by the symmetry of the situation, other firms form such anticipations. So again, to be one step ahead of the market, so to speak, firm i will attempt to forecast these latter forecasts $E_{i,t+1} \int E_{j,t+1} \int E_{k,t+1}(\theta_{t+1}) \, dk \, dj$, and so on. Thus described is an infinite regress problem in expectations.

It is argued in this section that this infinite regress problem necessarily emerges in the basic model if one is only willing to specify arbitrary initial prior beliefs on the part of firms about the parameter θ_t and about the beliefs of other firms. But, perhaps contrary to appearance, the infinite regress problem does have a solution, at least in principle, in an infinite-dimensional space. That is, there exists a dynamic competitive equilibrium with rational but disparate expectations. Taken up in the next section is a discussion of how to resolve the infinite regress problem, perhaps in a more natural way, by truncating the infinite regress.

The discussion of this section will be aided considerably by a small investment in notation. So let $\phi_{0t} = \theta_t$ for all t. Let the prior of firm i on θ_t at time t be termed its zero-order belief on θ_t with expectation $m_{0t}(i)$. Regard the economy-wide average of these forecasts $\int m_{0t}(j) \, dj$ as another variable ϕ_{1t}. Let the prior of firm i on ϕ_{1t} at time t be termed its first-order belief on θ_t with expectation $m_{1t}(i)$. Regard the economy-wide average of these forecasts $\int m_{1t}(j) \, dj$ as another variable ϕ_{2t}. Let the prior of firm i on ϕ_{2t} be termed its second-order belief on θ_t with expectation $m_{2t}(i)$. Continuing *recursively* in this manner, let $\phi_{nt} = \int m_{n-1,t}(j) \, dj$ for all integers $n \geqslant 1$.

Now define an infinite-dimensional vector of variables $\phi_t = \{\phi_{nt}, n \geqslant 0\}$. Let $m_t(i) = \{m_{nt}(i), n \geqslant 0\}$ be an infinite-dimensional vector of expectations on ϕ_t, and let $\Sigma(\phi_t)$ denote a doubly infinite dimensional matrix of covariances with $(k+1)$th row and $(n+1)$th column element $\sigma_{kn}(\phi_t)$. We shall suppose that firm i's beliefs about θ_t and about the beliefs of other firms are completely described by the infinite-dimensional normal distribution with mean $m_t(i)$ and covariance matrix $\Sigma(\phi_t)$. The covariance matrix is common knowledge. Thus, in this specification, means can vary across firms i, but covariances cannot. But both means and covariances can evolve over time. Beliefs at $t = 0$ are taken as an initial condition.

With this notation, the definition of a competitive equilibrium is now relatively straightforward.

Definition 1: A dynamic competitive equilibrium with rational but disparate expectations is a specification of a decision rule for each firm $i \in I$,

$$q_{it} = \sum_{n=0}^{\infty} \alpha_n m_{nt}(i) \tag{1}$$

a rule for economy-wide average output,

$$Q_t = \sum_{n=0}^{\infty} \beta_n \phi_{n+1,t} \tag{2}$$

laws of motion for the variables ϕ_t,

$$\phi_{0,t+1} = \rho \phi_{0t} + v_{t+1} \tag{3}$$

$$\phi_{k,t+1} = \delta_{k0}(t) P_t + \sum_{n=1}^{\infty} \delta_{kn}(t) \phi_{nt} \quad (k \geqslant 1) \tag{4}$$

laws of motion for the forecasts of the ϕ_t for each firm $i \in I$,

$$m_{k,t+1}(i) = \gamma_{k+1,0}(t) P_t + \sum_{n=0}^{\infty} \gamma_{k+1,n+1}(t) m_{nt}(i) \geqslant 0 \quad (k \geqslant 0) \tag{5}$$

and market clearing equation,

$$P_t = \phi_{0t} + \epsilon_t - b Q_t \tag{6}$$

such that the following hold.

(i) *Maximization:* The decision rule (1) is maximizing for each firm i given the average output rule (2) and market clearing condition (6).

(ii) *Statistically correct forecasting:* The laws of motion for forecasts (5) are statistically correct for each firm i given the average output rule (2), market clearing condition (6), and parameter laws (3) and (4).

(iii) *Consistent aggregation in output:* The average output rule (2) is consistent with the individual decision rules (1); that is, $\alpha_n = \beta_n$, $n \geqslant 0$.

(iv) *Consistent aggregation in forecasts:* The laws of motion for forecasts (5) over all i generate the laws of motion for variables (4); that is,

$$\gamma_{kn}(t) = \delta_{kn}(t) \quad (k \geqslant 1, n \geqslant 0)$$

The definition is self-explanatory in large part, but some additional comments seem appropriate. One notes in particular the separation between individual and average laws, both in output and in forecasts. That is, each i firm takes the average output rule (2) and laws of motion of parameters (3) and (4) as given in determining its own output and in making its own forecast. This keeps strategic interaction at a minimum. In fact, substituting (2) into (6) completely removes the dependence of the output decision of firm i on the average decision Q_t; just as in a standard rational expectations equilibrium, there is a kind of self-fulfilling distribution in prices.

An equilibrium may seem difficult to compute, but it is not. Essentially, all one needs to do is make the substitutions suggested in consistency requirements (iii) and (iv), and then search for the undetermined coefficients $\{\alpha_n\}$ in (1) and (2) and the undetermined coefficients $\{\gamma_{kn}(t)\}$ in (4) and (5). Moreover, these searches can be conducted recursively, as is now indicated. First, use (1), (2), and (6) to determine the $\{\alpha_n\}$. Under some mild regularity conditions, there exists a solution of the form $\alpha_n = (-1)^n a (ab)^n$, $n \geqslant 0$ (see Townsend, 1978, proof of Proposition 2). Second, consider the updating problem of firm i. Using (2) and (6) again, the posterior of firm i on the variables ϕ_t at the end of period t is a weighted average of its prior and the observation P_t; see Townsend [1978, equations (12) and (13)], for a similar calculation. The weights are determined by ratios of linear combinations of covariances, all in terms of the (known) parameters of $\Sigma(\phi_t)$, σ_v^2, σ_ϵ^2, a, and b. Now attack the system recursively. The law of motion for ϕ_{0t} is given in (3). So the posterior on ϕ_{0t} (just determined) and the law (3) give the updating formula of firm i for $\phi_{0,t+1}$, that is, (5) at $k=0$. Averaging over firms i produces law of motion for $\phi_{1,t+1}$, that is, (4) at $k=1$. Now take the expectation of firm i over $\phi_{1,t+1}$ and substitute the posterior formulas for all the ϕ_t. This yields (5) at $k=1$. Then average over all firms i to produce (4) at $k=2$. One can proceed in principle to compute all the infinite laws in this manner.

Thus, the infinite regress problem has a direct solution, at least in principle. But various potential drawbacks of this setup and its solution should be noted. First, it must be verified that the many infinite sums are well defined. Second, and related, in computing a solution one has to hope for closed-form solutions or hope that iterative procedures can be truncated after some point. Third, the coefficients in the equilibrium representation vary over time, an aspect that can only complicate econometric work; one hopes that these converge to constants over time. Fourth, and related, one hopes that the influence of the initial priors dissipates over time. In subsequent sections, all these hopes are fulfilled with alternative setups and solution techniques.

9.4.   Truncating the infinite regress: the gain from statistical decision theory

As noted, we might be happier for conceptual and computational reasons if the regress of the previous section could be truncated after some point. [Even Keynes (1936) stopped with third-order expectations in his observations on the stock market.] A sufficient way to truncate is for there to be *common knowledge of expectations at some (finite) order.* This section discusses various ways in which such common knowledge might occur.

To begin the discussion, imagine in the setup of the previous section that there is diversity at the beginning of period t regarding the forecasts of θ_t, that is, that the $m_{0t}(i)$ vary over i. But suppose for some reason or other that there is agreement on the extent of the disagreement, that is, that the average of these forecasts is known, known to be known, and so on, that is, $\int m_{0t}(j)\, dj$ is common knowledge. Then it can be established as a special case of the previous analysis that there exist equilibrium decision rules of the form

$$q_{it} = am_{0t}(i) - \frac{a(ab)}{1+ab} \int m_{0t}(j)\, dj$$

Moreover, in this case, because economy-wide output Q_t is known, statistical updating produces the result that $\int m_{0t}(j)\, dj$ will remain common knowledge in every period; see Townsend (1978, p. 487) for details.

It is problematical how common knowledge of some finite-order forecasts might be achieved. Surveys of expectations would surely help, but of course there are sampling and survey errors. In general, this is an area for future research efforts (Townsend, 1978, Section 6).

This brings us to perhaps the most compelling *modeling strategy* for truncating the infinite regress: statistical decision theory. Imagine that each decision maker's beliefs are not arbitrary but rather are the result of conditioning on a joint distribution on some specific observations. Then decision makers do not necessarily share common forecasts (conditional distributions). But they will have common knowledge of the *way* others are making their own forecasts (i.e., the statistical updating formulas), and *in some contexts this can be enough to truncate the infinite regress.* The following three sections, each of which is intended to illustrate a separate point, illustrate this gain to statistical decision theory in successively more complicated information structures.

9.5. Learning, convergence to rational expectations, and the existence of steady-state distributions: some conceptual issues

In introducing and developing the concept of rational expectations, Muth (1961) and Lucas and Prescott (1971) have argued that the notion of rational expectations is an *equilibrium* concept and should be regarded perhaps as the outcome of some unspecified process of learning and adapting on the part of economic decision makers. Recently, various authors have taken up this issue, asking whether or not models with learning converge to the rational expectations equilibrium outcome. This section addresses the convergence question.

To pose the issue of learning here, a limiting special case of the general model is considered first. Imagine that each of the parameters θ_t is equal to some constant θ, that is, that $\rho = 1$ and $\sigma_v^2 = 0$. In this context, a rational expectations equilibrium is a self-fulfilling price distribution; that is, a distribution of prices that, if taken as given by firms and used in their maximum problems, implies output decisions that, in turn, with market clearing under the random demand schedule, imply the initial distribution of prices. More specifically,

$$P_t(\epsilon_t) = \frac{\theta}{1+ab} + \epsilon_t \tag{7}$$

is such a self-fulfilling distribution. We may now ask whether or not there will be convergence to this distribution over time if for some reason initial guesses about the distribution are wrong but learning is allowed.

One way to proceed is to imagine that decision makers, firms in this instance, have in mind a relatively simple model that they use to make decisions and update beliefs, that is, learn about one or a number of parameters. Suppose, borrowing here and later from Cyert and DeGroot (1974), that each firm believes

$$P_t = \rho P_{t-1} + \epsilon_t \tag{8}$$

where $\{\epsilon_t\}$ is a sequence of independent and identically distributed (i.i.d.) variables, each with mean zero and variance $\sigma_\epsilon^2 = 1/r$. Each firm regards ρ as a fixed but unknown parameter about which it attempts to learn. That is, ρ is regarded as a normal random variable, with mean m_t and variance $1/h_t$ at the beginning of each period t. Thus, with contemporary observations on price, P_t,

$$m_{t+1} = \frac{h_t m_t + r P_{t-1} P_t}{h_t + r P_{t-1}^2}, \quad h_{t+1} = h_t + r P_{t-1}^2 \tag{9}$$

from standard statistical updating formulas (DeGroot, 1970). To close the model, note that for the representative firm, from (8),

$$E_t(P_t) = m_t P_{t-1} \tag{10}$$

But from the actual market clearing equation with $\theta = 0$ (as is now assumed),

$$P_t = -abE_t(P_t) + \epsilon_t \tag{11}$$

Thus, substituting (10) into (11),

$$P_t = -abm_t P_{t-1} + \epsilon_t \tag{12}$$

Here, then, the relatively simple model used by firms, namely (8), is not generally consistent with the actual distribution of prices (12); in the learning process, m_t moves around, and so parameter ρ in (8) is not fixed.

We might hope for consistency in the limit. In fact, if $m_t \to 0$, then we would have convergence to a strong-form rational expectations equilibrium. But the results reported by Cyert and DeGroot (1974) on their model are not comforting in this regard; the model oscillates and even explodes under some reasonable parameter specifications in various Monte Carlo runs.

What inferences can be drawn from the failure of Cyert and DeGroot's model to converge? Perhaps little. The failure to converge might be taken to indicate that decision makers were doomed at the outset by an incorrect view of the world and a limited statistical procedure: The model firms used was wrong and was never tested by them. This, of course, raises the question of how best to model inconsistent learning processes and to conduct stability analysis. As noted, a number of authors are attacking these issues.

An alternative to postulating relatively simple (incorrect) models that decision makers use in learning is to suppose that decision makers' models are consistent with the structure of the economy. It must be emphasized immediately that this is not so demanding an assumption as it might first seem, for one can still entertain all the rich variety of information structures and learning that statistical decision theory allows. There can be uncertainty about the nature of demand, the information and expectations of other agents, the decisions taken by them, and so on.

In the context of such a consistent structure, the convergence question can again be posed. In fact, it might be asked whether or not the period-by-period price distributions of the model of Section 9.3, with the *equilibrium* definition proposed there, would converge to the self-fulfilling price distribution described at the outset of this section. That is, would there be convergence to a (strong-form) rational expectations equilibrium? This question was answered affirmatively by Townsend (1978) for a special case, when industry output is observed period by period. More recently, Bray and Kreps (1981) have indicated that convergence (if not existence) results may be quite general. But it is argued here, as in Bray and Kreps (1981), that this particular convergence question is no longer of interest as a potential justification for rational expectations given that *rational expectations are imposed in the learning process*. To put it as bluntly as possible, such an imposition is tantamount to assuming what one wants to prove. The failure of the model to converge to a special configuration would seem to indicate little.

Of what use, then, are rational expectations models with rational learning? Again, the hope is that such models might mimic certain key features or stylized facts of the data. That is, do rational expectations models with learning have potentially testable implications, and, if so, are they consistent with data? This alternative issue leads in turn to yet another convergence question, one that *can* be answered in many contexts.

It seems unlikely a priori that a model with fixed shocks or parameter values can explain much of the interesting movement in economic time series even if there is learning and an absence of convergence. Thus, the model of this section, with θ_t shocks to demand fixed at θ for all t, loses its appeal. So we return to the more general structure in which demand is perpetually buffeted by new shocks v_t. That is, with $\theta_t = v_t + \rho v_{t-1} + \rho^2 v_{t-2} + \cdots + \rho^t \theta_0$, firms attempt to learn at the end of period t about the parameter θ_0 *and* past parameters $v_1, v_2, \ldots, v_t$. Equivalently, firms attempt to learn about the random variable θ_t at the end of each period t. See Townsend (1982) for a more detailed discussion of this equivalence.

Imagine that initially at $t = 0$ each firm has a common normal prior on the variable θ_0 with mean m_0 and variance Σ_0. Moreover, this prior belief is common knowledge. In addition, at the end of each period t each firm sees the market clearing price P_t *and* observation u_t, which is linearly related with noise to the demand shocks θ_t, namely,

$$u_t = \theta_t + w_t$$

where w_t is an i.i.d. normal random variable with mean zero and variance σ_w^2. In this context, we might hope to find an equilibrium that is consistent with considerable and interesting movement in economic time series and that is potentially testable.

The discussion will be aided considerably by redefining an equilibrium for this particular information structure. In doing so, it will prove helpful to let q_t and m_t denote the output decision and mean forecast of the representative firm, with Q_t and M_t the corresponding economy-wide averages.

Definition 2: A dynamic competitive equilibrium with rational and homogeneous expectations is a law of motion for θ_t,

$$\theta_{t+1} = \rho \theta_t + v_{t+1} \tag{13}$$

and observer equation,

$$u_t = \theta_t + w_t \tag{14}$$

a decision rule for the representation firm,

$$q_t = \alpha_0 m_t + \alpha_1 M_t \tag{15}$$

a rule for economy-wide average output,

$$Q_t = \beta M_t \tag{16}$$

a law of motion for the mean forecast of the representative firm,

$$m_{t+1} = \gamma_0 m_t + \gamma_1 P_t + \gamma_2 M_t + \gamma_3 u_t \tag{17}$$

a law of motion for the economy-wide average mean forecast,

$$M_{t+1} = \delta_1 P_t + \delta_2 M_t + \delta_3 u_t \tag{18}$$

and market clearing equation,

$$P_t = \theta_t + \epsilon_t - bQ_t \tag{19}$$

such that the following hold.

(i) *Maximization:* The decision rule (15) is maximizing given the average output rule (16) and market clearing equation (19).

(ii) *Statistically correct forecasting:* The law of motion (17) is statistically correct given the law of motion (13), observer equation (14), market clearing equation (19), average output rule (16), and average forecasting rule (18).

(iii) *Consistent output aggregation:* Rules (15) and (16) are consistent.

(iv) *Consistent forecast aggregation:* Rules (17) and (18) are consistent.
    It is hoped that what strikes one about this definition is its apparent simplicity. In particular, here we have a *finite number of state variables*

and *time-invariant coefficients.* Both these specifications are warranted; that is, an equilibrium with these properties can be constructed, as is now indicated.

First, note, from (18), that because M_0 is assumed to be known, and P_t and u_t are common observations, M_1 is known, and so on. This is what keeps the dimensionality finite. It only remains then to compute the undetermined time-invariant coefficients. Now equations (15), (16), and (19) are easily solved as before to yield $\alpha_0 = a$, $\alpha_1 = -a(ab)/(1+ab)$, $\beta = \alpha_0 + \alpha_1$. To compute the coefficients in (17), use is made of the incredibly powerful Kalman filtering algorithm (e.g., Bertsekas, 1976).[4] The system described here is a special case of a model with a linear law of motion for state variables

$$x_{t+1} = Ax_t + \bar{v}_{t+1}$$

and observer equations

$$y_t = Cx_t + \bar{w}_t$$

Here $x_t = \theta_t$, $A = \rho$, $\bar{v}_t = v_t$,

$$\bar{w}_t = \begin{bmatrix} \epsilon_t \\ w_t \end{bmatrix}, \quad y_t = \begin{bmatrix} P_t + b\beta M_t \\ u_t \end{bmatrix}, \quad \text{and} \quad C = \begin{bmatrix} 1 \\ 1 \end{bmatrix}$$

where

$$E\bar{v}_t = 0, \quad E(\bar{w}_t) = \begin{bmatrix} 0 \\ 0 \end{bmatrix}, \quad E\bar{v}_t \bar{v}_t' = M = \sigma_v^2, \quad E\bar{w}_t \bar{w}_t' = N = \begin{bmatrix} \sigma_\epsilon^2 & 0 \\ 0 & \sigma_w^2 \end{bmatrix}$$

Under mild regularity conditions that are satisfied here (Bertsekas, 1976; Kwakernaak and Sivan, 1977), for arbitrary prior distributions on x_0 with mean $E_0(x_0)$ and variance $\Sigma_{0|-1}$, the *updated posterior distributions converge,* so that the means satisfy the recursive relationship

$$E_t(x_t) = AE_{t-1}(x_{t-1}) + \bar{\Sigma}C'N^{-1}[y_{t-1} - CAE_{t-1}(x_{t-1})] \tag{20}$$

and the covariance matrices satisfy the recursive relationship

$$\Sigma_{t|t-1} = A[\Sigma_{t-1|t-2} - \Sigma_{t-1|t-2}C'(C\Sigma_{t-1|t-2}C' + N)^{-1}C\Sigma_{t-1|t-2}]A' + M \tag{21}$$

where

---

[4] Again, one could write out the entire history of observables and use standard formulas for conditional means and variances of normal random variables to forecast the entire history of innovations, and hence forecast θ_t. The Kalman filter is a recursive procedure that circumvents the dimensionality problems associated with this alternative.

$$\Sigma_{t|t-1} = E_t\{[x_t - E_t(x_t)][x_t - E_t(x_t)]'\}$$

and where $\Sigma_{t|t-1}$ converges termwise to a *time-invariant* matrix Σ. Then $\bar{\Sigma}$ in (20) satisfies

$$\bar{\Sigma} = \Sigma - \Sigma C'(C\Sigma C' + N)^{-1}C\Sigma \qquad (22)$$

and its terms are variances and covariances of beliefs on the state vector x_t at the end of date t. Clearly, (20), (21), and (22) can be used to deliver the time-invariant coefficients in (17). Then (18) is determined by $\delta_1 = \gamma_1$, $\delta_3 = \gamma_3$, and $\delta_2 = \gamma_0 + \gamma_2$. Finally, it will be noted that (20) can be viewed as in place even at $t = 0$ on the assumption that the system has an infinite past. This device of assuming an infinite past as the limiting case will be used again in a subsequent section. It is highly convenient for analytic and econometric purposes.

It is clear, of course, that the steady-state matrix $\bar{\Sigma}$ *in general* will not converge to zero, its value in a *period-by-period strong-form* rational expectations equilibrium, with θ_t known at the end of period t, so that $E_{t+1}(\theta_{t+1}) = \rho\theta_t$. At best, we can estimate or learn past innovations v_τ, $\tau < t$, arbitrarily well if τ is arbitrarily far in the past. But contemporary θ_t is continually buffeted by new shocks v_t about which little is known. The additional information in u_t will help in forecasting (i.e., reduce $\bar{\Sigma}$) but will not cause a degeneracy unless $\sigma_w^2 = 0$.

Thus, the failure of the system to converge to a period-by-period strong-form rational expectations equilibrium should not come as a surprise and is certainly not damning. In fact, the freedom that the model allows in specifying indirectly the steady-state forecasting variance $\bar{\Sigma}$ may be *useful for econometric purposes,* because in principle it allows a better fit of the model to actual data. It determines the extent to which forecasts respond to contemporary observations, and this in turn determines the extent to which the system itself moves around, say in response to relatively permanent shocks. In addition, a nontrivial forecasting variance $\bar{\Sigma}$ allows the system to respond to completely transitory shocks ϵ_t and to measurement errors u_t. Finally, it should be emphasized that this linear-normal system *can,* in principle, be taken to data by the methods described in detail by Townsend (1982, Section 10).

9.6.   Exploiting recursive structures with finite state space methods[5]

The information structure of the previous section allowed no diversity in forecasts; equilibrium was characterized by rational and homogeneous

---

[5] This specification was considered by Prescott and Townsend (1980). But again, the discussion here is marked by an alternative definition of equilibrium in the

expectations. This section and the next consider progressively more complicated information structures that do allow diversity. In this section we have a group of informed firms and a group of uninformed firms. It is established that such structures can be successfully attacked with statistical decision theory and the use of recursive procedures. Yet, despite the diversity, and in contrast to the analysis of Section 9.3, *there is no infinite regress problem.* Moreover, such structures can produce interesting time series.

To begin, imagine that at the beginning of period zero, all firms have a common normal prior on the variable θ_0, with mean $E(\theta_0)$ and variance $\text{var}(\theta_0)$. This prior is common knowledge. Now, at the end of each period t, $t \geq 0$, each of a set I of informed firms, fraction ρ_I of the set of all firms, observes a random variable $u_t = \theta_t + w_t$, where w_t is an i.i.d. normal random variable with mean zero and variance σ_w^2. Each of a set U of uninformed firms, fraction ρ_U, does not observe u_t. However, *all* firms do see the market clearing price P_t at the end of each period t. Industry output, on the other hand, is unobserved directly, though it may be inferred by some.

To attack this structure, we shall first uncover a *finite* list of state variables that will allow us to write down the decisions of firms and the evolution of their beliefs. All these state variables will be known in each period to the informed firms, but uninformed firms will know only a subset. Of course, θ_t remains unknown to all.

To begin, let $E_{It}(\theta_t)$ and $\Sigma_{It}(\theta_t)$ denote the beginning-of-period prior mean and variance on θ_t of informed firms. Now, for uninformed firms, $E_{It}(\theta_t)$ is unknown, because the u_t are unobserved by them. But we may suppose they regard $E_{It}(\theta_t)$ as an unknown variable π_t that is jointly normally distributed with the unknown variable θ_t; that is, $[\theta_t, \pi_t]$ is normally distributed, with mean $[E_{Ut}(\theta_t), E_{Ut}(\pi_t)]$ and covariance matrix $\Sigma_{Ut}(\theta_t, \pi_t)$. Then the state variables mentioned earlier are π_t, $\Sigma_{It}(\theta_t)$, $E_{Ut}(\theta_t)$, $E_{Ut}(\pi_t)$, and $\Sigma_{Ut}(\theta_t, \pi_t)$. Finally, note that $\Sigma_{It}(\theta_t)$ and $\Sigma_{Ut}(\theta_t, \pi_t)$ are assumed to be common knowledge.

We are now in a position to redefine an equilibrium with this state space.

Definition 3: A dynamic competitive equilibrium with rational but disparate expectations is a law of motion for θ_t,

$$\theta_{t+1} = \rho\theta_t + v_{t+1} \tag{23}$$

an observer equation,

more general setting in which θ_t's move around. Here, also, new Kalman filtering results are obtained, and a general method for attaching such structures is described.

$$u_t = \theta_t + w_t \tag{24}$$

a law of motion for π_t,

$$\pi_{t+1} = \xi_{1t} \pi_t + \xi_{2t} \theta_t + \xi_{3t} w_t + \xi_{4t} \epsilon_t \tag{25}$$

a decision rule for uninformed firms,

$$q_{Ut} = \alpha_1 E_{Ut}(\theta_t) + \alpha_2 E_{Ut}(\pi_t) \tag{26}$$

a decision rule for informed firms,

$$q_{It} = \beta_0 E_{It}(\theta_t) + \beta_1 E_{Ut}(\theta_t) + \beta_2 E_{Ut}(\pi_t) \tag{27}$$

laws of motion for forecasts and covariance matrix of beliefs of uninformed firms,

$$E_{U,t+1}(\theta_{t+1}) = \gamma_{1t} E_{Ut}(\theta_t) + \gamma_{2t} E_{Ut}(\pi_t) + \gamma_{3t} P_t \tag{28}$$

$$E_{U,t+1}(\pi_{t+1}) = \gamma_{4t} E_{Ut}(\theta_t) + \gamma_{5t} E_{Ut}(\pi_t) + \gamma_{6t} P_t \tag{29}$$

$$\Sigma_{U,t+1}(\theta_{t+1}, \pi_{t+1}) = \psi[\Sigma_{Ut}(\theta_t, \pi_t), \sigma_v^2, \sigma_w^2, \sigma_\epsilon^2] \tag{30}$$

laws of motion for forecasts and variance of beliefs of informed firms,

$$E_{I,t+1}(\theta_{t+1}) = \delta_{1t} E_{It}(\theta_t) + \delta_{2t} P_t + \delta_{3t} u_t + \delta_{4t} E_{Ut}(\theta_t) + \delta_{5t} E_{Ut}(\pi_t) \tag{31}$$

$$\Sigma_{I,t+1}(\theta_{t+1}) = \Phi[\Sigma_{It}(\theta_t), \sigma_v^2, \sigma_w^2, \sigma_\epsilon^2] \tag{32}$$

and market clearing equation,

$$P_t = \theta_t + \epsilon_t - b[\rho_I q_{It} + \rho_U q_{Ut}] \tag{33}$$

such that the following hold.

(i) *Maximization:* The decision rules (26) and (27) are each maximizing given the rules (26) and (27) and the market clearing equation (33).

(ii) *Statistically correct forecasting for informed firms:* The laws of motion (31) and (32) are statistically correct given the decision rules (26) and (27), market clearing equation (33), parameter law (23), and observer equation (24).

(iii) *Statistically correct forecasting for uninformed firms:* The laws of motion (28), (29), and (30) are statistically correct given the decision rules (26) and (27), market clearing equation (33), parameter laws of motion (23) *and* (25), and observer equation (24).

One comment is immediately in order. Unlike previous definitions, there is no distinction here between individual and aggregate decisions and forecasts. But it should be understood that the representative informed firm takes as given that the output decisions and forecasts of other informed firms are identical with its own, and similarly for uninformed firms.

An equilibrium is not difficult to compute. First, the coefficients α_1, α_2, β_0, β_1, and β_2 in (26) and (27) are computed by the method of undetermined coefficients, using property (i) of the equilibrium.[6] Second, the forecasting formulas (31) and (32) for informed firms are readily computed by Bayesian considerations; essentially, each informed firm is getting two independent observations on θ_t at the end of period t, through u_t and $P_t - b[\rho_{It} q_{It} + \rho_{Ut} q_{Ut}]$, and the law of motion (23) is known. For this purpose it is important to remember that q_{Ut} (and q_{It}) is expressed in terms of state variables that informed firms know. Now (25) follows immediately from (31), with $\pi_t = E_{It}(\theta_t)$. Finally, one has to attack the forecasting formulas for the uninformed firms. Using (33) with (31) and (27) [and (26)], uninformed firms are getting one observation θ_t and π_t through P_t – recall again $\pi_t = E_{It}(\theta_t)$. So the posterior $E_{U,t+1}(\theta_t)$ and $E_{U,t+1}(\pi_t)$ may be formed in the usual Bayesian way. Now the parameter laws of motion (23) and (25) for θ_{t+1} and π_{t+1} are known; so priors on π_{t+1} and θ_{t+1} at the beginning of period $t+1$ are readily calculated. This yields (28), (29), and (30).

An unfortunate aspect of the foregoing definition is the presence of time-varying coefficients – the coefficients are functions of period-by-period covariances that are allowed to move around. As it turns out, this is not a problem. First, steady-state Kalman filtering considerations can be used to remove the time dependence of Σ_{It}. This removes time dependence from (31) and hence (25). It then becomes apparent that the inference problem of uninformed firms can be cast as a classic optimal observer problem as well. To see this, consider the state vector $x_t = [\theta_t, \pi_t]'$. Then uninformed firms see $y_t = P_t + b\rho_U q_{Ut} + b\rho_I \beta_1 E_{Ut}(\theta_t) + b\rho_I \beta_2 E_{Ut}(\pi_t) = \theta_t + \epsilon_t - b\rho_I \beta_0 \pi_t$, so that

$$y_t = Cx_t + \bar{w}_t \tag{34}$$

where $C = [1 - b\rho_I \beta_0]$ and $\bar{w}_t = \epsilon_t$. Of course, x_t has the linear law of motion

[6] These undetermined coefficients are determined by the equations

$$\beta_0 = a[1 - b\rho_I \beta_0]$$
$$\beta_1 = a[-b\rho_U \alpha_1 - b\rho_I \beta_1]$$
$$\beta_2 = a[-b\rho_I \beta_2 - b\rho_U \alpha_2]$$
$$\alpha_1 = a[1 - b\rho_I \beta_1 - b\rho_U \alpha_1]$$
$$\alpha_2 = a[-b\rho_I \beta_0 - b\rho_I \beta_2 - b\rho_U \alpha_2]$$

It can be verified directly that these linear equations do have a solution.

$$x_{t+1} = Ax_t + \bar{v}_{t+1} \tag{35}$$

from (23) and (25), where

$$A = \begin{bmatrix} \rho & 0 \\ \xi_2 & \xi_1 \end{bmatrix}, \quad \bar{v}_{t+1} = \begin{bmatrix} v_{t+1} \\ \xi_3 w_t + \xi_4 \epsilon_t \end{bmatrix}$$

In the optimal observer system (34)–(35), the measurement error noise $\bar{w}_t$ and state excitation noise $\bar{v}_{t+1}$ are correlated. But Kalman filtering can handle this correlation – the covariance matrix of beliefs for uninformed firms converges to some constant, removing the time dependence from Σ_{Ut} and hence from (28) and (29).

It may now be noted how the hierarchical information structure and statistical decision theory allow a recursive attack on the system. First, it is supposed that there is a common prior distribution that is common knowledge. Informed firms know that the forecast of uninformed firms is the mean of their conditional distribution, the common distribution conditioned on variables that the uninformed firms *and* the informed firms see. So informed firms know the forecast of uninformed firms. Uninformed firms do not know the actual forecast of informed firms. But they do know that the forecast of informed firms is the mean of their conditional distribution, the common distribution conditioned on variables that the informed firms see, but that uninformed firms do not see completely. By Bayes's rule, then, uninformed firms know how the unobserved forecast of informed firms moves period by period, namely, as a function of the underlying unobserved state variables, observed and unobserved information variables, and the forecast of uninformed firms, which, of course, uninformed firms know. So uninformed firms can forecast the forecast of informed firms. There is no infinite regress problem: *Recursive structures are tractable by finite state space methods.*

As a final note, we might remark on the potential of recursive structures to generate interesting time series, as displayed in Table 9.1 and Figures 9.1 and 9.2. Suppose, for example, the industry is in a steady state at time t ($t=0$) and is subjected to a unit-variance shock ϵ_t, holding all other contemporary and future shocks at zero. All firms' forecasts of θ_t (which actually remains zero) will increase, thereby increasing industry output. Sustained increases of output (above the steady state of zero) for the first three periods keep prices low (below zero) for the first three periods, and uninformed firms come to believe that θ_t is actually negative. Consequently, uninformed firms reduce output (below zero), causing prices to go positive for periods four through seven. As a result, their forecasts go positive again for periods eight through ten, and prices go negative. This oscillatory pattern continues for some time, eventually

Table 9.1. *Response to a transitory ϵ_t shock*[a]

t	P_t	q_{It}	q_{Ut}	θ_t	$\pi_t = E_{It}(\theta_t)$	$E_{Ut}(\theta_t)$	$E_{Ut}(\pi_t)$
1	−0.30353	0.05970	0.31636	0.00000	0.36322	0.61102	0.17714
2	−0.26419	−0.16979	0.28703	0.00000	0.09439	0.56990	0.48685
3	−0.08535	−0.06082	0.09305	0.00000	0.02453	0.19823	0.44104
4	0.06403	0.07040	−0.07110	0.00000	0.00637	−0.12748	0.16707
5	0.10680	0.10845	−0.11813	0.00000	0.00166	−0.22883	−0.08042
6	0.06504	0.06547	−0.07191	0.00000	0.00043	−0.14487	−0.16611
7	0.00235	0.00246	−0.00260	0.00000	0.00011	−0.01026	−0.11149
8	−0.03357	−0.03354	0.03710	0.00000	0.00003	0.07003	−0.01330
9	−0.03282	−0.03281	0.03628	0.00000	0.00000	0.07142	0.04884
10	−0.01237	−0.01237	0.01367	0.00000	0.00000	0.02858	0.05319
11	0.00643	0.00643	−0.00710	0.00000	0.00000	−0.01243	0.02311
12	0.01284	0.01281	−0.01419	0.00000	0.00000	−0.02739	−0.00754
13	0.00853	0.00853	−0.00942	0.00000	0.00000	−0.01889	−0.01979
14	0.00095	0.00095	−0.00105	0.00000	0.00000	−0.00269	−0.01444
15	−0.00380	−0.00380	0.00420	0.00000	0.00000	0.00787	−0.00268
16	−0.00409	−0.00409	0.00452	0.00000	0.00000	0.00887	0.00542
17	−0.00175	−0.00175	0.00194	0.00000	0.00000	0.00400	0.00657
18	0.00060	0.00060	−0.00067	0.00000	0.00000	−0.00112	0.00319
19	0.00153	0.00153	0.00169	0.00000	0.00000	−0.00325	−0.00062
20	0.00111	0.00111	0.00122	0.00000	0.00000	−0.00244	−0.00233

[a] $\sigma_v^2 = 1.00000$; $\sigma_\epsilon^2 = 1.00000$; $\sigma_w^2 = 1.00000$; $\rho = 0.95000$; %inf $= 0.05000$; $a = 1.00000$; $b = 1.00000$.

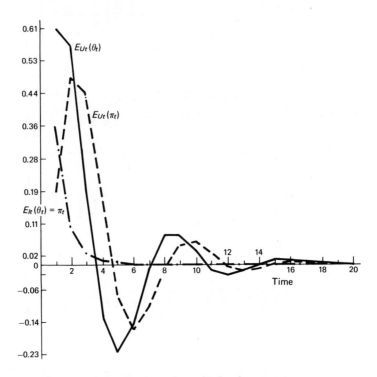

Figure 9.1. Response to transitory shock – forecasts.

converging to zero. Now, if one takes the difference between θ_t and $E_{Ut}(\theta_t)$ as a forecast error, then in this scenario, forecast errors oscillate, delivering the waves of optimism and pessimism that Pigou (1929) had in mind. This may be contrasted with the more conventional exponential decay of forecasts of informed firms (who figure out that the shock is zero within five periods, virtually).

It should be emphasized here that uninformed firms *do* take into account their own quantity movements in forecasting, but they remain uncertain about *informed* firms' outputs. It is thus that a series of low prices can cause them to put weight on θ_t being low. Of course, these forecasts themselves *are* the best possible given the uninformed firms' information set and their knowledge of the economy; that is, the forecast error of θ_t that uninformed firms expect or forecast at the beginning of period t given their information then *is* zero. It should also be emphasized in this regard that the scenario described here is not the only possible sequence of events that can take place in the economy, and unin-

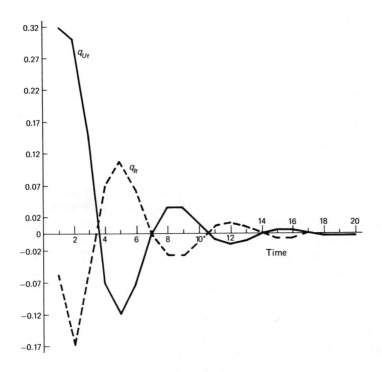

Figure 9.2. Response to transitory shock – outputs.

formed firms, as good Bayesians, put positive weight on other possible scenarios generating the random variable they see (in fact, innovation accounting experiments like the one described take place with probability zero, though they serve us well in characterizing the time series, here picking up a degree of volatility, for example).

Despite its simplicity, the present industry model can thus be used to *begin* an analysis of some of the observations made by Keynes (1936). In particular, factors that make no real difference to prospective profitability, such as completely transitory shocks, trigger oscillations in less informed opinion, this in turn causing fluctuations in the market price. Moreover, informed firms do take less informed opinion into account, though in this industry setting the latter influence is stabilizing. This can be seen from Table 9.1 and Figure 9.2. Again, after four periods, informed firms know the shock is completely transitory, but they continue to respond in a negative way to output decisions of the uninformed, ending up on the other side of the steady state, as it were.

9.7. Equilibrium in a symmetric but disparate information structure: the infinite regress problem again with a new solution[7]

As noted, the information structure of the previous section allows a recursive attack on the system. But imagine a symmetric information structure in which *each* firm receives its own information on the underlying state variable of interest, namely, θ_t. That is, suppose that, in addition to P_t, each firm i sees at the end of period t a random variable

$$u_{it} = \theta_t + w_{it} \tag{36}$$

where the w_{it} are regarded as normally distributed random variables, independent both across firms and over time, each with mean zero and variance $\sigma_w^2 \neq 0$. With industry output unobserved, each firm is getting observations on θ_t that are confounded through P_t with the forecasts other firms made on θ_t last period, which under (36) will not be known. Thus, to correctly forecast θ_t, each firm must forecast the economy-wide average forecasts of θ_t last period. Thus, each firm's forecast of θ_t depends on its forecast of the economy-wide average forecast of θ_t last period. Thus, the economy-wide average forecast of θ_t depends on the economy-wide average forecast of the economy-wide average forecast of θ_t last period. Now the economy-wide average forecast of θ_t last period must have a similar property. Thus, to correctly forecast θ_t, each firm must forecast the economy-wide average forecast last period of the economy-wide average forecast of θ_t two periods ago, and so on. It is apparent that there is an infinite regress problem here, despite the use of statistical decision theory.

This section describes a technique for overcoming this difficulty, a technique of undetermined coefficients, as in Townsend (1982). It is argued, moreover, that the information specification here, like the one in the previous section, has interesting implications for economic time series.

We begin by setting out the definition of equilibrium for this section in rather general terms. For notation, let Ω_{it} denote the information set of firm i at the beginning of period t. Let Ω_{it} contain at least past prices $P_{t-1}, P_{t-2}, \ldots$ and past information variables $u_{i,t-1}, u_{i,t-2}, \ldots$. Also, let $E(P_t \mid \Omega_{it})$ denote firm i's forecast of price P_t conditioned on the

---

[7] This section draws heavily on some recently developed techniques described by Townsend (1982). They are applied here to a model with *within-market interactions,* a feature missing from the work of Townsend (1982). Helpful comments from Lars Hansen on the procedures of this section are gratefully acknowledged.

information set Ω_{it}, and let $\bar{P}_t$ denote the economy-wide average of these forecasts. This yields the following definition.

Definition 4: A dynamic competitive equilibrium with rational but possibly disparate expectations is a law of motion for the parameter θ_t,

$$\theta_{t+1} = \rho\theta_t + v_{t+1} \tag{37}$$

an observer equation for each firm i,

$$u_{it} = \theta_t + w_{it} \tag{38}$$

a decision rule for each firm i,

$$q_{it} = aE(P_t \mid \Omega_{it}) \tag{39}$$

a rule for economy-wide average output,

$$Q_t = a\bar{P}_t \tag{40}$$

a forecasting formula for each firm i,

$$E(P_t \mid \Omega_{it}) = C(L)v_{t-1} + D(L)\epsilon_{t-1} + E(L)w_{i,t-1} \tag{41}$$

a specification of the economy-wide average forecast $\bar{P}_t$,

$$\bar{P}_t = A(L)v_{t-1} + B(L)\epsilon_{t-1} \tag{42}$$

and market clearing equation,

$$P_t = \theta_t + \epsilon_t - bQ_t \tag{43}$$

such that the following hold.

(i) *Statistically correct forecasting:* The forecast (41) is statistically correct given the parameter law (37), observer equation (38), information set Ω_{it}, the market clearing equation (43), average output rule (40), and the rule for economy-wide average forecast (42).

(ii) *Consistent aggregation in forecasts:* Formulas (41) and (42) are consistent; that is, the one-sided polynomials in the lag operator $A(L)$, $B(L)$, $C(L)$, $D(L)$, $E(L)$ satisfy $C(L) = A(L)$ and $D(L) = B(L)$.

Some comments are immediately in order. First, individual firm maximization and consistent aggregation in output have already been imposed, as is clear from (39) and (40). Second, the main task in the construction of an equilibrium is the simultaneous and consistent determination of individual and average forecasts. Note, in particular, that the average rule (42) is used by individual firms in the determination of (41).

The general procedure for the determination of an equilibrium is the

method of undetermined coefficients. One begins with an arbitrary specification of (42), that is, with coefficients in $A(L)$ and $B(L)$ unknown to
the modeler but assumed known to the firms. Then, in some manner, the
forecasting problems of individual firms are solved. This yields (41) in
terms of the undetermined coefficients. Then (41) is averaged over firms,
with the w_{it} disappearing (for this purpose, one should view the set of
firms as countably infinite). The average is then matched up with (42) to
determine the undetermined coefficients.

There is a potential dimensionality problem with the foregoing procedure. To see this, u_{it} and P_t can be written in terms of the economic
innovations ϵ_t and v_t, as well as the measurement error, w_{it}, namely,

$$u_{it} = \sum_{j=0}^{\infty} \rho^j v_{t-j} + w_{it} \tag{44}$$

$$P_t = \sum_{j=0}^{\infty} \rho^j v_{t-j} - abA(L)v_{t-1} - abB(L)\epsilon_{t-1} + \epsilon_t \tag{45}$$

Cast in this form, it appears that each firm should be forecasting *all* current and past shocks to demand. So, to simplify the problem, following
Chari's (1979) solution to his own (infinite) dimensionality problem, suppose in addition that the entire history of shocks and measurement errors
from $t-j$ on is known at time t. For example, let $j=2$; then v_{t-2},
$v_{t-3}, \ldots, \epsilon_{t-2}, \epsilon_{t-3}, \ldots$ are included in Ω_{it}. Then equations (44) and (45)
may be written as

$$u_{it}^* = v_t + \rho v_{t-1} + w_{it} \tag{46}$$

$$P_t^* = v_t + \rho v_{t-1} - abA_0 v_{t-1} - abB_0 \epsilon_{t-1} + \epsilon_t \tag{47}$$

where the variables with asterisks are defined implicitly.

There are two methods that can be used to forecast the innovations v_t,
v_{t-1}, ϵ_t, and ϵ_{t-1} from (46) and (47). Both are described by Townsend
(1982) and summarized here. For the first method, write out all current
and past observables that contain information on the unknown innovations; that is, write out (46) and (47) at t *and* $t-1$. Then use standard
formulas for conditional means and variances of normal random variables. This delivers the forecasts of the innovations in terms of observables and hence, by substitution, in terms of the innovations themselves.
This method is straightforward, but it is not recursive; a dimensionality
problem begins to arise as the lag to full information increases, that is, as
$j \to \infty$.

For the second method, the observer system (46)–(47) for each firm i
may be written as

$$
\begin{bmatrix} \epsilon_{t-2} \\ v_{t-2} \\ u_{it}^* \\ P_t^* \end{bmatrix} = \begin{bmatrix} 0 & 0 & L^2 \\ L^2 & 0 & 0 \\ (1+\rho L) & 1 & 0 \\ (1+\alpha L) & 0 & (1-\delta L) \end{bmatrix} \begin{bmatrix} v_t \\ w_{it} \\ \epsilon_t \end{bmatrix} \tag{48}
$$

or

$$
y_t = M(L)\xi_t \tag{49}
$$

where $\alpha = \rho - abA_0$ and $\delta = abB_0$. It is from this system that each firm i will attempt to forecast v_t, v_{t-1}, ϵ_t, and ϵ_{t-1} at the end of period t. (Note that only two undetermined coefficients, A_0 and B_0, are being carried into this forecasting problem.)

System (48) cannot be used for forecasting because the representation is not fundamental relative to firm i's information set. That is, the variables on the right-hand side are not in the space spanned by the current and past values of variables on the left-hand side. To see this, note that $M(z)$ is not of full rank at $z = 0$, a point inside the unit circle. But it is possible to convert (49) to a moving average representation that is fundamental, say

$$
y_t = M^{**}(L)\xi_t^{**} \tag{50}
$$

where

$$
M^{**}(L) = M(L)WB(L)\hat{W}B(L) \tag{51}
$$

$$
\xi_t^{**} = B(L^{-1})'\hat{W}'B(L^{-1})'W'\xi_t \tag{52}
$$

where the matrices W, $\hat{W}$, and $B(z)$ are orthogonal. This procedure is described in detail by Townsend (1982) and may be applied directly here. In fact, the matrices W, $\hat{W}$, and $B(z)$ are identical with those of Townsend (1982). System (50) can be used directly for forecasting via the Wiener-Kolmogorov formulas. This delivers forecasts of v_t, v_{t-1}, ϵ_t, and ϵ_{t-1} as linear functions of current and past ξ_t^{**}. Then (52) can be used to deliver these forecasts in terms of the unobserved shocks ξ_t. One can then proceed as indicated earlier.

It should be noted that *this procedure does not eliminate the infinite regress in expectations*. Forecasts of $\bar{P}_t$ will vary across firms, and thus one could compute an economy-wide average of these latter forecasts, and so on, perhaps indefinitely. *But it is no longer necessary to determine these forecasts to compute the equilibrium.*

A nice aspect of the foregoing procedure is that one can guarantee the existence of solutions for the undetermined coefficients via a fixed-point argument even though the equations in the undetermined coefficients are nonlinear. And one hopes, from Townsend (1982), that such solutions are unique and can be computed quickly via an iterative procedure. Arbitrary coefficients in the moving average representation (42) produce coefficients for firms' forecasts that in turn can be averaged to yield another set of coefficients in the representation (42). For Townsend (1982), such a procedure converged quickly to a unique solution, though the model was somewhat different.

As a special case of the model here, let $\sigma_\epsilon^2 = 0$, so that there is no transitory component to demand. Still, with economy-wide average output unobserved, at least not directly, firms face an apparently nontrivial signal extraction problem. But on the assumption of an infinite past, one can search for a moving average representation for the economy-wide average price forecast of the form (42). In fact, one can solve for the undetermined coefficients in the representation, namely, $A_j = \rho^{j+1}/(1+ab)$, $B_j = 0$, for all j. With these coefficients, the space spanned by current and past P_t's is identical with the space spanned by current and past v_t's; so the entire (infinite) history of the v_t's, and thus θ_t, is known to all firms at the end of period t [the observer equations (38) are redundant]. It is easy to verify then that this information specification yields a period-by-period strong-form rational expectations equilibrium, with $E(P_t) = \rho\theta_{t-1}/(1+ab)$.

More generally, though with $\sigma_\epsilon^2 \neq 0$, and of course $\sigma_w^2 \neq 0$, there will be diversity in forecasts, and economy-wide average output will not be inferred. Then the effect of ϵ_t shocks can produce interesting time series.

9.8.   Concluding remarks

This chapter began with the premise that equilibrium models with learning and with disparate but rational expectations will prove to be useful in describing aspects of reality. Of course, no model should pretend to describe reality completely. Thus, rather than being deterred by assumptions that can cause analytical difficulties, the emphasis here has been on specification strategies and solution techniques that make these models tractable. It turns out that the time series of these models do display interesting oscillations and can in principle be fit to data. So, consistent with the basic premise, an empirical application may soon be warranted.

One caveat is in order: Economic policy issues have not been considered. When considering the effect of a "new" policy, one must confront the "change-of-regime" issue and ask what determines decision makers' expectations; see Phelps (1980) and Sargent (1981b). To the extent that decision makers' expectations are arbitrary, one is led to an infinite regress problem. On the other hand, it may well be that statistical decision theory will prove to be a useful construct here as well, with priors of decision makers linked to government policy announcements, general political sentiment, and past experience.

References

Arrow, K. J., and J. R. Green (1973). "Notes on Expectations Equilibria in Bayesian Settings." Working paper No. 33, Institute for Mathematical Studies in the Social Sciences, Stanford University.

Bertsekas, D. P. (1976). *Dynamic Programming and Stochastic Control.* New York: Academic Press.

Blume, L. E., and D. Easley (1982). "Learning to Be Rational." *Journal of Economic Theory,* 26:340-51.

Bray, M. (1982). "Learning, Estimation and the Stability of Rational Expectations." *Journal of Economic Theory,* 26:318-39.

Bray, M., and D. M. Kreps (1981). "Rational Learning and Rational Expectations." Research paper No. 616, Graduate School of Business, Stanford University.

Chari, V. V. (1979). "Linear Stochastic Models with Decentralized Information." Unpublished manuscript, Carnegie-Mellon University.

Crawford, R. G. (1976). "An Empirical Investigation of a Dynamic Model of Labor Turnover in U.S. Manufacturing Industries." Dissertation, Carnegie-Mellon University.

Cyert, R. M., and M. H. DeGroot (1974). "Rational Expectations and Bayesian Analysis." *Journal of Political Economy,* 82:521-36.

DeCanio, S. (1979). "Rational Expectations and Learning from Experience." *Quarterly Journal of Economics,* 93:47-57.

DeGroot, M. H. (1970). *Optimal Statistical Decisions.* New York: McGraw-Hill.

Friedman, B. (1979). "Optimal Expectations and the Extreme Information Assumptions of 'Rational Expectations' Macro-Models." *Journal of Monetary Economics,* 5:23-42.

Friedman, M. (1957). *A Theory of the Consumption Function.* Princeton University Press for the NBER.

Frydman, R. (1981). "Towards an Understanding of Market Processes: Individual Expectations, Market Behavior and Convergence to Rational Expectations Equilibrium." Unpublished manuscript, New York University.

Futia, C. A. (1981). "Rational Expectations in Stationary Linear Models." *Econometrica,* 49:171-92.

Hansen, L. P., and T. J. Sargent (1980a). "Formulating and Estimating Dynamic Linear Rational Expectations Models." *Journal of Economic Dynamics and Control,* 2:7-46.

(1980b). "Linear Rational Expectations Models for Dynamically Interrelated Variables." In: *Rational Expectations and Econometric Practice,* edited by R. E. Lucas, Jr., and T. J. Sargent, pp. 127-56. University of Minnesota Press.

(1981). "Exact Rational Expectations Models: Specification and Estimation." Federal Reserve Bank of Minneapolis, Staff Report No. 71.

Hayek, F. A. (1939). "Price Expectations, Monetary Disturbances and Malinvestments." In: *Profits, Interest, and Investment.* London: Routledge; reprinted (1944) in *Readings in Business Cycle Theory,* pp. 351-65. Philadelphia: American Economic Association.

Jovanovic, B. (1978). "Job Matching and the Theory of Turnover." Ph.D. dissertation, University of Chicago.

Keynes, J. M. (1936). *The General Theory of Employment, Interest, and Money.* New York: Harcourt Brace & World.

198   **Comment by J. B. Taylor**

Kwakernaak, H., and R. Sivan (1977). *Linear Optimal Control Systems.* New York: Wiley.

Kydland, F., and E. C. Prescott (1981). "Time to Build and Equilibrium Persistence of Unemployment." Unpublished manuscript, Carnegie-Mellon University.

Lucas, R. E., Jr. (1972). "Expectations and the Neutrality of Money." *Journal of Economic Theory,* 4:103–24.

——— (1975). "An Equilibrium Model of the Business Cycle." *Journal of Political Economy,* 83:1130–44.

——— (1976). "Econometric Policy Evaluation: A Critique." In: *The Phillips Curve and Labor Markets,* edited by K. Brunner and A. H. Meltzer, Carnegie-Rochester Conference Series on Public Policy. Amsterdam: North Holland.

Lucas, R. E., Jr., and E. C. Prescott (1971). "Investment Under Uncertainty." *Econometrica,* 39:659–81.

Meltzer, A. H. (1981). "Rational Expectations, Risk, Uncertainty, and Market Responses." Manuscript prepared for the NYU Conference on Crises in the Economic and Financial Structure, November, 1981.

Muth, J. F. (1960). "Optimal Properties of Exponentially Weighted Forecasts." *Journal of the American Statistical Association,* 55:299–306.

——— (1961). "Rational Expectations and the Theory of Price Movements." *Econometrica,* 29:315–35.

Phelps, E. S. (1980). "The Trouble with 'Rational Expectations' and the Problem of Inflation Stabilization." Unpublished manuscript, Columbia University.

Pigou, A. C. (1929). *Industrial Fluctuations,* 2nd ed. London: Macmillan.

Prescott, E. C., and R. M. Townsend (1980). "Equilibrium Under Uncertainty: Multiagent Statistical Decision Theory." In: *Bayesian Analysis in Econometrics and Statistics: Essays in Honor of Harold Jeffreys,* edited by Arnold Zellner, pp. 169–94. Amsterdam: North Holland.

Sargent, T. J. (1978). "Estimation of Dynamic Labor Demand Schedules Under Rational Expectations." *Journal of Political Economy,* 86:1109–44.

——— (1981a). "Interpreting Economic Time Series." *Journal of Political Economy,* April, pp. 213–48.

——— (1981b). "Stopping Moderate Inflations: The Method of Poincare and Thatcher." Unpublished manuscript, University of Minnesota and Federal Reserve Bank of Minneapolis.

Townsend, R. M. (1978). "Market Anticipations, Rational Expectations, and Bayesian Analysis." *International Economic Review,* 19:481–94.

——— (1982). "Forecasting the Forecasting of Others." Unpublished manuscript, Carnegie-Mellon University, (to be published in *Journal of Political Economy,* 83).

Comment

JOHN B. TAYLOR

Implicit in almost all practical applications of the rational expectations method are two strong assumptions. First, it is assumed that *people know the model* of the economy used in the analysis and that they form expectations using this model. Second, it is assumed that *people know that all other people know the model* and form expectations in the same way. These two assumptions seem to restrict the range of applications of rational expectations methods. They suggest that the methods are most realistic in situations where economic events are recurrent – such as business cycles – and where policy rules are in operation for a long time. As with most hypotheses used in economic analysis, however, these assumptions should be judged not only by their apparent realism but also by how successful they are in describing and forecasting economic behavior and by how they compare with alternative assumptions. As yet, there have been few attractive alternatives available.

In this elegant and constructive chapter, Robert Townsend proposes alternative, less restrictive assumptions that have the potential of broadening the range of economic problems to which rational expectations analysis can be applied. Moreover, he develops a methodology through which tractable results can be obtained using these alternative assumptions and shows how the methods work in some representative economic applications. In my view, these alternatives deserve careful consideration by those using rational expectations in situations where the more restrictive assumptions seem inappropriate, and, as Townsend suggests, they ought to be tried out in some practical economic policy problems. In these comments I shall discuss how the Townsend assumptions represent a generalization of existing expectational assumptions and consider the types of applications where some experimentation with the methods might be useful.

Rather than assuming that economic agents know the parameters of the model, Townsend assumes that some of these parameters are unobservable and evolve over time. For example, firms are assumed to be unaware of the intercept (θ in the chapter's notation) of the demand curve that they face. Instead, they know that this intercept moves according to the probability law

$$\theta_t = \rho\theta_{t-1} + v_t$$

and can only be observed with error $u_t = \theta_t + w_t$ [see equations (23) and (24) of the Townsend chapter]. The firms use this information structure to forecast future values of the intercept and thereby form expectations of future prices and make production decisions.

It is not difficult to imagine applications where this assumption might be more appropriate than assuming θ was known. In a commodity demand equation, the parameter θ could represent tastes that change gradually and that can be estimated with error through survey methods. In a money demand function, such an assumption could represent technological change in transactions technology that can be tracked only up to some measurement error. In a fiscal or monetary policy reaction function, such an assumption could be used to capture gradually shifting economic policies that are never fully announced or believed. In this case, the probability law would represent how policy was evolving through time, and u_t could be a current policy announcement that is only imperfectly correlated with actual policy. Note that in each of these three examples Townsend's assumptions require that agents know the model that underlies these shifts: a model of taste change, a model of technological change in financial markets, or a (political?) model of policy change.

In a number of situations the Townsend assumptions might not be appropriate as an alternative to the "agents-know-the-model" assumption. For example, an important modeling task is to describe economic behavior during a transition from one policy regime to another.[1] After a change in policy regime it would be inaccurate to assume that economic agents immediately understand the new policy. Instead, they might learn about the policy gradually as they observe policy decisions over a period of time. More generally, a structural parameter of the model might change, and agents would have to learn about this change through observation. In terms of Townsend's notation, these types of problems could be represented in terms of the parameter ρ of the autoregressive process. If θ were the money supply growth rate, then a switch to $\rho = 0$ could represent a fixed monetary growth rate. People would learn about ρ only as they observed actual money growth rates. Because in Townsend's models people are assumed to know the process generating θ, this type of problem cannot be handled.

Learning about the parameters of the model in this latter sense has proved to be a quite difficult phenomenon to model adequately.[2] There are three reasons for this difficulty. First, because agents must make decisions based on estimates of parameters, their actions cannot be considered exogenous to parameter estimation. The actions form the data on which the estimates of parameters are made. Because most conventional econometric procedures require that the data be exogenous, or endogenous in particularly restrictive ways, these market interactions with data generation require different techniques for analysis. Second, there is a possibility that, as agents gradually learn about the parameters, their

---

[1] See, for example, J. B. Taylor (1975). "Monetary Policy during a Transition to Rational Expectations." *Journal of Political Economy,* October, pp. 1009–21, and L. H. Meyer and C. Webster, Jr. (1982). "Monetary Policy and Rational Expectations: A Comparison of Least Squares and Bayesian Learning." In: *Carnegie-Rochester Series in Public Policy,* edited by K. Brunner and A. Meltzer, Amsterdam: North Holland.

[2] Chapter 6 by Margaret Bray in this book considers such a problem in a simple one-parameter learning situation.

actions will converge to some constant value that does not generate enough new information about the parameters. In the demand-curve example, a firm might begin selling the same quantity each period based on its estimate of the expected price; this prevents quantity from varying enough to get reliable estimates of the demand curve.[3] In some instances, estimates are inconsistent, but few results are yet available. In any case, the analysis necessarily becomes quite complicated, even without the market interactions previously mentioned. The problem is much worse in a multiparameter situation, and this is one reason why many studies have focused on one-parameter examples.[4] Third, the possibility that agents might affect how much information they can obtain about the parameters changes the nature of the optimal control problems in fundamental ways. A simple example is that of a firm experimenting with its prices, temporarily deviating from its best guess of the optimal price, in order to obtain information to be used in the future. Even in one-parameter partial equilibrium problems, this "dual-control" or "joint estimation and control" problem leads to significant complications. Solutions that may have been linear in a model where the parameter was known do not even have a closed form when the parameter is unknown.[5]

Because of these computational difficulties with existing approaches to modeling learning, Townsend's approach, although assuming that the laws governing parameter movement are known, may be a satisfactory alternative. For some applications, the distinction made here between knowing parameter values (θ) and knowing the probability law generating the parameter values (ρ) may be sufficiently fine that Townsend's more tractable approach could be used.

Thus far, I have discussed situations, as in Section 9.5 of the chapter, where expectations are assumed to be homogeneous. In Sections 9.6 and 9.7, Townsend considers ways to avoid this assumption and allow for heterogeneous, or disparate, expectations. With disparate expectations,

---

[3] This argument can be made more general with exogenous shifts in the functions. See T. W. Anderson and J. B. Taylor (1976). "Some Experimental Results on the Statistical Properties of Least Squares Estimates in Control Problems." *Econometrica,* November, pp. 1289–302, for a discussion of the problem and a demonstration of how this problem leads to a situation of extreme "multicollinearity" and poor parameter estimates.

[4] A proof of convergence and asymptotic normality is given for a partial equilibrium one-parameter example by J. B. Taylor (1974). "Asymptotic Properties of Multiperiod Control Rules in the Linear Regression Model." *International Economic Review,* June, pp. 472–84.

[5] See E. C. Prescott (1972). "The Multiperiod Control Problem under Uncertainty." *Econometrica,* November, pp. 1043–57.

an infinite regress problem arises in which agents must not only forecast but also forecast the forecasts of others, and so on. Townsend deals with this infinite regress problem head-on, by augmenting the state variables to include forecast of forecasts – the second-order expectation, as well as third- and higher-order expectations. There is a modeling choice, however, about where to truncate the infinite regress, or whether to truncate it at all. An element of judgment is required here, but perhaps the decision could be made empirically. As Townsend has shown in an earlier study, the regress problem has implications for the serial correlation properties of the errors in statistically estimated decision rules.[6] It would be interesting to examine whether, for example, the second- or third-order expectation truncation fits the data better than the first-order truncation that is conventionally used. But, in general, because it is impossible to know which truncation to assume, this may leave an element of arbitrariness in situations where there are other reasons for serial correlation. Clearly, some empirical work is necessary before we can say whether or not Townsend's higher-order expectations model is an improvement over the first-order methods now in use.

[6] See R. M. Townsend (1982). "Forecasting the Forecasts of Others." Unpublished manuscript, Carnegie-Mellon University (to be published in *Journal of Political Economy*, 83).

CHAPTER 10

Keynesianism, monetarism, and rational expectations: some reflections and conjectures

AXEL LEIJONHUFVUD

To what extent is Keynesianism discredited? Is there anything left? Did Monetarism score a total victory? Must Rational Expectations make New Classical economists of us all? Every teacher of macroeconomics has to wrestle with these questions – hoping against hope that some new cataclysm will not let some fantastic supply-side doctrine or whatever sweep the field before he has been able to sort through the rubble of what once he knew. I am going to sort some of my rubble. The object of the exercise is to make some guesses at how the seemingly still usable pieces might fit together.

My starting points are as follows. Keynesianism foundered on the Phillips curve or, more generally, on the failure to incorporate inflation rate expectations in the model. The inflation, which revealed this critical fault for all to see, was in considerable measure the product of "playing the Phillips curve" policies. But the stable Phillips trade-off was not an integral part of Keynesian theory.[1] Its removal, therefore, should not be (rationally) expected to demolish the whole structure.

Monetarism made enormous headway in the economics profession and with the public when the misbehavior of the Phillips curve and the inflation premium in nominal interest rates became obvious for all to see. And few observers could continue to doubt the strong link between nominal income and money stock as the Great American Inflation went on and on and on. The monetarist "victory"[2] was impressive enough

---

I have profited from discussions with Carlos Daniel Heymann and from comments on earlier drafts by Earlene Craver-Leijonhufvud.

[1] I know, of course, that to some people Keynesianism means little else than Phillips-curve stability, but I ask indulgence in using my own definition of the term.

[2] "Victory" and "defeat" are terms that belong, perhaps, on the sports pages rather than to the history of science. Here, however, no epistemological meaning but only sociology of knowledge connotations are intended: To "win" means to attract the best new, young talent. In this sense, the monetarism of

that the profession's interest turned elsewhere. But it was not total.[3] The Phillips curve and Gibson's paradox both were late-coming issues to the monetarist controversy. The *original* issues were not settled, but rather more or less forgotten. Chief among these was the old bone of contention, namely, the hypothesis that the money stock is exogenously determined, so that the correlation between money and nominal income can be interpreted as a causal one-way street.

In the contest between Keynesians and monetarists over the Phillips curve and Gibson's paradox, the neoclassical anticipated inflation model (AIM) played a pivotal role. The monetarists pushed it; most Keynesians were reluctant to grant it empirical relevance. The monetarists were seen to have been empirically more nearly right on the issues where this model had provided their theoretical ammunition.

The AIM was again pivotal when the rational expectations group shouldered the monetarist aside. The full logical implications of the model for the monetarist position were not entirely welcome: If exogenous money supply changes are known to be the only aggregative shocks worth worrying about, and if exogenous money is neutral, then anticipated (recognized) money supply changes will not have any real effects. Thus, rational expectations methodology applied to the monetarist position produces New Classical economics. This development has put the monetary theory of nominal income within an (unanticipated) inch of conversion into a short-run neutrality proposition that could not explain cyclical fluctuations in real magnitudes and hence could not give a plausible account of the monetary history of the United States, from (say) 1867 to 1960.

This brief recapitulation of recent controversies suggests an agenda of four items: (1) the treatment of expectations in macromodels, (2) the anticipated inflation model, (3) the forgotten issues of the monetarist controversy, and (4) the question of equilibrium or disequilibrium theory.

10.1. Expectations

Consider how the expectations business looks from the standpoint of politicians and civil servants who have to take some measure of responsibility for macroeconomic policies and their consequences.[4] The disarray

Friedman and Brunner "won" over American Keynesianism only to "lose" soon afterward to the New Classical economics of Lucas and Sargent.

[3] Rejection of the stable Phillips curve does not suffice to establish the natural-rate-of-unemployment hypothesis (Leijonhufvud, 1981*a*, pp. 182–7).

[4] From here on, I borrow heavily from my response to Joint Economic Committee (1981) questions on the role of expectations in economics.

among macroeconomists is apparent to them. Whose advice do they rely on?

From what they are told, the role of expectations in macroeconomics must be the crux. On the one hand, they have the "Old Keynesian" macroeconomics that once looked so solid and reliable, that had very little to say about expectations – and that now, apparently, is thoroughly discredited for its lack of attention to such ephemeral matters. On the other hand, they have the "New Classical" economics that looks so paradoxical and speculative, that has very little to say except about expectations – and that now, obviously, gets all the attention from economists. In between, they have the already "Middle-Aged monetarism" that used rational expectations arguments to undermine the one-time Keynesian belief in a stable Phillips trade-off – but that balks at the new rational expectations doctrine that fully anticipated money stock policy is totally ineffective. The "Old" advise that monetary policy alone is no way to cure inflation; the "Middle-Aged" have it that only monetary policy will do, but the safe way is slow and gradual; the "New" urge a quick, clean, indubitable end to inflationary money growth.

For policymakers who have been around for that long, the heyday of Keynesianism must seem like the good old days. Those were the days when macromodels disgorged policy options in the form of readily understandable quantitative predictions: If you do a, GNP will rise by x dollars per annum, employment will grow by y percent, and prices will go up by z percent. And so on. Nowadays, economists tell them that the effects can be this or that, depending on the state of expectations. Unless one can ascertain (in some quantitative manner) what the state of expectations is or will be, therefore, it would seem that one cannot know what it is that one is doing. Unfortunately, measures of expectations do not inspire trust. Their unreliability (or unavailability) makes direct tests of all the novel propositions about the influence of expectations difficult (or impossible). So, again, whom are policymakers to believe? And, if they cannot know what they are doing, how are they to choose from the alternative policies that different factions clamor for?

They may hope to escape from this predicament in various ways. The first hope, perhaps, is that there will be many instances where expectations will not matter after all. The second would be that in most of the remaining cases, economists will be able to measure expectations so that their influence can be taken into account.

Vain hopes. In macroeconomics, expectations always matter. Sensible policy judgments cannot be made at all if their influence is ignored. They cannot be accurately measured for econometric purposes. Significant

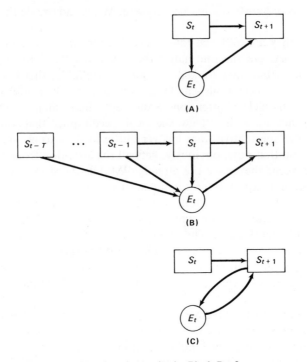

Figure 10.1. What is going on in the Black Box?

progress on their measurement, moreover, is unlikely.[5] For present purposes, we may as well think of them as *unobservable*.

There is a third possible avenue of escape from the expectations predicament. Expectations might be "well-behaved" (let's call it). Expectations are well-behaved if linked in a stable manner to the system of
observable variables.

In the simplest imaginable case (Figure 10.1A), we would have one-to-
one correspondence between the unobservable, E, and the contempora-
neously observable aspects, S, of the state of the system. The unob-
servability of expectations then would not matter. It would not prevent
us from developing reliable macromodels. (If the world generally were to

[5] This is not to say that expectations cannot be made the subject of very worthwhile research. See, in particular, Jonung (1981). We may be able to obtain
good data on short-term inflation expectations. What we theoretically require,
however, is the entire "term structure" of inflation rate expectations relevant to
multiperiod decisions to be made currently. For some purposes, moreover,
some measure of the dispersion over agents (period by period into the future) of
these expectations is also needed. It is this task that seems to me hopeless.

conform to this simplest case, of course, the proposition that behavior is governed by expectations would be a moot point of Austrian philosophy, supported by no empirical evidence other than introspection.)

A problem first arises when each vector of observable state variables may be combined with any one of many unobservable states of expectation. With one state of expectation, a policy of demand stimulation might, for example, reduce unemployment; with another, it might produce nothing but inflation. So it matters. One may then resort to the past history of observables for the clues that will differentiate one state of expectation from another (Figure 10.1B). The search is for a one-to-one correspondence between *sequences* of observable states and states of expectations. If that hope is fulfilled, reliable prediction is again possible.

In Keynesian theory, (long-term) investment expectations are not necessarily well-behaved, and Keynesian macromodels had, in fact, not much success in predicting investment. But for the rest, both Keynesians and monetarists – following Koyck (1954) and Cagan (1956) – did pretty well by assuming expectations to be well-behaved in this manner. Well enough so that the "old" macroeconomics in its time did not need to trouble us much by hedging all its predictions on the unobservable state of expectations. Its time ran out with the arrival of the Great American Inflation.

It is the Great Inflation of the last fifteen years that has destroyed faith in macroeconomics. By the same token, it is not expectations in general that have been the problem here but specifically expectations about inflation. Why should expectations about the future of the price level give us more trouble, more serious trouble, than expectations about other things?

It is tempting to jump to the conclusion that, perhaps, price level expectations are ill-behaved, that is, not related in any stable manner to observables. Then the system can in principle not be modeled in a reliable way, and making policy is simple and unavoidably a dangerous business. But it cannot be true in general that price expectations are ill-behaved. If that were the case, we would not have had to wait until the decade of the 1970s to discover that we were in trouble.

Inflation expectations in the 1970s were not well-behaved in either of the two ways that the older macroeconomics habitually sought to rely on. Clearly, people did not form their expectations about the future of the price level just from observing the present state of the economy. Extrapolating from the immediate past, as we know by now, would have been irrational. If these linkages to the *present* and the *past* will not do, there is only one way left: Assume that people's expectations match the macro-model's predictions about the *future* (Figure 10.1C).

The costs of not accepting this rational expectations development are apparent.[6] If we have to give up on making expectations well-behaved, we must either start faking expectations measures or else condemn ourselves to an indefinite future of doubletalk: "The effect will be either this or that." Of course, disassociating oneself from macroeconomics is also a way out, and one that many colleagues have found the most attractive of late.

When would this last-ditch method to make expectations behave be needed? If monetary policy were itself well-behaved, so that base money creation were some stable function of present and past observables, agents would be able to base their short-term price level expectations on the history of those variables. So this rational expectations twist becomes important when monetary policy is ill-behaved, that is, when it is not predictable on the basis of past performance.

What limits to rational forecasting should be built into our macromodels to fit such conditions? What is it that people can and cannot know about the future of inflation? We have two clues. First, if the outside modeler must treat the state of expectations as unobservable, then inside agents will not be able to observe each other's expectations. Second, if the system poses a difficult predicament to policy makers (who can call on all the modelers for advice), it must be worse still for agents who have to cope with the added uncertainty of not knowing what actions will be taken by policy makers who do not know what they are doing.

Phelps's chapter in this book begins the exploitation of the first clue. I have been trying to get some mileage out of the second (Leijonhufvud, 1980, 1981b).

10.2. The anticipated inflation model

Let us define a *monetary regime* as a system of expectations that governs the behavior of the public and that is sustained by the consistent behavior of the policymaking authorities. The reaction of the public to any particular policy action (such as a change in the growth rate of base money) will depend on the regime that is believed to be in effect. Consequently, each regime requires its own applied macrotheory; models that do reasonably well for one regime may break down badly for its successor. We can choose among the different possible monetary regimes by choosing behavior rules for the fiscal and monetary authorities.

What consistent behavior on the part of the policymaking authorities

---

[6] The novelty of this solution is sometimes exaggerated: This is how Keynes dealt with short-term (sales and real income) expectations in his *General Theory*.

would sustain the expectations assumed in the anticipated inflation model? If the public unanimously predicts a particular constant inflation rate (to continue indefinitely), then it must be because the authorities are bound to produce it. Rational agents will not anticipate a result that no one is even trying to bring about. The model presupposes a believable precommitment by the government to create money at precisely the pace required to produce the anticipated inflation rate. The authorities operate, in effect, under a most rigid monetary discipline, having forsworn all discretionary options to "make policy" in the future in light of the then existing conditions.

If we define a *monetary constitution* as a set of rules, binding in the short run,[7] that specify the conditions under which (base) money will be created or destroyed, then the anticipated inflation model presumes an exceedingly restrictive monetary constitution to be in effect. All meaningful constitutions must put limits on the exercise of discretionary authority. This one, however, eliminates discretion altogether.

The representation of the inflation expectations of the public by a single number, *the* anticipated inflation rate, seems reasonable in this instance. Individual agents who expect a higher or lower inflation rate will be taught the errors of their ways in a most systematic and pedagogical manner by suffering losses in the marketplace. Individual expected inflation rates should converge, therefore, on the constitutionally dictated rate. If the regime is operated with great precision, the variance of each agent's subjective expectations should also be small. Obviously, expectations are exceedingly well-behaved under this regime.

Now, if all of this be true, it doth follow that the only welfare costs of inflation are the trivial ones associated with a tax on money balances (Bailey, 1956). Contrary to a widespread opinion among economists, this kind of inflation can be stopped at even smaller cost. If, initially, "greenbacks" are depreciating in real purchasing power by k percent per year, we simply create a new "blueback" currency and make it, by law, appreciate relative to greenbacks by k percent per year. Bluebacks grow in their legal capacity to extinguish greenback debt at this k percent rate. This currency reform does not force any redistribution of wealth. All outstanding contracts will be discharged in exactly the real terms originally anticipated by the parties. Because the inflation tax on greenbacks is k percent and zero on bluebacks, the former will disappear from circulation. People will demand larger real balances of bluebacks than they

---

[7] Consider, for example, a constitutional law that can be changed or amended only by majority votes in two consecutive sessions of the legislative body, the two sessions to be separated by a general election. The U.S. Constitution is too difficult to amend, I would think, for the purpose here discussed.

held of greenbacks. To the extent, therefore, that the steady-state demand for money is interest-elastic, the monetary authorities must allow for the creation of a larger initial stock of bluebacks than the stock of greenbacks that is being retired, so as to avoid the emergence of deflationary pressure on the blue price level. If this aspect of the transition is only handled right, there should be not the slightest blip in the unemployment rate. We end up, painlessly, with a zero inflation rate in the blueback currency.

The anticipated inflation model implies that the social problem that we have agonized over for fifteen years could be gone by Monday. That implication is false. So the model, for all its pedagogical virtues, makes bad theory. This conclusion is of some consequence because of the model's pivotal role in the macrotheoretical controversies of the 1970s.

For want of a better name, I have called the present American monetary regime the random-walk monetary standard (RWMS). This is a somewhat halting metaphor, not a technical description, but it will have to do.

Under the RWMS, the authorities decide one period at a time whether to accelerate, keep constant, or decelerate the rate of money stock growth. Only current economic conditions and immediate political pressures enter into the decision. Future money growth rates are left to the future; they will be chosen at the last minute on the basis of what seems most pleasant and convenient to whoever happens then to be in charge.

In contrast to a Friedman rule (for example) that is unconditional, money creation in this regime is conditional on a great but unspecified number of things, most of which cannot be predicted very far in advance. Consider the term structure of an individual agent's inflation rate expectations. How could he predict the rate of money growth in the first quarter of 1992? Suppose he already has a forecast for the last quarter of 1991. That given, he needs to predict the acceleration or deceleration chosen by the authorities in the next quarter. But he does not know what the economic conditions and the political situation will be, or what people will be in charge, or even what economic theories they will believe in. For dates this distant, therefore, he may as well regard money growth rates (and inflation rates) as picked by a random device.[8] The individual's expected price level for 1991 is a subjective forecast entertained with very little confidence. It is likely to be an *ill-behaved* expectation, that is, one not itself predictable from current and past values of the observable variables of some macromodel.

---

[8] He cannot be confident, however, that drawings from this urn will be made at fixed intervals. Moreover, the distribution in the urn is presumably not stationary.

Because there is no scientific method to forecast price levels in the relatively distant future, the distribution over all agents of individual subjective expectations is likely to show very considerable dispersion. Period by period, policy will shower profits on those who most nearly behaved as if they had anticipated it and losses on those who failed so to behave. But the profits and losses produced by frequent turnarounds in monetary policy will not teach people to make better ten-year forecasts. Consequently, individual long-term forecasts will not converge. For brevity, we shall refer to this as an *incoherent* state of long-term nominal expectations.

As we consider forecasts over successively shorter terms, more and more of the determinants of monetary policy will begin to seem predictable to the transactor. Such predictions – about who will be in office, what economic theory he will favor, and what conditions he will face, five, three, two, one year hence – will vary among agents, and so will the models by which they generate price level forecasts from such predictions. Nonetheless, the state of expectations should become more coherent and more nearly well-behaved for shorter and shorter time horizons. In the very shortest end, behavior might approximate that of the New Classical model: Agents watch contemporaneous base money growth and, insofar as they believe the state of expectations to be coherent,[9] let it affect their pricing decisions but not their immediate output and employment decisions.

This does not mean that random-walk (RW) monetary mismanagement has "neutral" consequences. On the contrary, the regime will reduce productivity, discourage productivity growth, and lower the rate of capital accumulation. Longer-term commitments will be the most adversely affected. RW inflation will also exacerbate social tensions and undermine popular confidence in inherited political institutions and social arrangements. But these costs and consequences of random-walk inflation I argue elsewhere (Leijonhufvud, 1977, 1981*b*).

None of the three types of theory under discussion has done much to further our understanding of the costs and consequences of the Great Inflation. But, of the three, the Keynesian has clearly been the most grievously wrong about inflation. It was wrong about the "ineffectiveness" of money stock policy in changing nominal income, wrong about nominal interest rates and culpably wrong in supporting the "playing-the-Phillips-curve" policies that led to our present lamentable regime. In each respect, monetarism was the better guide in an era of developing monetary instability. As the economy learned to adapt, finally, to the

---

[9] That is, insofar as they believe that others generate their inflation expectations as they themselves do.

incessant discretionary manipulation of a fiat money totally without anchor, the lags in responses of prices and nominal short-term rates shortened. In this respect, the rational expectations version of the monetarist model came to look better. At the same time, however, the state of longer-term nominal expectations became increasingly incoherent and ill-behaved, with the result that neither agents nor modelers can rationally expect to do very well at predicting the relationships between money, prices, and real activities.

It is not possible to have a macroeconomic science that can predict well in all possible worlds. If expectations are unobservable (or unmeasurable) and ill-behaved, macroeconomics will predict badly, policymakers will not be able to precalculate the effects of what they are doing, and agents will not have well-founded ideas of what policies to expect or of each other's expectations. It is possible, however, to change the world to fit (more nearly) what macroeconomics can do – and, incidentally, make its inhabitants better off in the process.

This is accomplished, of course, by putting constitutional constraints on monetary policy. Some social institutions exist because they rationally solve problems of conjectural interdependence that cannot be left simply to the rational expectations of individual agents. The right-hand driving rule saves a lot of speculation on average opinion every morning before you hit the freeway. It also saves those who did not get it right. A monetary standard is another example. It provides a target on which individual expectations can converge. As the state of expectations coheres around the time path implied by the standard, individual agents can plan on the basis of the justified supposition that average expectation is not far off from their own. Economic activities will be more efficiently coordinated as a consequence.[10]

Suppose, then, that we would have a presently unanticipated return to monetary stability – as much stability, for instance, as the Bretton Woods regime at one time supplied. How would we rate the various macrotheories in such a setting? The judgments of their relative merits given earlier make the 1970s (as experienced in the United States) the exclusive test of a macrotheory's worth. To do so is very much in tenor with the literature of recent years. But the issues on which monetarism vanquished Keynesianism only to be outflanked by the New Classical economics are rather defused by the supposition of a return to stable money. Would our assessment of Keynesian theory be more favorable if we were to see it in the context of a framework for monetary stability such as

---

[10] Compare the discussion of "coordination games" by Schotter (1981); see also Sowell (1980).

might have been constructed by J. M. Keynes (to pick a largely irrelevant name not altogether at random)?

At this point, I am at the end of my reflections. Here start the conjectures.

10.3.   The forgotten issues of the monetarist controversy

Keynesian theory failed to incorporate inflation expectations. In a world of high and volatile inflation this is a fatal flaw. But for a long time, before the Great American Inflation got under way, a majority of economists found the theory an adequate guide to reality. Events did not reveal the flaw. But how could this be so if the disturbances causing business fluctuations were predominantly of a nominal nature? Can the monetarist hypothesis be the general explanation of fluctuations in a world where the Phillips curve maintains the appearance of stability?

When we come to reconsider the macrotheory of constitutional monetary regimes, the "real" theory of business fluctuations will, I conjecture, make a comeback. The hypothesis of Keynes and most pre-Keynesian business cycle theorists that medium- and long-term real expectations tend to misbehave will regain, I think, a measure of qualified acceptance. Two subsidiary conjectures: (i) the interpretation of correlations between M_2 and income for such regimes will shift back to a renewed emphasis on the endogeneity of inside money, and, correspondingly, (ii) Gibson's paradox will once more be seen as a procyclical pattern of real interest rates reflecting underlying movements in profit expectations. These are the matters on which I think the "Old" Keynesians were more nearly right than they are currently given credit for.

The Great Inflation has held the truths of monetarism before our eyes for some fifteen years without a break. But several developments in economics during this same period have actually weakened the case for a "Middle-Aged" monetarist interpretation of nominal income fluctuations in stable monetary regimes. One has been the rationally expectant youth movement's stress on deficient information about changes in outside money as *the* (implausible) source of business fluctuations in monetarist theory. Another has been the monetarist balance-of-payments model for small, open economies with its demonstration of the endogeneity of money stocks for at least $n-1$ countries in a fixed-exchange-rate world. A third, perhaps, has been the apparent difficulties that some central banks have had in hitting their money stock targets with any consistency.[11]

---

[11] For some reason, however, early converts to money stock targets do not seem to have as much difficulty as the last central banks to profess abandonment of interest rate targets.

Some motivation for these conjectures needs to be sketched in conclusion. We should consider a monetary constitution that has much smaller long-term price level uncertainty than the present RW regime but comparable short-term uncertainty. For concreteness, think of a managed gold exchange standard where, over the longer term, the price level is determined by the requirement to maintain fixed exchange rates, but where, in the short run, the central bank can expand or contract by letting its reserves vary. Another possibility is a money stock rule with a band within which the central bank is allowed discretion.[12]

In this constitutional (MC) system, agents will know the longer-term, "permanent" trend (or level) of prices.[13] They will have inelastic expectations about this permanent price level. The Fisher premium in long-term nominal interest rates, if any, should be constant. Knowing the price trend, MC agents will be able to distinguish periods of "high" and periods of "low" prices. When such periods occur, they will expect reversion to the constitutional mean. Now, suppose for the sake of argument that this system exhibits "cyclical" alternations of "high" and "low" prices and that real activity levels fluctuate correspondingly.[14] How do we explain it? Well, it depends. We are back with the half-forgotten issues of the original monetarist controversy, before inflation expectations became the center of it.

The monetarist and the Keynesian hypotheses regarding the cause of business fluctuations need not, of course, be mutually exclusive. It is useful, however, to proceed, to begin with, *as if* they were.

Take first the monetarist hypothesis that the fluctuations in nominal GNP are caused by changes in the exogenous money stock. For simplicity,

[12] I have in mind a rule specifying a constitutional *level* of the money supply for each date after the constitution goes into effect and a bandwidth of $x\% \pm$ around this target. A growth rate rule with a band defined as $z\%$ plus/minus the constitutional rate is a different possibility.

[13] And, if this trend is only implied rather than stated in the constitution, they could use some autoregressive scheme to learn it.

[14] It is tempting to go on to say that prices must be "sticky" because they move with less amplitude than nominal income and that this "explains" the real income movements. But the implied suggestion that prices (and/or wages) "should" move proportionally to nominal income is misleading when the shock is not a purely nominal one. Nor does it help much to substitute speculation on the basis of "inelastic price expectations" for involuntary constraints on price setters – as in Leijonhufvud (1968, Chapter II). Note that while rational agents in the MC system should have inelastic expectations about the price level over the longer run, it is not obvious that the monetary stability contributed by the constitution sketched earlier would instill inelastic price expectations over the short run.

suppose we have a central bank that sets up a sine wave in base money around the path that will maintain the constitutional price trend over the longer run. This is a purely nominal, systematic disturbance to the economy. It is difficult to see why the system should not learn to find the rational expectations equilibrium path: In each period, nominal prices should be proportional to the base, and the short-term nominal interest rate should reflect the anticipated price change until next period. The short-term rate should trace out its own sine wave around a constant long-term nominal interest rate. But then output and employment should not react to this monetary "policy," and so the real cycle is left unexplained.

The nominal disturbance may, of course, be less predictable than in the sine-wave example. But agents do not need to predict it accurately, if they can be quite confident that movements in the nominal base are exogenously caused. As pointed out by Ben Eden (1979), they could simply index-link all contracts to the base so as to obtain "real" transactions prices from which nominal disturbances have been purged.

The class of hypotheses that combine exogenous monetary impulses with the inability of agents to disentangle real from nominal disturbances to explain the cycle seem to be implausible, therefore. In this monetarist world with a constitution, short-term nominal expectations can be kept on track by simply watching the money supply, and long-term nominal expectations are kept well-behaved by the constitution.

Second, then, consider a "real" cycle hypothesis. In order to have a clean-cut opposite extreme to the purely monetarist theory, suppose that the monetary base obeys a Friedman constitution (but that we still have business fluctuations, although perhaps of "moderate" amplitude). All agents know, therefore, that no disturbances emanate from the central bank. But investment expectations are not necessarily well-behaved. Forward markets for the goods that will be produced with the capital goods to be bought today are missing. (Tired old refrain?) It is possible, therefore, for agents individually to invest on the basis of expectations that are inconsistent with aggregate ongoing investment.

To keep the story close to those in the recent equilibrium cycle literature, where agents usually are pure price takers in all markets, we may redo the "shifting marginal efficiency of capital" story into one in which producers mistake the future relative price of their products.[15] In the boom, the majority of producers think that the price of their product is going to go up relative to the general price level,[16] so that, by producing

[15] This suggestion is due to C. D. Heymann.
[16] Some subset may be optimistic instead that they are going to cut their real costs.

today for sale tomorrow, they can earn a return (intramarginally) higher than the real rate of interest. In recession, most producers make the opposite error.

The perception of higher profits in prospect may be caused, initially, by innovations in certain industries, by government spending, or by political events abroad, and so forth. (Because the process never duplicates itself exactly at the individual "island" level, transactors will not learn never to be fooled again.) The producers who first start betting on improved real profits for themselves will bid for more inputs. The expansion of the industries first affected improves business conditions in general. Prices edge up as real supply inelasticities begin to make themselves felt. The increase in the volume of transactions is financed, we may imagine, primarily through an all-around expansion of trade credit. Bank credit could be a critical component of this credit expansion but is not necessarily of predominant quantitative importance. In any case, the money supply expands endogenously.

The upswing will peak for several reasons. Real interest rates will creep up as the banking system runs out of excess reserves. As the stock of nonbank trade credit outstanding grows in relation to sales, the rate of credit growth tapers off. Rising money prices will make the present employment of "marginal" factors seem increasingly costly in relation to prospects of future revenues (at constitutional prices). But, mainly, producers discover that not everyone's real terms of trade can improve relative to everyone else's. As this starts to dawn on more and more people, prices that are high in relation to the constitutional mean will tempt inventory liquidation. When this gets under way, sales revenues will be used to reduce accounts payable rather than to maintain production. The volume of credit outstanding contracts and the inside money stock falls as the recession develops.

This, of course, is simply an attempt to paraphrase the kind of story told innumerable times in the Keynesian and pre-Keynesian business cycle literature.

Repeated episodes of this sort, in the MC setting, might generate observations such that an impressively stable Phillips curve could be fitted to them. For the sake of argument we might suppose that alternating periods of high prices/low unemployment and low prices/high unemployment produce a Phillips scatter with all points virtually on a line.[17] If so, that curve still does *not* hold out the promise of a permanent policy trade-off. It is not exploitable because the points on the locus are not stationary equilibria; instead, these historical observations record states

---

[17] A series of counterclockwise loops is more likely, actually.

in which the expectations held are bound to be revised in the light of outcomes. An attempt to exploit the apparent stable trade-off will, if pursued far enough, destroy the monetary constitution without gaining its object of permanently lowering unemployment. Once the MC system is swept away, the stable Phillips curve disappears. But we have been through that, I think.

In a trade cycle of this kind, discretionary fiscal and monetary policy could possibly have a useful role in trying to reduce its amplitude and to prompt the upswing. If this is correct, my further conjecture is that such policy will be maximally effective when fully anticipated. Note, however, that we are presupposing continued adherence to a monetary constitution that regulates the monetary base and, therefore, the price level over the medium and longer run. Monetary policy in such a setting is reduced to short-term credit policy, and one expects it, naturally, to use interest rate targets. Its "effectiveness" is likely to be limited.

For simplicity, we have dealt with the monetarist and the "real" (or Keynesian) hypotheses as if they were mutually exclusive. In a purely monetarist case, where real aggregative disturbances are known not to occur, rational agents need only watch the appropriate monetary aggregate and price their wares proportionally to stay out of trouble. In a purely Keynesian case, where exogenous monetary shocks are ruled out, monetary aggregates move with more general movements in real credit; credit, moreover, expands and contracts with real output. Pricing proportionally to bank credit will not do; the safe strategy is to revise prices in response to market excess demand.

The two types of disturbances are not, of course, mutually exclusive but may be present at the same time. When, in addition, they interact, transactors will have a difficult time sorting nominal from real shocks. Suppose, for example, that the central bank is in the habit of supplying an "elastic currency," that is, that it participates in the all-around expansions and contractions of credit so that the base will move pro-cyclically also in Keynesian processes. This, I believe, creates an information problem for the private sector that may give a more plausible reason for short-run nonneutrality of money than does the "islands" story. When the base is seen to expand, is it an extension of "real credit" by the central bank (that will reduce real rates of interest)? Or is it a nominal scaling up of all values in the system, so that one's prices should be marked up proportionally? Uncertainty on this score could produce stickiness of nominal prices in the face of monetary expansion.

The relationship between money and credit in the business cycle, however, is a large and difficult topic that cannot be pursued further here.

10.4.   Equilibrium or disequilibrium theory?

One last question: Suppose the conjecture is right that the Keynesian "real" disturbance hypothesis is due to be readmitted on at least a co-equal basis with the monetarist "nominal" shock hypothesis. Would this have any implications for current squabbles concerning the merits of equilibrium versus those of disequilibrium approaches to business cycle theory? I do not pretend to have a firm answer to this question. But it ought not to be evaded altogether.

Monetarist theorists have, on the whole, rested content with the equilibrium method. In the older, Friedman, version, monetary disturbances may cause temporary deviations from the natural rate of unemployment. In the newer, Lucas version, changes in unemployment are interpreted as movements between temporary equilibria. In either one, the coordination of economic activities is taken on faith. In Keynesian economics, it is problematic.[18] The problem, moreover, is essential in the Keynesian view of business fluctuations – an integral, not an optional, part of the inquiry.

The most heated discussion of the issue has centered on the "clearing" of labor markets. The New Classicists have made the (telling) point that fix-price assumptions imply that agents allow perceived gains from trade to go unexploited; if, in contrast, one assumes all perceived gains to be exhausted, the implication is that the labor market "clears." At this point, the discussion easily gets derailed into unproductive arguments about the "voluntary" or "involuntary" nature of unemployment. That thicket had better be avoided on this occasion.

"Speculative" pricing, based on temporarily given information sets, seems to me also preferable to more or less arbitrary fix-price constraints as the theoretical rationale for short-run wage "stickiness." So far, so good. But the matter does not end at this point. Price flexibility in this qualified sense does not by itself guarantee that the time path of the economy will be a sequence of temporary Walrasian equilibria. A Keynesian theorist would proceed to consider how the trades actually realized at the speculatively set prices this period might affect the feasible set of trades for next period. In the standard example, reservation wages are set too high, so that labor's realized income is reduced with further consequences for consumption. And so forth.

What eliminates such income-constrained state sequences from the New Classical theory is not just the assumption that fix-price constraints are absent. The assumption that all agents have the same information

[18] In cruder versions of Keynesianism, admittedly, coordination of activities is not problematic either – just impossible. An article of a more pessimistic faith.

sets is just as crucial. If all agents in a market receive the same news and evaluate it using the same theory, they will all agree on what change in price is indicated. The volume of transactions will not be affected by disagreements among transactors. Taking the old Keynesian example again, if the news causes revisions in the demand price and supply price of labor of equal magnitude, neither side will be surprised by, or disappointed in, the volume of transactions realized.

It is not easy to come up with a context in which the assumption of universally shared information sets seems more reasonable than in the monetarist case of purely nominal shocks. Even so, it eliminates the Friedmanian temporary deviations from the natural rate of unemployment. These departures from equilibrium come about because firms learn of changes in the inflation rate before workers do, so that there is a transitory information asymmetry between the two sides of the market. Once workers catch on, the information asymmetry vanishes, and employment returns to the natural rate. The New Classical assumption does not allow the asymmetry to develop.

The labor market focus of the debate over the new equilibrium business cycle theory has been unfortunate. Preoccupation with the stickiness of money wages comes naturally to monetarists: If you believe that all aggregative shocks are purely nominal, the failure of nominal prices to adjust appropriately must be the key to the explanation of unemployment. Keynesians do not believe that exogenous nominal shocks are the only disturbances, or even the typical disturbances, to worry about. Traditionally, they have been concerned about the intertemporal coordination of saving and investment decisions. In the latest round of the solemn, farcical muddle that is modern macroeconomics, we have been treated to a spectacular bout in unemployment theory featuring, in one corner, New Classicists blaming the failure of nominal interest rates to adjust to changes in money and, in the other, Old Keynesians blaming the rigidity of nominal wages in the face of changes in real intertemporal opportunities.

The Keynesian case for a disequilibrium approach is best considered in an intertemporal context. The real rate of return on investment is not just some given constant. We have to presuppose that political events and technological developments, for instance, can change the real returns in prospect for broad sectors of the economy. A change in the returns perceived to be in prospect, in the unfashionable terminology of Keynes, causes a change in the marginal efficiency of capital (MEC). Such changes are real shocks – "real" in the sense that system adjustments to them require changes in the allocation of resources and in the relative price vector and not just some scaling up or down of nominal values. We now have (at least) the following possibilities:

(A) There is nothing in all this for macroeconomists to talk about. Real disturbances cause reallocations of resources between sectors but no movements in macroeconomic aggregates – unless monetary shocks are also involved. In the latter case, the macroeconomic effects are all attributable to the latter.

(B) A real equilibrium business cycle: Utilization of both labor force and manufacturing capacity fluctuates but does so optimally in response to correctly perceived changes in the real rate of return. The labor market is continuously in equilibrium. People choose to work more when the real rate on savings is high, ceteris paribus – intertemporal substitution à la Lucas. In this case, we assume that everybody has the same information and the same theory. They act, therefore, on the basis of mutually consistent beliefs,[19] and these beliefs are correct. The rate of capital accumulation fluctuates, but saving equals investment (*ex ante*) throughout.

(C) A real business cycle that is a sequence of temporary equilibria. Mutually consistent beliefs again, but we allow for the possibility that what everyone believes will still be wrong. Again, saving equals investment in every period. When expectations are found to have been inaccurate, both savers and investors revise their expectations to the same extent and at the same time ("between innings").

(D) A Wicksell-Keynes disequilibrium cycle wherein the market real rate of interest fails to coordinate saving and investment decisions appropriately. In cyclical expansions, investment tends to exceed saving (market rate below natural rate); in contractions, these inequalities are reversed. There are any number of variations on this theme.[20] All have in common the assumption that the expectations of entrepreneurs taken collectively are inconsistent with those held in the financial markets.

Of these four possibilities, (A) is the only one that is fully consistent

[19] No great matter of principle hinges on it, but I happen to prefer this terminology (i.e., consistent or inconsistent beliefs). See "The Wicksell Connection: Variations on a Theme" (Leijonhufvud, 1981*a*).

[20] The collection of variations discussed in "The Wicksell Connection" (Leijonhufvud, 1981*a*) is not by any means complete, but should suffice to try the patience of all but dedicated antiquarians with the general idea. Note also that the broad-brush taxonomy painted in the text will be judged incomplete (E) by Cambridge Keynesians who do not believe the interest rate can equilibrate saving and investment, (F) by old-time Keynesians who do not think the equilibrium exists, and (G) by post-Keynesians who do not think the equilibrium can be defined. We have already passed over the modern muddled Keynesians who think Keynesian theory has nothing to do with saving and investment but

with the New Classical economics. New Classical theory is made up, however, from monetarist theory and rational expectations method. (B) and (C) are nonmonetarist, but are clearly compatible with the rational expectations equilibrium approach to modeling. (B) is probably the most appropriate benchmark for discussion of "real" cycle theory.[21] A formal version of (C) would be a real counterpart to Lucas's monetarist equilibrium cycle model (Lucas, 1975). The problem comes down to the various versions of (D).

Whether (D) can be modeled using a rational expectations equilibrium approach depends on how stringently the latter is defined. Phelps's "islands" parable, formalized by Lucas in a study that has been central to the entire rational expectations development, should be adaptable to the representation of such Keynesian processes (Phelps, 1970; Lucas, 1972). Each producer is his own island in regard to his expectations of future profit from present investment. There are no archipelago-wide (futures) markets to ensure the consistency of these expectations with the plans of consumers and with aggregate ongoing investment. If the MEC on the home island falls below what the producer thinks is obtainable elsewhere, he will cut back on investment and pile up his retained earnings in liquid form, and so forth. From there the Keynesian story develops as usual (Leijonhufvud, 1981a, pp. 197–9).

If, however, by "equilibrium approach" we mean modeling the economy as if it behaved like an Arrow-Debreu contingency market general equilibrium system,[22] it is clear that Keynesian processes must fall outside its purview. An Arrow-Debreu economy works like a "clockwork" going through the Markovian motions of a system in which all allocation decisions were made and reconciled at the beginning of time. Agents may have trouble predicting states of "nature,"[23] but they have no trouble with each other. Coordination of activities, given the state of nature, is not a problem. All agents have the same information on the probability distributions for future states of nature. There is no room, in this framework, for the inconsistencies of belief or expectation that are essential in Keynesian theory.

has sticky wages as its analytical fulcrum. There are more kinds of Keynesians than one can shake a stick at! Believe me – I've tried.
[21] My "Wicksell Connection" uses (A) as the benchmark. It would have been more relevant to current debates if I had used (B).
[22] This is the position taken by Lucas (1980) more recently.
[23] Monetarist cycle theory can be cast in this frame, it would appear, only by classifying central bankers as "ravages of nature" rather than as open market "traders."

222   **Axel Leijonhufvud**

It is, perhaps, necessary in conclusion to insist that the incompatibility of the rational expectations equilibrium method and the Keynesian hypothesis is totally irrelevant to the scientific appraisal of the latter. It merely indicates the limitations that the unanimity-of-beliefs postulate builds into the method.[24]

References

Bailey, M. J. (1956). "The Welfare Costs of Inflationary Finance." *Journal of Political Economy,* April, pp. 93–110.
Cagan, P. (1956). "The Monetary Dynamics of Hyperinflation." In: *Studies in the Quantity Theory of Money,* edited by M. Friedman, pp. 25–117. University of Chicago Press.
Eden, B. (1979). "The Nominal System: Linkage to the Quantity of Money or to Nominal Income." *Revue Economique,* January, pp. 121–43.
Koyck, L. M. (1954). *Distributed Lags and Investment Analysis.* Amsterdam: North Holland.
Jonung, L. (1981). "Perceived and Expected Rates of Inflation in Sweden." *American Economic Review,* December, pp. 961–8.
Joint Economic Committee (1981). *Expectations and the Economy.* Washington, D.C.: U.S. Government Printing Office.
Leijonhufvud, A. (1968). *On Keynesian Economics and the Economics of Keynes.* New York: Oxford University Press.
(1977). "Costs and Consequences of Inflation." In: *The Microeconomic Foundations of Macroeconomics,* edited by G. C. Harcourt, pp. 265–312. London: Macmillan; reprinted in Leijonhufvud (1981*a*).
(1980). "Theories of Stagflation." *Revue de l'Association Française de Finance,* December, pp. 188–201.
(1981*a*). *Information and Coordination.* New York: Oxford University Press.
(1981*b*). "Inflation and Economic Performance." In: *Money in Crisis,* edited by Gerald P. O'Driscoll. Cambridge, Mass.: Ballinger.
Lucas, R. E., Jr. (1972). "Expectations and the Neutrality of Money." *Journal of Economic Theory,* 4:103–124; reprinted in R. E. Lucas (1981). *Studies in Business-Cycle Theory.* Cambridge, Mass.: M.I.T. Press.
(1975). "An Equilibrium Model of the Business Cycle." *Journal of Political Economy,* 83:1113–44; reprinted in R. E. Lucas (1981). *Studies in Business-Cycle Theory.* Cambridge, Mass.: M.I.T. Press.
(1980). "Methods and Problems in Business Cycle Theory." *Journal of Money, Credit, and Banking,* November, pp. 696–715; reprinted in R. E. Lucas (1981). *Studies in Business-Cycle Theory.* Cambridge, Mass.: M.I.T. Press.
Phelps, E. S. (1970). "Introduction." In: *Microeconomic Foundations of Employment and Inflation Theory,* edited by E. S. Phelps et al., pp. 6–7. New York: Norton.

[24] The argument that the agents will act so as to exhaust apparent gains from trade that the new classicists have used against fix-price modelers is simply irrelevant in the intertemporal context chosen here as the appropriate one for discussing the Keynesian case. With incomplete intertemporal markets, the interactions required to generate information about, and exploit, these potential gains from trade do not take place.

Schotter, A. (1981). *The Economic Theory of Social Institutions*. Cambridge University Press.

Sowell, T. (1980). *Knowledge and Decisions*. New York: Basic Books.

Comment

FRANK HAHN

Profesor Leijonhufvud's chapter considers "the solemn, farcical muddle that is modern macroeconomics." In doing so he makes a number of interesting and important observations and offers some useful conjectures. But he does not at all dig down to the source of the muddle, and here and there he seems himself touched by it. Over his essay there looms the imposing and dangerous Lucas, who seems to have one of the foremost scholars of Keynes in so mesmerizing a grip that he forgets what Keynes had to say. But Lucas to some extent and the Lucasians almost wholly are responsible for the muddle that Leijonhufvud discerns, and so it is not too helpful to be under the sway of these economists. The rest of these remarks constitute an attempt (probably premature) to convince the reader of this.

I start in praise of Lucas. He not only realized that it was impossible to believe that there are two separate subjects called macroeconomics and microeconomics, but he acted on this realization. This is not the project of providing microeconomic foundations for macroeconomics. Such a project is absurd – What exactly are we asked to provide foundations for? If we are interested in the behavior of aggregates, then we must use economic theory to help us, and the only theory we have is one of rational and self-seeking agents. On this matter, then, three cheers for Lucas.

After this insight, however, everything went wrong, and I cannot resist the temptation to say that this may well be due to the way economic theory is often taught, namely, as science rather than as a provisional tool for organizing our thoughts. However that may be, Lucas (and the Lucasians) proceeded on the basis that economic theory, to be recognizable as such, had to be Walrasian equilibrium theory. It is true that even for him the Arrow-Debreu version was too extreme, so that a sequential structure was favored that then necessitated the well-known move regarding expectations that I shall comment on later. But fundamentally, macroeconomics was turned into Walrasian equilibrium economics.

Now, the first point I wish to make is this: If you decide that one should and can study an economy as if it were always in Walrasian equilibrium, then you had better be prepared to justify this on the basis of first principles or you should keep silent on Keynes. For, plainly, once the hypothesis is granted, Keynes makes no sense at all.

The arguments that are offered in support of the view that we can treat the world as if it were in continuous Walrasian equilibrium are so appallingly bad and so much at variance with the Lucasian resolve to pursue serious and rigorous economics that they are barely worthy of consideration. One is told that not only will all Pareto-improving possibilities be exploited by markets but also they will be exploited the instant they arise. (No distinction is made between perceived and actual possibilities, and no attention is paid to the manner in which agents communicate.) There is the even more disreputable argument that some three or four log-linear econometric equations not immediately at variance with the microeconomics of a single agent and economy-wide equilibrium "work." Then, of course, there is the "street light" defence, which says that because the Walrasian equilibrium theory is the only fully developed theory we have, we had better use it. But the drunk searching for his keys under a street light, when he lost them in a dark alley, will certainly not find them. Ptolemaic theory was the street light before Kepler.

Now, in fact, there are first principles from which Walrasian equilibrium can be deduced, but they are not the ones invoked by the Lucasians. They have to do with particular games played by a very large number of agents under some pretty strong informational assumptions. This work tells us at a glance that there is no reason to suppose that any actual economy satisfies the conditions required. More important, this careful work leaves half the story unaccounted for: It provides no theory derivable from first principles of how Walrasian equilibrium, when it is the appropriate equilibrium, comes to be established.

It is for all of these reasons that I have always held the view that the Walrasian theory in all of its manifestations is an important theoretical benchmark but that a vast and unruly terrain had to be traversed before one understood (leave alone predicted) the behavior of an actual economy. No economist and certainly no theorist should be ignorant of the Walrasian theory, and no economist and certainly no theorist should pronounce on actual economies and policies on its basis alone. There is a lot to be said for Wittgenstein's: "Whereof you cannot speak thereof you should be silent."

But these are not my main concerns now. What I think is plain is that we cannot discuss Keynesian insights and pronouncements simply on the ground that they are inconsistent with Walrasian equilibrium analysis. One can discuss the claim that two plus two is five by appealing to the rules of arithmetic, which are necessary truths and inconsistent with the claim. One can dismiss a promise to walk on the waters as inconsistent with laws of physics that are pretty well established both inductively and theoretically. But Walrasian equilibrium theory is not like arithmetic or physics, and my first response to someone noting its inconsistency with Keynes is to ask, So what? My second response is more constructive. It is to ask whether or not the Keynesian opus can be firmly based on what I hold to be a fundamental prop of all economic theory: the rational and greedy agent. If this enterprise fails, and only then, can one claim to have found a serious inconsistency, although of course it will still be far short of an actual refutation, because the "fundamental prop" is not at all beyond dispute. Moreover, should one wish to do the job without this prop, then one would be committed to a departure from what we can now plausibly hope to do, which is probably too large to be credibly accomplished at one go.

As a leading example of the kind of issue that is at stake, consider involuntary unemployment. Professor Leijonhufvud writes that he is concerned to avoid unproductive arguments about the "voluntary" or "involuntary" nature of unemployment. That from the student of Keynes! Professor Lucas has also recently pronounced on the same subject in a manner that would have done credit to Marie Antoinette: "The unemployed worker," he writes, "at any time can always find *some* job at once" (Lucas, 1978). Mr. Goodhart, who labors at the Bank of England, has also recently criticized me for being concerned with involuntary unemployment on the grounds that it is not an operational concept. And so on. In recent years, only the neo-Ricardians have produced more muddle and nonsense than this.

Involuntary unemployment has nothing to do with any metaphysical conundrum about "free will." It is a technical term used to describe a certain kind of (Walrasian) market failure. In the macroeconomic context it denotes a state in which the market wage of "labor" exceeds its shadow wage. In a more agreeable context it means that there are individuals for whom the expected utility of some jobs, which it is known they can do, exceeds their expected utility from their present position. That need not be one of unemployment. Thus, imagine Professor Lucas dismissed from his post because of serious malinvestment by his university. We find him washing up in a hamburger parlor. He is likely to be involuntarily unemployed as an economist. (Of course, this means an unexploited Pareto-improving move that, it is argued, can never arise. The claim that he may be involuntarily unemployed is a counterclaim to that general proposition.)

So the first thing to do is to get rid of two muddles. First, forget all about free will *et sub specie aeternitatem* and concentrate on the definitions. Second, do not ride your macroeconomic horse of "labor" and your microhorse of different jobs and workers at the same time. There surely may "always be some jobs at some wage," but this has nothing whatsoever to do with the issue.

When these two muddles have been got out of the way, strengthen your understanding by seeing what is wrong with what Professor Leijonhufvud has to say on the Phillips curve and Keynesians and with what now appears on this matter in macroeconomics texts. You will read that it has now become clear that there is no permanent trade-off between unemployment and inflation, a trade-off (you will be told) the Keynesians "believed in." But it so happens that it is difficult to think of a "Keynesian," and certainly impossible to think of Keynes, believing anything like that. What was argued was that inflation might lower the rate of *involuntary* unemployment. For this the arguments are quite strong in the context of a theory that does not rule such unemployment out of court axiomatically. But the baneful power the Lucasians have over current thinking is so strong that a scholar who must know Keynes and Keynesians much better than I do does not even pause to consider this matter. In any case, "the" natural rate of unemployment is associated with what Keynes and Keynesians (e.g., Beveridge) called "full employment," and I shall give Professor Leijonhufvud a hundred dollars if he finds Keynesians advocating inflation to get employment levels higher than full employment. As for Phillips curves that shift all over the place and that Professor Leijonhufvud regards as counterevidence against the poor Keynesians, all one can say is that that could happen to anybody. Stable functions cannot be posited either by theory or by econometrics. That this behavior of the curves led to important and useful theorizing concerned with expectations is of course quite correct, and I shall return to it. But no one was more concerned with expectations than was Keynes, and it seems to me that his inevitable vulgarization at the hands of textbook writers, civil servants, and politicians has nothing to do with the fundamental issue of whether or not Keynes's denial of the Lucasian axioms allows a coherent theory.

But consider the view that the notion of involuntary unemployment is not operational. Again, philosophy, gleaned at second hand, clouds the issue. "Is it not the case," the philosopher-economist asks, "that there is no way of distinguishing the pain of a terminal cancer patient from that caused by the pimple on my nose?" "How can we know what goes on in people's minds?" he goes on, adding, "provided, of course, there is some way in which we could say that there *are* other minds." It was one of the great virtues of Keynes that he had a direct, Johnsonian approach. He saw people queuing at labor exchanges, he saw them marching and protesting, and he drew the natural conclusion that they would prefer to be employed at the current wage. Considering the assumptions we are all in the habit of making, this one seems mild and eminently reasonable.

But in any case, the claim that one could never distinguish between the two kinds of unemployment is false. Go to a labor exchange, where you will find, say, an unemployed carpenter with an impeccable work record. You can from the records discover $(\lambda < 1)$, the proportion of laid-off carpenters who have been finding jobs as carpenters. Let w be the prevailing (average) carpenter wage, w_1 the wage in the Lucasian job that the carpenter can have on demand, and w_2 the unemployment pay. Then, if our carpenter has turned down no carpentry job and is still looking for one, it must be, on usual assumptions, that $w\lambda + (1-\lambda)w_2 > w_1$. The shadow wage w^* with concave utility functions and $w > w_2$ will be less than $w\lambda + (1-\lambda)w_2$ and so less than w. Moreover, even if the carpenter takes the Lucasian job, we can deduce that $w^* < w$ when $\lambda < 1$. Much more sophisticated methods could be used. So what Lucas and Goodhart, assuming they are not engaged in amateur philosophizing, have in mind is that the two kinds of unemployment cannot be distinguished on the basis of the statistics they are in the habit of using. But that is their problem, and it carries no Popperian moral.

From the point of view of policy, the possibility of involuntary unemployment is of great importance, for it means that an expansion accompanied by *lower* real wages may be consistent with equilibrium. Indeed, that is what Keynes maintained. To make sense of this, one needs to have equilibrium concepts that are non-Walrasian, and one must recognize that these (just as Walrasian concepts) are not often unique. I have quite recently written at some length on this (Hahn, 1982) and will not repeat the arguments here. Even "fully anticipated" monetary expansion can have lasting real expansionary effects provided the public has not been dragooned into believing that the Lucasian (homogeneity) outcome is the only one. (To check this, consider an economy with constant returns and involuntary unemployment.)

Professor Leijonhufvud considers the recent inflation of the seventies to have "done in" Keynes and to have shown the monetarists right. This, I think, is a widely held view, and I find it incomprehensible. I do so for the same reason as I would the claim that the twenty-five years after the war when the West was Keynesian and "never had it so good" proved Keynes right and the monetarists wrong. These are after-dinner remarks. To test one theory against another, one has to do some testing, and that means model choice done econometrically, and on that we have no final verdict at all.

Lastly, in this connection I cannot but regret that so considerable a connoisseur of the ironies of our subject as Leijonhufvud has not commented on, indeed has adopted, the custom of referring to all non-Walrasian economics as "disequilibrium economics." In its own way, this nomenclature is as mendaciously partisan as, say, is Marxian "exploitation." It has the implication not only that this kind of theory is not "quite proper" but also that such a state of the economy will not persist. In any event, it is sloppy. An equilibrium state is one where all agents take the actions that in that state they prefer to take, and these actions are mutually compatible. At least that is what the term traditionally means. It does not *define* equilibrium as a Pareto-efficient state, nor does the term apply only to Walrasian economies. Fixed price models are neither equilibrium nor disequilibrium models until a theory of price is proposed. If an agent finds it optimal to set a price independent of the state of demand for his product, or if a group of agents (union and employer) find this optimal, then that has as much claim to the title of equilibrium price as does the Walrasian "market clearing" price. Names matter, and the muddle that Leijonhufvud discerns is often grounded in simple illiteracy.

On rational expectations, Leijonhufvud has a number of good things to say. The whole enterprise is founded on the intuition that sooner or later rational agents will learn what is the case ("the true model"), and, of course, on the simple fact that it sidesteps the embarrassing circumstance that we know next to nothing of how actual people form actual expectations. But the intuition is by no means secure, not because there is empirical counterevidence to quote, but because it is not logically well grounded.

Take the usual definition of a rational expectations equilibrium for a Walrasian economy. It is a vector-valued function $p(s)$, that is, prices as a function of the state of nature, such that if agents plan and act in its light the prices will be market-clearing if the given state occurs. At least that is an appropriate definition when all agents have the same partition of the set of the states of nature. In suitable circumstances such an equilibrium exists. But there may be many of them. This now raises the important point that I must have a view of which of the equilibria other agents think the economy is in before I can formulate "the true model." Of course, one can simply say that by some divine fluke we always all agree on the equilibrium that the economy will be in, but that is, to say the least, a little awkward to justify, and it leaves the original intuition nowhere. In fact, having "the true model" will in general be quite insufficient to tell me what will be the case given any state of nature.

Now, rational expectations econometricians of the good sort are aware of this difficulty. Their first step in dealing with it is to demand that every rational expectations equilibrium have the steady state as an asymptote. Because it is not immediately obvious why this should be acceptable or reasonable – after all, rational expectations equilibria that are not viable for infinite time may be so for ten million years – they often justify their procedure by an appeal to "transversality conditions." To this there are two decisive objections: First, no one in a capitalist economy performs the Ramsey maximization for that economy, nor does that economy plausibly behave as if someone were doing so. Second, the move does not help, because for many economies one can show that there is a continuum of rational expectations equilibrium paths *all* of which seek the steady state. (The latter is not, in general, a saddle point in the full-dimensional phase space.) Of course, all these paths have the homogeneity property of the elementary textbook. However, it is boldness verging on madness to make *that* the basis of an "ineffectiveness proposition" for such economies.

But back to Keynes. He was not at all averse to the idea of rational expectations equilibria – he called them bootstrap equilibria. In the good old days, the good old Keynesians used (in England) to like setting the following (Robertsonian) examination question: "The rate of interest is what it is because it is expected to become other than it is. Discuss." The right answer would have been approved by Lucas – with one proviso. For Lucas and his followers, the agent discovers what the world is "really like" independent of the beliefs of other agents. Not so for Keynes. Azariadis and Shell, in their recent demonstration of rational expectations equilibria conditioned on "sunspots" and cycling, are much more in the Keynesian court. It is true that infinite equilibria seem incompatible with (exponential) bubbles, but that, for obvious reasons, is not damaging to the Keynesian vision.

That vision we are only now beginning to understand in the language of rigorous theory, to which Keynes, to his and our loss, was so averse. Put generally, it turns on some essential externalities, or, if one prefers, on an essential Nash-like element. Everyone, whether in Chicago or not, knows about situations (games) with many Nash equilibria, some of which can be Pareto-ranked. A cooperative solution dominates a set of noncooperative ones, and that is the externality. Diamond has produced a simple search model with just such features – there are many equilibria that can be Pareto-ranked. For Keynes, the importance of the effective demand notion was that he thought that more would be produced and more people would be employed if collective action assured to each agent that extra output could be sold. For the individual agent – given the actions of others – it was not worthwhile to expand. All of this can be made quite precise and correct provided we do not insist that an economy is always in Walrasian equilibrium.

For rational expectations theory, the story is only just beginning, for the anonymity of "large" Walrasian economies is entirely fictitious. In practice, agents have to forecast quantities and also the *actions* of others. It would be interesting to hear from the new macroeconometricians what the evidence is, for instance, that firms in deciding on their output and investment plans are concerned to forecast only the price level and the money stock. To me, this seems extravagantly implausible. Even in the world that they are supposed to inhabit, agents might worry about the forecasts made by others.

To this must be added the crucial observation that we all have only half a story as long as we do not have actual agents setting prices. The fish market is not a good paradigm for macroeconomics. This observation then leads to the idea of conjectures and rational (or reasonable) conjectures. Here we are at a very uncertain beginning of understanding. It is both rash and unattractive to write as if this problem did not exist or had been settled.

So, all in all, I was saddened by Professor Leijonhufvud's chapter. It was, as it were, up to date on inflation and "all that" and certainly up to date on the new macroeconomics. But there are many "practical" and busy economists who are also in this position of skimming on the surface of a subject they have not really mastered. From Professor Leijonhufvud I expected a magisterial insight into the foundations: *Felix sunt qui potuit rerum cognoscere causas.* I did not experience this happiness from reading his chapter.

References

Hahn, F. H. (1982). *Money and Inflation.* Oxford: Blackwell.
Lucas, R. E. (1978). "Unemployment Policy." *American Economic Review,* May supplement, pp. 353–7.

Index